INSIDE
THE AUSTRALIAN
PARLIAMENT

DAVID SOLOMON

SYDNEY
GEORGE ALLEN & UNWIN
LONDON BOSTON

First published in 1978 by
George Allen & Unwin Australia Pty Ltd
Cnr Bridge Road and Jersey Street
Hornsby NSW 2077

National Library of Australia
Cataloguing-in-Publication entry:

Solomon, David Harris.
  Inside the Australian parliament.

  Index.
  Bibliography.
  ISBN 0 86861 352 5 Paperback
  ISBN 0 86861 344 4

  1. Australia. Parliament. I. Title.

328'.94

Library of Congress Catalog Card Number 77-78557

Set in 10 on 11 point Times by G.T. Setters, Sydney

Printed in Australia by Hedges and Bell, Maryborough

INSIDE
THE AUSTRALIAN
PARLIAMENT

Contents

Introduction

This is a book about Parliament House Canberra and about the Australian Parliament. It provides a description of the more important procedures of the two houses of the parliament and it also attempts to explain what lies behind many of the formal trappings which envelop parliamentary activity in Canberra. It is concerned with examining the extent to which parliament carries out the functions it is supposed to carry out. The book is also concerned with those events outside the two chambers of the parliament which affect the workings of the parliament.

The emphasis of the study is on what does happen inside Parliament House, not on what is supposed to happen. The aim is to see how and where parliament fits into the Australian political system. I have sought to provide an inside view of Parliament House, an insight into the politics of the Australian Parliament. I have attempted to look beyond the formal standing orders and formal purposes to what actually happens—how ministers, members, governments and oppositions approach and are affected by the various procedures and proceedings in both parliament and Parliament House.

This is not a historical study of the parliament, though such a study would be useful to explain why the parliament has developed the way it has, adopting some of the procedures of the British Parliament but not others. Nor is it a comparative study. Australians probably know even less about the workings of Westminster than they know of parliament in Canberra. Comparisons are certainly desirable, but they can only be made when there is a clear understanding of what happens in Canberra.

Unfortunately, not much academic attention has been paid to the Australian Parliament. Writers of general textbooks devote the mandatory chapter or two to it, but a full-length study has not been published. It may be that political scientists have taken little interest in it because they have assumed there has been little to learn from studying it—that what needs to be known, is already known.

It is because I do not hold that view that I have written this book. It is written from the viewpoint of a journalist who has spent a decade in Parliament House, first as a reporter and commentator on parliament, then as a political correspondent, and finally as a member of the staff of a Prime Minister.

The book was made possible by the grant of a Visiting Fellowship in the Department of Political Science, Research School of Social Sciences at the Australian National University. I am indebted to the head of the department, Professor R. S. Parker, to Dr C. A. Hughes, Dr Peter Loveday and Dr Patrick Weller, and to other members of the department, for encouragement and assistance in the planning and preparation of the book. I also thank the many members of the parliament and its staff, public servants and members of the Press Gallery (particularly Laurie Oakes and Michele Grattan) who contributed information and assistance. Professor Henry Mayer, of the University of Sydney, provided invaluable advice on the structure and content of the book.

1 The Australian Parliament, 1978

Parliament was essentially irrelevant to the development and implementation of the plans of the first Fraser government (1975-77). The government had a solid majority in both houses and could plan its legislative program in the certain knowledge that bills would be passed when, and in the manner, the government desired. The only parliamentary question which concerned the Prime Minister was the timing of elections. Within the limits set by the constitution, he had complete freedom of choice on election dates: he had no need to consult the parliament, nor could it force a date on him.

It was all very different throughout the Whitlam Labor government (1972-75). At no stage did the Labor government have control of the Senate, so its legislative program was constantly under threat. In those three years the senate rejected more legislation than it had in its previous 71-year history. The government could never be certain that any particular bill would be passed, or even when it would be considered, by the upper house. This led to political as well as legislative problems for the government whose term could be threatened (and was eventually ended) by actions of the Senate. The timing of elections was largely dictated by questions of parliamentary tactics and by the government's opponents. There were two double dissolutions of the parliament, the first of which left the government still without a majority in the Senate.

The Liberal-National Country Party-controlled Senate demonstrated between 1972 and 1975 that a government must have a majority in the Senate if its very existence were not to be at risk. This had not previously been the case. Many governments had survived in the face of hostile Senates. Their legislative programs might have been (and often were) subject to harrassment, but most proposed laws were passed. While the Senate was aware that it probably had the power to force a government to the polls, this power was rarely discussed and the threat of its use never made. Throughout the life of the Whitlam government, the opposition constantly threatened to use this Senate power and of course in the end did so.

This newly-demonstrated power of the Senate to force a government to the polls before the expiry of its term of office sits alongside the traditional power of the House of Representatives to determine which party or parties should form the government. In the first eight years of the Australian federation, shifting party alliances in the House of Representatives were more responsible than the elections for determining which party would form the government. And in 1941 the Fadden government was brought down when two independents voted against its Budget. A Labor government (headed by Curtin) was then supported in the House by the independents until the elections were duly held in 1943, when Labor was returned to government with a majority in its own right.

Thus only the House of Representatives can give a government life, but both houses can administer the death penalty, although the Senate may take a long time to put its wishes into effect. The government may appeal from the parliament to the people through an election. (In 1975 the House of Representatives passed a vote of no confidence in the Fraser government that had been installed by the Governor-General, Sir John Kerr, on 11 November. Yet that government remained in office until the elections on 13 December, when it scored a massive victory.) But even where the Senate succeeds in forcing the government to hold an election, the result may be indecisive. The circumstances may be such that there cannot be an election for the Senate, but only for the House of Representatives, that is, the time may not be (constitutionally) ripe for a Senate election or the preconditions for a double dissolution may not be present. Or the voting may be such as to return the government with a majority in the House of Representatives but still without a majority in the Senate (as in the 1974 double dissolution).

These vital life-and-death powers over government are far from the be-all and end-all of parliament's activities. If they were, there would be little point in parliament meeting for sixty or seventy days each year during a period when the government had a comfortable majority in each chamber. It would be a complete waste of time. Yet only a few MPs or Senators, even in their worst moments of opposition-depression, regard it thus—though it should be noted that Dr J. F. Cairns, a former Labor Deputy Prime Minister, is among those who recently have publicly voiced this attitude.

It is not that the vast majority are kidding themselves about their importance in the system. Above all else, being a member of the parliament teaches a man or woman that a backbencher has virtually no place in the government of the day, little influence over policies and only very occasionally any access to a share of real power. Few fall into the trap of thinking that parliament and government are synonymous. Almost all put their hearts on being in government, but most have to make do with just being parliamentarians. That doesn't mean that what they do as backbenchers, or what the parliament does under the thumb of the government, is irrelevant. But it is different from what most of their electors probably think they should be doing while they are "up in Canberra"—running the country.

In fundamentally different ways, the Senate and the House of Representatives have in the past decade or so demonstrated that they have to be taken seriously as parliamentary and political institutions. To ignore either one is to ignore an important aspect of the Australian polity.

The House of Representatives is a stage for the leaders of the government and the opposition to confront one another on the political and legislative issues of the day, though not necessarily the most important one. A study of the news coverage by radio, television and the press of events in the House suggests this function of providing a forum is not as important as the political clashes between government and opposition that are contrived by the various public media—particularly television current affairs programs.

While they may not be all that important for the public, the theatrical clashes of the parliamentarians in the House are absolutely vital for the politicians themselves. One may argue that it is how a leader performs on television, rather than in the House, that really matters (in terms of electoral fortune). That argument was largely accepted by the Liberal Party in 1968 when it chose the superior television performer, John Gorton, over three other contenders to replace Harold Holt as Prime Minister. The Liberals then saw Gorton flounder as he tried to adapt his Senate debating style to the more rough-house mauling confrontations that occur in the House. Whitlam easily bested Gorton, and his successor McMahon. He so effectively destroyed Snedden on the floor of the House that he made it inevitable that Fraser would be successful (the second time round) in his bid to take over the opposition leadership. And then, during 1976 and 1977, Fraser established an ascendancy over Whitlam in parliament. Just as in the late 1960s and early 1970s the morale of Liberal MPs had slumped with every Whitlam victory in the House, so in the mid-1970s Labor's morale was lowered with Whitlam's. The Labor Party parliamentarians were convinced that at any election in which they were led by Whitlam, they would be unable to disturb Fraser's hold on government. Fraser too was convinced of this, and one of the factors which prompted him to hold elections in December 1977 rather than at a later date was his conviction that the Labor Party would replace Whitlam with Hayden early in 1978—and that this would present him with a far more difficult challenge.

Leaders are not the only people judged by their performances in the House. Ministers who in question time are easily able to provide answers which will be reported in the media in a satisfactory manner have a more difficult task persuading their parliamentary colleagues that they are on top of their jobs. How an answer is reported is only one of the criteria by which a minister is judged by his colleagues, his subordinates and his leader. On the Labor side parliamentary performances are extremely important as an MP has to get the voting support of his colleagues if he is to be elected to the ministry or shadow ministry. It is impossible to quantify the importance of parliamentary performances and the way in which they affect party morale and personal reputations. What is certain however is that such performances do matter, they do affect political developments outside the parliament and they help determine the progress of individual MPs.

Senators are not generally judged in the same way by their performances in the chamber (though Gorton owed some of his reputation to his handling of the VIP aircraft affair in the Senate in 1967). Politicians do not regard the Senate as the political equal of the House of Representatives. While it may have almost as much power as the House, and shares with it the ability to destroy a government, the Senate is regarded as a second-class political chamber. Political leadership is concentrated in the House of Representatives, not the Senate. Although the House is only twice the size of the Senate, four times as many ministers are drawn from the House as from the Senate. In any ministry, senators never fill the top two positions (Prime Minister and Deputy Prime Minister) and usually take only one or two of the top dozen ministerial posts. The media also emphasises the political significance of the House. Fifty or more journalists will watch question time in the House of Representatives, perhaps half a dozen will watch the Senate. And very rarely will the Senate produce any question time stories.

To build up its reputation, the Senate has concentrated on parliamentary activities, and in particular, in the past decade or so, on committee work. From the mid-1960s there was a deliberate campaign led by the then ALP Senate leader, Lionel Murphy, who was closely assisted by the Senate Clerk, Jim Odgers, to expand the nature, activities, reputation and importance of Senate committees. The highlight was the committee sponsored by Murphy and eventually headed by Tasmanian Liberal Peter Rae, which inquired into the Australian Securities industry and produced weeks of headline reports about manipulation of the stock market through the use of mineral exploration companies. In recent years the Senate has completed the formal establishment of a network of committees covering the whole range of governmental activities. Estimates committees give Senators a twice-a-year opportunity to pry into the spending of every Commonwealth department. Every department is also covered by one or other of the Senate standing committees on legislation and administration. Any particular policy issue which emerges as politically interesting can be referred to a committee, as can any piece of legislation or even any petition. Select committees may also be established to look at any problems that are considered by the Senate to require more detailed investigation and analysis that can be supplied by a standing committee.

The committees all have full power to call witnesses, and demand the production of any documents they want to see. Their inquiries can be carried out in great secrecy (protected by parliamentary privilege) or in the full glare of television lights, depending on the whim of the committee. Ministers can be called upon to face up to the committees and can be cross-examined with a thoroughness which demonstrates the inadequacy of the regular question time proceedings in both houses.

The Senate also has the ability to subject legislation to a scrutiny which, because of the nature of our political parties, simply does not happen in the House of Representatives. The Senate's criticism of bills can be constructive or destructive, depending on the political composition of the Senate *vis-à-vis* the House of Representatives. As a result of the 1977 elections, the Senate from 1978 to 1981 (and probably thereafter) is closely divided, and contains representatives of minor parties who are anxious to use the power of the Senate to demonstrate their own importance. Also present are likely to be a few government backbenchers who are prepared to use their votes against the government on particular issues they consider not to be matters of "confidence", so as to promote the Senate's importance.

These aspects of the House of Representatives and the Senate demonstrate why meetings of the Federal Parliament affect politics, even if the government of the day has an overwhelming majority in both chambers, as occurred between 1975 and 1977. The less certain that majority is, the more political importance the parliament takes on. But under any circumstances, what happens in parliament cannot be ignored if the observer wants to understand why politicians, governments and oppositions behave the way they do.

2 The Environment: Historical, Geographical and Social

In 1927 the Australian Parliament took possession of a new building in the new national capital, Canberra. During the first twenty-six years of the federation, the national parliament had met in the buildings of the Victorian Parliament, in Melbourne. The move to Canberra affected the development of the Australian parliamentary system, because it made more intimate the relationship between government and parliament, normally two distinct elements in the political system.

The then new Canberra Parliament House was a three-storey brick building rendered with cement and painted white. It was set in the middle of a paddock in the geographic heart of a capital which had a population of about 7000 people. The nearest shops, commercial offices and houses were several kilometres away. Within walking distance were some newly-built offices for the public service and some accommodation intended mainly for parliamentarians. Parliament House was as isolated within Canberra as Canberra itself was from the major centres of population and civilisation of Australia.

The physical circumstances drove ministers to set up their offices within Parliament House. Before parliament moved to Canberra, the only minister who had even a temporary office within the building used by the parliament was the Prime Minister. At that time all the commonwealth public service departments as well as the parliament were located in Melbourne and most had their headquarters within a few hundred metres of the Victorian parliamentary building in Melbourne's Treasury Place.

When the parliament was transferred to Canberra a cabinet room was built in West Block, a few hundred metres from Parliament House. Because the public service departments had not yet been transferred to Canberra, ministers were given temporary offices in the Parliament. According to Frank Green, at one time Clerk of the House of Representatives, there were plans to build a large administration block near Parliament House to house the ministers. (The story is told in "Changing Relations between Parliament and the Executive", *Public Administration* (Sydney), Vol. 13, June 1954, pp. 65–75.) Work began but was halted for financial reasons. The building was not finally completed until the mid-1950s, almost thirty years later. In the meantime the government had established itself in Parliament House on a permanent basis. A few months after the transfer to Canberra in 1927 the cabinet ceased using the room provided for it in West Block, and held its meetings in a cabinet room in Parliament House which was originally intended only for emergency meetings.

The move by the ministers into the parliament building was undertaken only after the government had sought the approval of the Speaker of the House and the President of the Senate. They, nominally, were the landlords, representing the institution of parliament. Parliament was supposed to own the building, not the government. Fifty years later, however, most of the pretence that Mr Speaker and Mr President are in charge of the building and that it is primarily for the use of parliament, has been abandoned. A major expansion of Parliament House in 1972–73 was limited to providing improvements for ministers and their staffs. A new cabinet room was constructed to replace the old "emergency" room with a suite less capable of being "bugged". It is roomier and has an ante-room equipped with a kitchen. Accommodation arrangements for ministers by this time were under the control of the Minister for Administrative Services, not the presiding officers of the houses who were responsible only for accommodation for backbenchers and the leader of the opposition.

Parliament House has in fact become the centre of government in Australia as well as the place in which parliament meets. Only rarely do cabinet or any of its committees meet outside the Parliament House—if they do it is in Sydney or Melbourne. Most ministerial work is conducted from the suites which all ministers possess inside Parliament House. The Prime Minister works mainly from his office in Parliament House. While he has an official residence, the Prime Minister's Lodge, it in no sense resembles No. 10 Downing Street, or the White House. It is a residence only (and a small one) in which the Prime Minister might do some entertaining, and hold some private talks, but which is quite unsuitable for office work.

The fact that the Prime Minister works mainly from Parliament House encouraged other ministers to centre their activities there as well. A network of telephone lines gives all ministers direct push-button contact with the Prime Minister as well as their own departments. Facsimile transmission machines in the mid-1970s provided ministers with almost instant documentation, whether the central office of their department is located in Canberra, Melbourne or Sydney. Security phones (with scramblers) are provided for those ministers who need them.

Most ministers have offices provided for them in their departments, offices which are spacious and generally lavishly furnished. Many ministers, on their appointment, resolve that they will use their departmental offices because they believe they will have more immediate and more frequent consultation with their departments. The resolution rarely holds for long. Ministers cannot escape from Parliament House while the parliament is sitting, and they quickly build up files within the cramped quarters they have in Parliament House. They find their departmental advisors are quickly on tap (it takes only fifteen minutes for the officers of any department in Canberra to drive to Parliament House). During parliamentary recesses ministers tend to operate from offices in their home cities if they are not required for meetings in Canberra.

Australian governments use Parliament House as they would an executive office building. They host conferences there, even within the sacrosanct chambers of the House of Representatives and the Senate. They provide entertainment there. When the state Premiers and their officials visit Canberra for the Premiers' Conference, they use the chamber of the House of Representatives, which is stripped for the occasion of the books, dispatch cases and other paraphernalia which decorate the centre table while the House is in session. The Premiers are allocated the rooms of parliamentary office-holders (such as the Speaker and the Senate opposition leader) while government officials who are managing the paperwork of the conference take over the government whip's office. Until 1976 drink and food were provided in the government party room. The arrangements rarely intruded on ministerial offices.

Nearly all national political events which occur in Canberra tend to occur in Parliament House. Not infrequently the word "House" is dropped from media reports about these events, with the result that all forms of national political activity tend to be associated with "Parliament". The activity of the House of Representatives and the Senate for the most part is the least newsworthy of these events in "Parliament". The fact that the Canberra political bureaux of all national news media organisations are located within Parliament House itself adds to the confusion of identity. As far as political activity is concerned, Parliament (meaning Parliament House) has become synonymous with Canberra, and Canberra with national politics. In the states it is common for politicians and newspapers to rail at what "Canberra" is doing to them: they might be referring to decisions of the national government, or to Acts of the federal parliament.

Parliament House was erected as a "provisional" Parliament House—more than temporary but less than permanent—because the construction had to be completed in less than three years. It cost £348 000 and was supposed to have a life span of just fifty years. The building was extended from time to time to take account of the needs of the library and refreshment services, as well as of members and ministers. By the mid-1970s it had almost doubled its original size and the annual maintenance cost was approaching the original capital cost. Governments and parliaments had been dickering with the idea of constructing a "new and permanent" Parliament House for almost ten years, and had managed to agree on a location for it after seven years of squabbling (about the time it took to select the site of the national capital at the beginning of the century). With very few dissentients, it was agreed that the new Parliament House would house the executive on a permanent basis. The idea of the government and the parliament being so closely associated had, over a fifty-year period, become both acceptable and respectable.

The provisional Parliament House in the 1970s was a very crowded and self-sufficient world. More than 1000 people worked and lived inside Parliament House when parliament was in session and perhaps 700 when it was not. As well as the 188 or so parliamentarians, there were over 150 ministerial staff, almost 300 on the staff of the two chambers and over 200 employed on joint house services, more than 100 in the library, about 75 in the Hansard staff and more than 150 in the press gallery, along with innumerable drivers, public servants, lobbyists and hangers-on who would be visiting the parliament at any given time. The parliament provides for them several refreshment rooms, two main bars, and some billiard and table tennis rooms. Outside the building there are tennis and squash courts. Inside, for the use of MPs only, is a sauna. There were also a barber, committee rooms, several television studios, a post office, and a library. The multiplicity of facilities means, however, that there is very little space for anything.

Through the 1960s and most of the 1970s, many MPs had to share office space in Parliament House, and sometimes new MPs were three to a room. In 1974 the parliament began transferring staff out of the building to various annexes around the city, though mainly to the old Hotel Canberra, a few hundred metres away from the parliament. A limit was put to the expansion of the press gallery—which occupied an area branded by officials as a fire trap. By ruthlessly transferring all non-essential committee, support and library staff out of the building, the presiding officers were able in 1978 to provide a separate office (specially equipped with a wash basin) for every MP and Senator.

There are a few elegant areas—the President of the Senate has a suite bigger than that of the Prime Minister, and has his own dining room and entertainment area (but that was excused because he was supposed to entertain the monarch there when she visited parliament). For the most part, however, it is fortunate for the public image of government that visitors are denied any sight of ministerial and members' offices and are confined to the King's Hall and the two Chambers where reality is obscured by the paraphernalia and the portraits and the pieces of historical record (like a copy of the Magna Carta, or the desk on which the Constitution Act was assented to).

MPs and Senators who are not members of the ministry spend less than one day in five in Parliament House each year. While parliament is in session they devote only Tuesday, Wednesday and Thursday to their parliamentary business; there is generally a two-week break after every three sitting weeks, a three-month break in summer and at least two months' break in winter. During a sitting week, most members fly to Canberra on Tuesday morning and leave on Friday morning. Senators arrange things better—they can generally get out of Canberra on Thursday night.

While they are in Canberra, most MPs and Senators see little outside Parliament House or their bedrooms. Most nights the House does not adjourn until 11 p.m. and after that there is little entertainment available in Canberra, except in the form of parties inside Parliament House. Most eat their meals at lunch and dinner time in the House: a few venture 200 metres to the Lobby Restaurant; very few would travel three kilometres to eat in the city. Once every two weeks they might get an invitation to a "national day" celebration at one of the embassies in Canberra, but most never accept these invitations.

Most parliamentarians will readily agree that Parliament House is an unreal world. In 1970 this feeling led the Members of the House to experiment with new sitting times. The experiment required two four-day sittings in successive weeks, and then a week's break. The sitting days were arranged Tuesday to Friday in week one, Monday to Thursday in week two. The aim was to persuade MPs to spend the weekends between weeks one and two in Canberra. This was supposed to give them the opportunity to see some of the other inhabitants of Canberra outside the parliament—diplomats, public servants and others, as well as enabling a greater concentration on parliamentary business. It was supposed to cut down on travel. The experiment lasted less than a year. The Standing Orders committee reported to the House of Representatives on 19 August 1971:

Your Committee was informed that experience had shown that the present sitting pattern had not proved as efficient or convenient as anticipated and that the large majority of Members favoured a return to the pattern of sittings previously in use. (House of Representatives Standing Orders Committee. Report together with Recommendations.)

What had happened was that most members had continued to fly out of Canberra as soon as they possibly could. Only MPs in Western Australia and the Northern Territory or distant parts of the other states were forced to remain in Canberra over the weekend. No travelling time was saved, and there was precious little additional contact made with Canberra. There wasn't any parliamentary business for those who stayed behind to attend to. Their secretaries and offices, as well as their families, were back in their electorates. The lure of the electorate and home was sufficient to persuade most MPs to waste half a day on Saturday travelling home, and to waste a similar time on Monday morning returning to Canberra. However in 1978 the government decided to resume the 1970 experiment: its main argument was that the four-day sittings would mean that MPs would spend fewer weeks of each year in Canberra.

For the average MP or Senator life within Parliament House is not particularly exciting. The ministry dominates the parliamentary village, both inside the chambers and out. Only ministers have the space to provide hospitality. Ministerial staff tend to treat MPs and Senators as lesser mortals and the media representatives treat them at best on a basis of equality. But the worst aspect of the place is that there is nowhere else to go, nothing else to see. MPs read far more newspapers than they would back in their electorates and they read mainly about politics. They talk and breathe politics with all the other inhabitants. It is a common bond which makes for incestuous living in a familial society which appears self-sufficient but is quite cut off from the real world.

Most of the people inside Parliament House recognise and disapprove of the isolated life they lead, but the last thing they want is to be excluded from its society. It encourages them to seek promotion within the system, not to escape it. One Senator, a year after he was elected, recalled that his first impression was that Parliament House was like a boarding school. In a more cynical mood he imagined it as a penitentiary, the inmates bearing stabwounds in the back, serving their sentences after being convicted of ambition. "Discipline", he reported, "is enforced by a system of bells which exert total psychological control over the inmates, and monitored by specially privileged old lags called 'whips' ... talking is mandatory. Behaviour is generally bad."

The "bad behaviour" aspect of Parliament House is not much discussed except as internal gossip. It is well known among the inhabitants of the place that some members regularly drink too much, that others pay no attention to their parliamentary duties (apart from voting when required), that still others spend a deal of time seducing, or being seduced by, other denizens of Parliament House. But any public suggestion of such behaviour is frowned on. Any member who speaks out against the conduct of his fellows is likely to be frozen out— witness the treatment meted out to the brash, young Andrew Jones in the 1960s who publicly criticised (unjustly perhaps) his fellow MPs' behaviour. All the inhabitants of Parliament House (including the press gallery) close ranks against any suggestion that their behaviour is anything but proper (or normal).

Many MPs and Senators find that their attendance at parliament puts strains on their family life. While most wives accept the necessity of acting as unpaid secretary to their husbands, many are unhappy at the regular separations necessitated by parliamentary and committee sittings. Some MPs and Senators spend long hours on the telephone each day, talking to their wives and being briefed on the latest family crises. Others make no secret of the fact that they enjoy the freedom that parliament gives them. Yet most clearly resent the time they have to spend in Canberra where attractions other than work appear non-existent because of the daily 9 a.m. to 11 p.m. schedule they must adhere to.

Personal questions aside, MPs and Senators often object to having to be in Parliament House because while they are in Canberra they are separated geographically from the trade unions, manufacturers, commercial or farming interests with which they tend to identify and upon whom they may rely or remain in contact with to formulate their political attitudes.

Most politicians in Parliament House probably devote at least as much effort to manoeuvring for power and influence among their fellows as they do to engaging in political activity directed at the external, public world of inter-party competition. A politician's effort to advance his own cause may involve him in trying to impress others in parliament (in opposition parties as well as his own), or journalists, or ministerial or parliamentary officers, or public servants. It may involve him in concentrating his efforts inside the parliamentary chamber, or in the party room, or in the library or the bar.

The political games that people play in parliament are not always directed towards politically logical ends. Personal antagonisms or ambitions not infrequently prompt a politician to take actions which directly or indirectly are meant to damage leaders or colleagues and which can have the side-effect of also damaging his party. Just what politicians are seeking to do at any given time is not always obvious; it does not always appear relevant to a political goal; and it may not be.

Under the influence of the Parliament House atmosphere, MPs will freely discuss both the faults and abilities of their own leaders and fellow party members, as well as of their opponents. Parliament House is always full of tales about the performances of individual ministers within cabinet—a supposedly secret body. Rumours generally originate with people who are in a position to know telling their views about rivals within their own parties to friends in opposing parties. Mostly this is done discreetly. But one senior Liberal once told a formal lunch where there were about twenty Labor Cabinet ministers and a few other Liberals that the performance of his own party was so bad that he hoped it would be decimated in the next election. (He was not reprimanded for his outspokenness.)

It is rarely possible to grasp all or even most of the political developments occurring within the walls of the parliamentary building in Canberra. Parliamentary proceedings and public posturing by politicians can be used to disguise or conceal the real direction of political activity. Any thorough understanding of the political process in the parliamentary institution must be based on an understanding not only of the procedures of the parliament but also of the way in which they may be manipulated. It must take into account not only what politicians do and say in the House of Representatives or the Senate, but also their activities in other parts of the building and their relations with its other inhabitants.

3 Functions of the Australian Parliament

In the ten years after Sir Robert Menzies retired from the parliament in 1966, Australia had six different prime ministers from three political parties. For nine of the ten years, the government of the day did not control a majority in the Senate. The period saw the establishment of scores of select committees and a network of Senate standing and estimates committees. The Governor-General became directly involved in the political and parliamentary processes of the nation by dismissing a government which controlled the House of Representatives and ordering a dissolution of both houses of the parliament. Two double dissolutions of the Parliament occurred as did the first-ever joint sitting of the two Houses. The Commonwealth gradually expanded its legislative power, with the approval of the High Court, while the states directly participated in actions designed to change the political composition of the Commonwealth Government. In 1977 the Liberal–National Country Party government proposed constitutional changes to close some of the loopholes which had helped it to achieve government in 1975 and which it had previously opposed at referendums.

In the light of these and other changes, what could be said of the functions which could be ascribed to the Australian Parliament?

Providing the national government

One of parliament's basic functions is to provide Australia with a government. This function is largely carried out by the Australian electorate, when voters choose the members of the House of Representatives. The leader of the party or group of parties which gains a majority of seats in the House is automatically sworn in as Prime Minister before the House is called together. Ministers are selected or elected from the members of the governing party or parties in both the House of Representatives and the Senate. Under normal circumstances, the government will remain in office until a House of Representatives election provides the Opposition with a majority of seats. The House of Representatives could (and did in 1941) force a change of government in mid-term. This would only happen when independents hold the balance of power and switch their allegiance, or when a split occurs within the governing party that is large enough to dissolve its majority.

If the government controls the House of Representatives but not the Senate, it will form the government for as long as the Senate majority decides to permit it to remain in government. By various devices, such as refusing supply, a Senate can force the dismissal of a government and/or an early election for the House or for the House and the Senate. This can happen at a time of the Senate's choosing (unless drastic changes are made in the way in which parliament votes supplies to the government).

Where a government does not control the Senate, it may find that the Senate will determine not only whether the government as a whole survives, but also whether individual ministers should retain their portfolios. This last power has not yet been invoked by the Senate, but there seems no logical reason to expect it to desist from doing so forever.

Monitoring the government

Parliament has developed many means by which individual back-benchers and the opposition generally can examine government administration and focus attention on administrative errors. Most recently, the parliament has used committees to perform this function, through the Senate's estimates committees and the House's expenditure committee. The committees, however, can do little more than skim the surface. Public servants and ministers rarely have to produce much of the information they are prepared to disclose if required.

Embarrassing questions and mistakes are mostly fobbed off. Essentially what comes out at these committees is what the government and its leading public servants want to come out. Parliamentarians generally do not have enough information on which to base a thorough probe of the administration—and when they do it will generally be declared a "policy" area where the government may decline to reveal everything, and public servants will refuse to say what kind of advice they have given ministers. The concept of ministerial responsibility is used as an excuse for limiting the amount of information which parliament is given.

Apart from using committees, MPs and Senators can use question time, grievance debates, adjournment debates, private member's motions or bills and urgency debates to draw attention to the government's administrative deficiencies. However, they again generally lack access to the type of information which is likely to embarrass governments, and unless they take very special steps to alert journalists to what they are planning to say, their words will normally remain buried in Hansard.

Public servants and ministers are normally anxious to dampen any criticism of their policies or administration. They do this by restricting information; when genuine complaints do emerge they treat cases as individual ones, and do not look for possible faults in the system. Ministers are ready enough to deal with grievances that are raised outside the chambers by MPs and Senators in order to reduce any criticism to which they might be subjected. (It is common for an MP airing a grievance to praise the way the minister intervened when it became clear that the particular complaint was sound.) MPs like their complaints dealt with in this way because they can then explain to their constituents what fine work they have personally done by intervening with the minister in the interests of the constituent. Grievances are reduced to a personal level and are treated on an individual basis.

Gathering information

Committee investigations and questions on notice are the major methods by which parliamentarians gather information. Questions without notice are rarely treated as a serious information-gathering process by either government or opposition. The success of parliamentary committees in gathering information depends on the extent to which they know what information they want. If they are staffed by experts in the paricular fields in which they are interested (not a common phenomenon), the prospects of getting most of the relevant information in the field are increased.

The parliamentary library research service is used less for gathering hard-to-get information than for assembling easy accessible facts. Contacts between the Library and Commonwealth departments provide a potentially useful way of obtaining information, but again the problem is that parliamentarians often don't know what questions to ask. Those who employ research assistants to help them in policy areas are likely to be better equipped in this task. Research assistants may also enable the MPs to process better the information which governments do make available to them through reports and papers presented to parliament. Few MPs try to digest very much of the information, and most rely on the press to locate anything of political significance and to summarise it. The press has extraordinary pressures of time, staff and space, that prevent it from doing this at all adequately. (For example, journalists have six hours to digest the significance of everything in the eight or nine booklets of the annual budget, and to write their reports. There is little combing of these documents after the publication of the budget, because by then the information is dated—even though much of the material might not have been properly analysed.)

Legislating

The Constitution assigns one major function to the parliament—making laws. However while laws are processed through the parliament, law making is effectively carried out before proposals reach the parliament. Legislation normally originates with the public service or with the cabinet. A legislative proposal will have to gain approval in general terms from the cabinet, and be approved in its specific terms by the cabinet's legislation committee. At least 90 per cent of legislation passed by parliament is in the form approved by the legislation committee.

What happens to the legislation after it passes through cabinet depends on which party is in government, and whether it controls the Senate. When Labor is in power, legislation has to be approved by the full caucus, often after detailed examination by specialist caucus committees. Thus the Labor majority of a parliament has to give its approval before the parliament gets the bill—and changes after the bill formally goes into parliament are rare. When the Senate is controlled by non-government parties, passage through the upper chamber is not guaranteed: amendment or rejection of the bill depends on the opposition's political evaluation of it. Whether a government has a "mandate" for a bill is used in the political argument about it but is in no way decisive.

Legislation in the form of regulations may be disallowed by either House of Parliament. These regulations are usually generated by the public service and then approved by the minister or by cabinet. A Senate committee which is guided by the part-time assistance of a lawyer looks at regulations and ordinances to ensure that they don't exceed the boundaries that the Senate has decreed for subordinate legislation. Parliament rarely approves legislation proposed by backbenchers.

Parliament has not created any machinery to review the effectiveness of the legislation that it passes.

Providing and auditing finance

The provision of money for government is a special case of parliament's legislative function. Special constitutional requirements give the government sole authority to initiate spending and taxation proposals. However the Senate's power to reject financial legislation, and in particular its power to reject the budget or supply bills, gives the Senate the means by which it may force a government to the polls.

Standing orders and constitutional requirements make difficult any detailed tinkering with budgets presented to the parliament, but opposition-controlled Senates may force political confrontations with governments over specific policy issues by requesting cuts or additional funds for particular departments or policy proposals.

The main function of checking the government's financial books has fallen on the Auditor-General, whose office was established by parliamentary legislation. He, and the Parliamentary Public Accounts Committee which follows up his reports, look to see whether the government has spent money in accordance with the requirements of legislation and regulations. Estimates committees in the Senate and the expenditure committee in the House are also concerned with checking the government's finances.

Publicising issues

Parliament provides a forum in which the major political parties can argue about the most important political issues of the day and draw attention to vital national and international problems. Most of the standing orders and procedures of the parliament appear designed to encourage this publicising of issues. Ministers may make statements about any policy matter to which they wish to draw attention; oppositions may reply. Governments may concentrate attention on specific policy proposals by legislating for their implementation; the opposition's ability to move amendments encourages it to develop its responses and allows it to present its alternatives in concrete forms. If an opposition wants to draw attention to governmental errors, it can move urgency motions. If it wants to present carefully thought out proposals in legislative form it can do so through private member's bills introduced on general business days. Debates on financial legislation allow opposition and government to speak about any subject of public affairs. So do debates on the address-in-reply at the opening of parliament.

Other parliamentary activities are also readily adapted to the business of publicising issues. Question time can be manipulated by either government or opposition to focus attention on particular issues or views. Finally, the opposition can move no-confidence motions to point up deficiencies in government administration or policies.

All these devices are used from time to time. Indeed many of them are frequently used. However, it is rare for a government or opposition to succeed in using parliament to develop and publicise particular issues. Any parliamentary day is likely to see the opposition and the government trying to cover half a dozen issues which are, or are sought to be made, topical. But in terms of what is featured on radio and television news bulletins and what appears in the morning press, it is rare for either government or opposition to have much success in focusing attention on their particular views of a particular subject.

Publicising issues depends less on what is done or said inside parliament than on what is done to persuade the media to give the issue public exposure. In recognition of this, ministers spend less time making statements to the House than they do holding press conferences or issuing statements to the media. The opposition rushes to put out press releases and to hold media briefings to answer the government: replying in parliament is of secondary importance. Which issues will be taken up on a particular day will often depend on what will "make the best television" or provide the best radio interviews. Current affairs programs find it easier to stage debates between politicians than to research issues—the former has its built-in balance between the political sides, the latter takes time and effort, and can lead to charges of bias. The result is an emphasis on personalities rather than policies, long a characteristic of Australian politics. Media proprietors and editors have encouraged their political (and general) reporters to concentrate their attention on the human drama of politics, on the personalities of governments and oppositions, on the personal idiosyncracies of political leaders. Editors seem to find it difficult to provide the space necessary to treat issues and arguments in any depth. Commercial radio and television rarely even try. Politicians, aware of the preferences of the media, play up to them.

Parliament's compressed sitting schedule makes its task of focusing public attention on political issues even more difficult. After time is taken up on the generalised debates on the budget, supply bills and addresses in reply, governments find they have to pass, on average, four or five bills through each house each day. While many bills are minor, the prospects of any important bill being debated for more than a day are low.

The speed with which bills have to be pushed through parliament reduces the possibility of an opposition producing sound alternative policies. An opposition might have to deal with a dozen new bills each week, and it will normally have only a week between the time it receives each bill and the time it has to debate it in which to analyse the bill, decide whether to support it or not, and decide what amendments, if any, it will propose. This schedule tends to force serious policy making outside the parliament. Party organisations take over the responsibility for developing policy programs for opposition parties. Those policies are produced at times when the parliament is not sitting. The parliamentarians have a large say in what policies are determined party leaders or spokesmen announce the policy and lead the debate on them; but this takes place away from the parliament.

Developing political leadership

Parliament attracts many men and women who want to be political leaders. The only way to become the prime minister or a minister is to become a member of parliament. Once there, an MP or Senator finds that he has to impress his fellows and/or his leader if he is to gain promotion to the front bench. That is achieved in various ways: by making thoughtful speeches in the parliament, the party room or in the electorate generally; by scoring political points in the parliament or in the media; by forming friendships and performing favours; by drinking in the right circles; or by demonstrating diligence. Little of it has much to do with parliament, which is only one of the forums in which an MP or Senator may choose to perform. Of course, it helps not to make mistakes in parliament, but brilliant performances don't necessarily earn promotion.

But then, brilliant parliamentary performances do not necessarily indicate whether a man or woman is a good minister or not. A minister has to be very poor indeed to make a mess of question time, and that is the most testing period he is normally likely to face. And long years in parliament don't provide much of a preparation for ministerial duties: at best they will teach an MP some verbal dexterity. It is more likely that he will learn that saying as little as possible is the best way to avoid being caught out. It is possible that he might, through his parliamentary experiences, come to place some positive value on lying and deceit.

Occasionally MPs gain promotion to the ministry without serving an apprenticeship on the backbench. They often seem awkward in their appearances in the House for some time afterwards. But a few months is all it takes for them to learn the various tricks of the trade and become accepted. Lack of parliamentary apprenticeship never seems to make any difference to their handling of their portfolios.

Parliament is also supposed to allow the opposition to show that its leadership team is a satisfactory alternative to the government of the day. Oppositions tend to take little notice of this aspect of parliament's role, even if editorialists sometimes do. Oppositions tend to be more concerned with demonstrating their capacities to the public through the media, rather than through the parliament.

Other functions?

Parliament, it appears, does have one very positive function: it determines who will be the government. This occurs mostly through the verdict of the electorate when it chooses the House of

Representatives. When the electorate has also chosen a Senate of a different political colour, the process of sorting out the government until the electorate next has a say can be bitter and bloody.

The other functions of parliament seem less significant if one is to judge from the way parliament performs. It is not very good at monitoring the government; its record on gathering information is poor; it contributes little to the legislation it passes at the behest of the executive; its handling of financial matters is no more effective than its handling of other legislation, but of course provides the way in which it may dispose of governments; it has taken second place to the media in determining what political issues should take the public's attention; the training it provides for political leadership is rudimentary and for administration non-existant.

Many of the parliamentary-type activities of MPs and Senators take place outside the parliamentary chambers. Legislation is affected and amended to a greater extent by representations of government MPs in ministers' offices, or in party committees or in meetings of the government party or parties, than it is in parliament itself. Ministers face more intensive questioning about the administration of their departments from individual MPs in letters and in personal interviews than they get in the parliament. Information about government activities and policies is more likely to be passed "on the quiet" than in the parliament.

According to Section One of the Commonwealth Constitution, the parliament consists of the Queen, the Senate and the House of Representatives. When the executive government and the two houses are under the same political control, the parliament seems of little importance—it is what the government says and does that matters. Parliament simply does as the government tells it. Parliament appears to be important as an institution in its own right only when its various elements are not in harmony, when the government is not able to determine what one of the houses will do. Thus the way in which parliament functions depends largely on the balance of the political forces in the three elements which together constitute the parliament of the Commonwealth of Australia. In that sense, parliament is wholly political in the way it functions: it has no important function independent of politics.

4 Government v. Parliament

The Prime Minister and his cabinet are the most important members of the parliament. They have the power of government. Insofar as the term "parliamentary government" has any meaning these days, it is in terms of government by these parliamentarians: parliament itself does not govern. It is not intended to discuss at length here whether it is more accurate in Australia to talk in terms of cabinet government or prime ministerial government (a debate which is unresolved in the British context). The position in Australia depends largely on whether there is a Liberal–National Country Party or a Labor Government, and varies to a lesser extent with the particular personality of the Prime Minister himself.

There can even be variation in the degree of prime ministerial dominance of the government under a given Prime Minister. Mr Fraser in his first two years was a very strong Prime Minister but after the 1977 election his position was even stronger. The lessening in the standing of his deputy leader, Phillip Lynch (including his removal from the Treasury), the strengthening of the Prime Minister's Department and the filling of senior public service positions with close associates of the head of the Prime Minister's Department, together with the fact of Mr Fraser's second overwhelming election victory left Mr Fraser probably the most powerful Prime Minister in Australia's history. While Labor leaders, like Mr Whitlam, might aspire to the same kind of power that Mr Fraser accumulated, the system tends to prevent this.

A Liberal Prime Minister decides which of his colleagues will be ministers, and is able to exercise a veto power over any National Country Party MPs who are put forward as ministers. (Mr Fraser exercised this power in 1977 to prevent Senator Sheil from becoming a minister, after his appointment had been announced and after he had been sworn in as an Executive Councillor—because Mr Fraser disapproved of statements Senator Sheil had been unwise enough to make about apartheid—statements which conflicted with Mr Fraser's views on that subject.) Liberal Prime Ministers also decide how big their ministries will be and whether to admit all ministers into the cabinet (since 1956 cabinet has been restricted to about a dozen ministers, approximately half the total ministry). They also have complete freedom in allocating portfolios among ministers, although the Liberal deputy leader can usually lay claim to whichever portfolio he wants (though this did not happen in 1969 and 1977).

Labor leaders share little of this power. Their ministers are chosen for them by the whole parliamentary Labor party (caucus) voting by secret ballot. Caucus decides how big the ministry will be. Caucus also determines whether the cabinet should be coextensive with the whole ministry (it bound Mr Whitlam to a twenty-seven-man cabinet). The Labor leader has the power only to determine which portfolios his various ministers should hold.

Because Labor's ministers are elected by the whole caucus and not selected by the Prime Minister, they tend to be more independent of prime ministerial control. They can resist a Prime Minister's encroachment into areas they consider fall within their own ministerial responsibility. Liberal ministers are less able to do so. In any conflict, a Labor minister can appeal to caucus for support as Dr Cairns unsuccessfully did in 1975; a Liberal minister may only resign, and plot to overthrow his leader, as Mr Fraser did in 1971.

The ministerial system thus requires different qualities of the leaders of the two parties. A Labor leader should ideally be a good chairman, and a good conciliator, who is able to get his team working, preferably in an agreed direction. A Liberal leader may adopt this approach, but he is more likely to impose the direction and enforce discipline among his team.

The near-irrelevance of parliament in the process of government is illustrated after each election. The votes for the House of Representatives electorates are counted and the party or coalition gaining the majority of seats is determined. If the winner had previously been in opposition, its parliamentary leader is called on by the Governor-General to form a government. Depending on the leader's wishes, the formal swearing in may take place within a few days of the election (as in 1972) or it may be delayed for a few weeks. The Parliament is not called together to make any decisions before the government is formed. Indeed, even the members of the winning parliamentary party may not be called together until after the formation of the new government. In 1972 Mr Whitlam had himself and his Deputy, Lance Barnard, sworn in as a two-man government, together occupying all twenty-seven ministerial positions. This was done before the Labor caucus met, and without the prior approval of the caucus. Had caucus considered the question, it would probably have disapproved Whitlam's actions. It was only after this interim government was formed that the parliamentary Labor party met to formally confirm Mr Whitlam as its leader and Mr Barnard as Deputy, and to select the other twenty-five men who would form the full Labor ministry.

In 1977 Mr Fraser did not hesitate to announce a twenty-eight man ministry to form his government despite the fact that by law his ministry was limited to twenty-seven. His extra minister (Sheil, see above) was sworn in as an executive councillor, and would have carried out his functions as a minister in the (obviously correct) anticipation that parliament would amend the Ministers of State Act to provide for the additional position.

At no stage does parliament have any say in who the Prime Minister should be, or which person should fill any particular portfolio. At best it has a veto power: it can vote no-confidence in the government as a whole or in a particular minister. Such a vote by the House of Representatives ought to require the resignation of the government or the particular minister, though Mr Fraser's interim ministry did not resign on 11 November 1975 when a vote was carried against it in the House of Representatives. The circumstances on that occasion were extraordinary, but then they are always likely to be extraordinary in a situation where no confidence is voted in the government of the day.

The relationship between the government and the parliament (in particular the House of Representatives, but sometimes the Senate also) is one of master and servant—the government being the master. In recent decades, Australian governments have set up special apparatus to better control the parliament and the work it does. This organisational hierarchy is directed particularly at controlling the operations of the House of Representatives—the Senate is considered as subsidiary to the House with regard to planning parliamentary business such as the timing of legislation and ministerial statements, and the planned answering of difficult questions. Though it may seem to demonstrate a lack of political common sense, it is nevertheless true that from 1967 to 1975, even when governments did not control the Senate, they made few arrangements to specially monitor events or plan for contingencies there, even though it was in the Senate that they were obviously going to face most parliamentary problems. This blind-eye approach to the Senate had particularly disastrous consequences for the Labor Government in late 1975 (which will be dealt with in a later chapter). Liberal governments have shared a similar disdainful attitude towards the Senate, though when Mr Gorton (a former

Senator) was Prime Minister, he did spend a little of his time courting the opposition Senate leadership and Senate independents.

The Leader of the House is the man responsible for the Government's planning of parliament's activities, including tactical decisions. This is a part-time job for a senior minister in the Cabinet, though during parliamentary sittings it can take most of the minister's time. Under the Labor Government in 1972-75 the job was handled by Fred Daly, who was given a comparatively light portfolio (Minister for Administrative Services) so that he could devote a greater proportion of his time to parliament. Under Fraser, the Leader of the House was the Country Party Deputy Leader and Minister for Primary Industry, Ian Sinclair. The Liberal Government's Senate Leader, Senator Reg Withers, took over Daly's old portfolio together with responsibility for conduct of the government's business in the Senate.

The opposition also designates a senior man to "shadow" the Leader of the House. Before 1972 the job was handled by the Labor Deputy Leader—Whitlam in the early 1960s, then Barnard. After 1975 the job was given to Gordon Scholes, who was Speaker in the House for most of the last year of the Labor Government. (Obviously a confusion of terminology can arise in talking about the "Leader of the House" on government and opposition sides, particularly as the positions are not held by the Leader of the government or the Leader of the opposition. There is no accepted title given to the opposition equivalent of the Leader of the House.)

More than most "shadow" ministers, the opposition's equivalent of the Leader of the House has an active role to play in the running of the House. He talks regularly with the Leader of the House in arranging the business of the House, deciding when bills and statements are to be debated. He has the leading role in determining the opposition's response to government initiatives in the Parliament, and in developing opposition tactics to harrass the government.

The government's Leader of the House has the assistance of a senior public servant, seconded from the Prime Minister's Department, to help him with both the routine work of scheduling parliamentary activities, and the more important political task of devising parliamentary strategy and tactics. The Parliamentary Liaison Officer, as this person is officially called, can in turn call on the resources of the parliamentary branch of the Prime Minister's Department for research and any other aid he needs.

The office of PLO was created in 1946, but it was only in the mid-1950s that the job took on its present significance. The Leader of the House took on the full running of the House at about the same time, when Harold Holt had the job. The first minister to be given the title of Leader of the House was Sir Eric Harrison in 1951. (A Senate PLO was first appointed in 1972, but for several years he had very little influence.)

The PLO acts often as a runner between the Leader of the House and his opposition opposite number, adjusting the parliamentary timetable to suit the convenience of both sides. He is the only official to have a permanent seat among the six places for officials on the government side of the chamber in the House of Representatives. He generally occupies it throughout question time, and whenever there is any uproar in the House which might require the Leader of the House to change the government's contingent planning for the day.

The determination of parliamentary tactics is essentially a matter for the Leader of the House and his opposition counterpart, in both Chambers. In the House of Representatives, the freedom given to the Leader of the House on tactical questions will vary with the interest the Prime Minister of the day has in such matters. Liberal Prime Ministers tend to leave the whole subject to the Leader—this was certainly Fraser's inclination. When Whitlam was Prime Minister he was consulted by Daly, his Leader of the House, several times a day while the House sat, but they did not discuss tactics with other ministers except where those ministers were directly involved on a particular issue. Parties in opposition tend to leave tactics to their Leader in the House—the man responsible for making arrangements with the government. But matters such as urgency motions and censure motions are generally decided by the full executive of the opposition party.

Since 1950 Australian governments have given responsibility for the supervision of legislation before its introduction to parliament to a special legislation committee of the cabinet. The committee is most frequently chaired by the Leader of the House (except, as in the case of the Whitlam government, when the Prime Minister puts himself on the committee). It generally contains the Leader of the Government in the Senate or the minister in charge of government business in the Senate (if the government has differentiated between the two functions), the Attorney General and other ministers with legal training. Officials always present at its meetings include two or three parliamentary draftsmen (the Parliamentary Counsel and his deputy, and the officer who drafted the particular bill) and the officers of the Prime Minister's Department including the two Parliamentary Liaison Officers. Officials are frequently drawn into discussions on questions of detailed drafting and scheduling.

The committee reviews the progress of proposed legislation through its various stages: bills which the legislation committee has not seen but which are due for introduction in the current or next session; bills which have been before the committee but are being redrafted; bills which have been cleared by the committee which have not yet been introduced into the parliament; and bills which have been introduced into one or other of the Houses and are in various stages of passage. But its main job is to review draft bills to see that they are satisfactory and in accordance with the government's general policies and the specific instructions approved by cabinet for the particular piece of legislation. After clearance by the legislation committee, bills are printed and prepared for introduction to the House at times decided either by the committee or by the Leader of the House. The Parliamentary Liaison Officer provides the Prime Minister and the Leader of the House with regular reports on the progress of legislation through the legislation committee and its schedule for introduction into, and passage through, the House.

It can be seen that Australian governments in the 1970s have adopted the view that running the parliament—or at least that part of it which is directly controllable, the House of Representatives—is too important and political a business to be left to chance—or to the parliament itself. The Speaker and the employed officers of the House have no say at all in the arrangement of the business of the House. The Leader of the House (helped by a government official, the PLO) determines what happens during the period devoted to government business (over 80 per cent of the House's sitting time) and also what happens in most of the remainder of the time the House sits. The time for government business is taken up essentially with the discussion of legislation. Statements by ministers on matters of government policy are not counted as "government business'. Nor is question time, which of course is entirely devoted to questioning ministers about their conduct of the government. The only times available to the opposition and backbenchers to use as they wish are the adjournment debate (usually the last forty minutes of the day's proceedings—it is not broadcast and gets little publicity), about an hour once every fortnight for general business, and such urgency debates on matters of policy as the opposition decides on and the government permits (generally a maximum of two a week taking a total of two hours). There is no Australian equivalent to the House of Commons' thirty or so opposition-days each year.

Mr Fraser tightened the government's management of the parliament after he became Prime Minister. In 1976, his cabinet formally decided that it would by-pass parliament as much as possible by relying heavily on executive authority and the use of regulations. The cabinet directed the Parliamentary Counsel to

> give particular attention in drafting bills to the possibility of leaving to regulations details that are liable to frequent change.

It required departments to examine

> existing Acts and Acts of a recurring kind administered by their
> ministers to see whether matters dealt with by the Acts but
> requiring frequent change could be left to regulations.... As far as
> possible, and bearing in mind the need for flexibility in special or
> unforeseen circumstances, not more than one bill to amend a
> particular Act be introduced in any one year. Parliamentary
> Counsel keep constantly in mind the possibility of combining
> related bills, in particular amending bills, but exercising his
> discretion having regard to the interests of the public, their
> advisors and the courts.

Cabinet further agreed

> not to limit the bills to be introduced in a particular year by
> determining limited programs, but that ministers, where appropr-
> iate, develop and introduce concurrently their legislative
> proposals so as to facilitate the use of cognate debates to the
> maximum possible extent.

The cabinet decision was leaked to one newspaper. But when the
story was printed, it drew not a single parliamentary protest. In
practical terms, MPs recognised that reducing the number of bills
which went before parliament, having legislative details spelt out in
regulations rather than Acts, and providing for simultaneous debates
on related bills (already a common occurrence) were not going to affect
the way the Australian Parliament approached its legislative function.
Reformers more concerned with asserting the superiority of parliament
over the administration, or concerned with the growth of delegated
legislation (a matter of concern as long as forty years ago) might have
hesitated to make these changes which the Fraser Government
accepted. However as a practical politician, Fraser was prepared to act
on the assumption that parliament's concern with legislation was more
political than legislative—that as long as parliament had the chance to
debate the principles or politics of each bill, it was mostly prepared to
leave the details to the "experts" in the public service (for later
amendment, if necessary).

The House of Representatives accepts its subordination to the
government of the day. Government backbenchers see their primary
duty as being to support the government—and that is probably what
the people who elected them want them to do. They are not, like
American congressmen, expected to have their own policies or their
own ideas about legislation. They are not expected to expose the faults
of the government they were elected to help put in office. Government
backbenchers do not regard themselves as supporters of the
government, they regard themselves as part (if a minor part) of the

government. There is no encouragement given to the idea that there
might be a higher duty—to the parliament itself—to tempt members
on either side to line up against their own party.

5 Party Discipline

In 1970 a group of Liberal and Labor backbenchers interested in parliamentary reform held a clandestine meeting in Parliament House. Their aim was to try to develop a bipartisan policy to create a new system of parliamentary committees, modelled on those being introduced into the Senate at that time. Behind the meeting was the knowledge that backbenchers outnumber those in the ministry plus the opposition front bench. It was thought that backbenchers on both sides sometimes had more in common with one another than with the leaders of their own party. And in particular it was believed that backbenchers could properly combine their efforts to develop a policy which would increase parliament's power and importance and which would give those on the backbench a worthwhile job of work to do in the everyday proceedings of parliament.

The scheme failed. It was not because the backbenchers could not agree on a common policy: they could and did. What they could not do, however, was buck the machine. They were talked out of their plan of action by their leaders. Although the Speaker of the House, Sir William Aston, came up with a workable proposal for committee reform behind which the backbenchers could unite, the leadership on both sides managed to prevent the implementation of the proposal. Had the backbench revolt succeeded, the parliament would have become a very different place. Its failure meant that the prospects of a future parliament being reformed against the wishes of the government of the day were so small that for practical purposes they did not exist.

After 1970 about the only subject on which backbenchers from different parties were able successfully to lobby their leadership was on parliamentary salaries—helped no doubt by the fact that the leadership as well as the backbench benefits from any increase in parliamentary salaries. Improvements in conditions for backbenchers have resulted not from backbench action but from government initiatives. (See Chapter Seven.)

Backbenchers have had slightly more success in lobbying their leaders for changes in their own party structures than they have in uniting to force changes which might benefit backbenchers from both sides. The 1970 revolt, for example, was headed off on the Labor side by diverting the efforts of the Labor backbenchers into (successfully) reforming the caucus committee system. On the Liberal side backbenchers were encouraged to (unsuccessful) efforts to have the Liberal ministry partly elected by the party instead of being wholly selected by the Prime Minister.

What prevented reform in 1970 was that the backbenchers accepted that, in the House of Representatives, voting against one's party was simply not done. No government need fear that its backbenchers will cross the floor to vote for an opposition measure or against a government proposal. On the Liberal side there is an occasional defection from the ranks in the Senate (Senators are elected for six years, not three as in the House, and different preselection methods allow Senators with strong State Executive support to enjoy a tiny bit more freedom than their straight-jacketed fellow Liberals in the House of Representatives). But in the House, dissent is simply not tolerated on either side.

Tight control over the government party or parties is maintained irrespective of the importance of the particular issue. The most trivial matter is deemed important to the prestige of the political parties. Even if an opposition discovers a patent error in a bill, an amendment in the House will not succeed unless the minister in charge of the bill decides to accept the amendment. Most ministers, faced with that situation, prefer to correct their errors by introducing their own amendments, generally when the bill reaches the Senate. They argue with backbench supporters who want to vote for an opposition improvement to a bill that the government and the Parliamentary Draftsman will need to look at the matter to see whether other clauses might also be affected. But the basic emotional argument, which so completely pervades Parliament House in Canberra that it rarely has to be voiced, is that the government will somehow suffer damage if a vote goes against it— irrespective of the issue on which the vote is taken. That feeling goes so deep that no party will allow its members a "free" vote (a vote according to their individual consciences) on non-party matters such as the siting of a new Parliament House, or abortion law reform, unless the other major party also agrees to have a free vote on the issue. Party discipline has virtually become an end in itself.

The Labor Party is generally blamed for the introduction of this state of affairs. When its first members were elected to the colonial parliament of New South Wales in 1891 they decided that only unity would give them the parliamentary strength to gain policy concessions from the major groups which then exercised power. They agreed on a "pledge" which committed them to vote together on subjects where they had determined an attitude jointly by majority vote. The "pledge" in form does not appear all-encompassing: each candidate for parliamentary election pledges

> on all occasions to do my utmost to ensure the carrying out of the principles embodied in the Labor Platform, and on all such questions, especially on questions affecting the fate of a Government, to vote as a majority of the Labor Party may decide in a caucus meeting. . . .

Caucus, however, takes a stand almost on every question before the parliament and members abide by those decisions. The habit extends to following the lead of the executive member handling a particular debate or procedure in the House on virtually all matters, whether they involve amendments to bills or procedures of the parliament.

Disciplined voting was apparent in non-Labor parties in the early 1890s and it extended to cover the whole field of parliament in step with the Labor approach. The Liberals have no "pledge", but their voting pattern in the House of Representatives shows almost the same degree of cohesion as the Labor Party's. In the Senate a few Liberals have been able to sustain a limited degree of independence; they have occasionally voted against their party leadership over legislative matters. But their example has not proved to be catching. A Liberal Senator has to have a strong power base in his own state party, or be so well known that his absence from the party ticket risks costing the party votes (or even be able to muster enough support to gain election as an independent), to risk his party's wrath by voting against it. It is probably no coincidence that the rebels tend to come from the smaller states, where the Senators may become well known and capable of building up personal electoral support. A show of independence, whether carried through into a vote or not, can condemn a Senator or MP to the backbench while his leader selects less difficult (though perhaps less able) people for advancement.

While the Labor Party set the example, the media have been largely responsible for turning party discipline into a virtue—or at least establishing that the absence of strictly disciplined behaviour in the parliament (and elsewhere) is a cardinal vice. The press and the political parties appreciate that numbers matter, particularly in a situation where parliaments are comparatively small. Party majorities are frequently very small—a government in the Commonwealth or State Parliaments will not infrequently have a majority of one after providing a Speaker. In such situations discipline is essential to the continued life of the government. Parties simply cannot afford to tolerate members who do not toe the voting line. MPs may be allowed some eccentricities, but voting against the party is generally not one of them.

In this political atmosphere, any MP or Senator who votes differently from his party (even to the extent of deliberately abstaining from voting) can expect reports of his deed to be emblazoned across the front page of the daily press, and broadcast on radio and television. Almost no other action he can take as a backbencher can guarantee him such substantial media coverage as voting against his party. The action will be characterised as a revolt, a party split or a defection, depending on the style of the news medium concerned. The merits of the case do not matter. The report will concern itself mainly with the fact that the individual or group of backbenchers voted against their party and with the political implications of this action. The issue involved will generally take second place to the fact of the defection from party ranks. It makes little difference whether the vote is on an amendment to minor legislation or on a question of national political significance.

The fact that the action will have resulted in publicity which is damaging to the party (it is a basic tenet that a party is damaged by any suggestion that there is a difference of opinion within its ranks) means that any MP or Senator who votes against his party knows that his action will damage his party. It is no excuse to suggest that a Senator might have been attempting to improve legislation brought forward by his own government. That, according to the parties and the press, is not as important as maintaining party solidarity. Members of parliament are not primarily parliamentarians, they are politicians. A member's first duty is to his party, not to the parliament, and if he forgets it both the party and the media will quickly remind him of their view of the proper priorities.

This tight discipline reduces the significance of party whips in the parliament. In Britain the whips have to work hard to keep attendances high and defections to a minimum in key divisions. In Australia the whips' jobs are far easier and essentially just mechanical. In the House, the two major parties both have a Whip and a Deputy Whip, and the Country Party just a single Whip. In the Senate each party has just a single Whip. The main job of the Whips is to count the votes and mark off division lists whenever the chamber divides. As part of this function whips co-operate across the chamber to arrange "pairs" of members who wish leave to be absent from the parliament for a particular division or a particular period. The Australian Parliament is marked by very high attendance records of its

members—though MPs and Senators are only seen in force at the start
of the day for question time and in divisions. For members of the ALP,
attendance at parliament and in divisions is compulsory. The caucus
rules state:

> 3(a) It shall be the duty of each member to attend and vote in his
> House in support of the propositions upon which the Party
> has established a collective attitude unless he has obtained
> leave from the Leader or a person authorised by him.

Discipline in the Lberal Party is not formally as strict as this, but the
Liberals' obligation to be present is made abundantly clear to them.
For example in 1976, when the Liberal and Country Parties had their
largest majority ever in the House of Representatives, on one occasion
half a dozen Liberals missed a division which was called unexpectedly
after a luncheon adjournment. Although the government still had a
majority of about thirty, each of those absent from the division
without leave received a letter from the party Whip noting his absence
and warning that any future absence would be reported to the Prime
Minister.

Ministers sometimes have to be absent to attend meetings with state
or foreign counterparts, and normally they are readily granted "pairs"
with members of the opposition who wish to be away on political or
private business. The Prime Minister and Leader of the Opposition
operate a permanent "pair" which allows them to be absent from most
divisions. If they wish to be present, because of the importance of the
vote, or because one of them has proposed the particular motion, they
make sure the other is aware that the "pair" will not operate for that
division. There is no natural "balance" between the number of people
from both sides wanting to be absent at any one time, and it is the
function of the Whips to provide the balance, to ensure that a member
who is present in parliament does not come into the chamber when a
vote is being taken if he is "paired" for that division, or that day.
Members who are paired to an absent MP don't necessarily take a
holiday—they are paid attendance money, which is geared to their
presence in the chamber at some time during the day, not to whether
they vote.

The work of the Whips ensures that in both chambers, the results of
divisions normally reflect quite precisely the overall state of the parties
in the two houses. The Whips ensure that governments are not
accidentally defeated on bills. If accidents do occur, a government can
recommit the particular clause or stage of the bill—but that takes time
and trouble and it is often as much in the interests of the opposition as
the government to see that everything is kept tidy. If a pair is broken
accidentally, it is likely to be noticed while the count is on: the

particular MP or Senator will be told by his Whip and then will seek leave (which will be given) to withdraw from the division before it is concluded.

The other function of the Whips is to compile lists of speakers for the various bills and other matters being debated in the chambers. Sometimes this will mean cutting down on some of the volunteers wishing to participate in a particular debate (to keep numbers within the limits set by the Leader of the House); at other times it will mean co-opting reluctant MPs to take on a subject they know nothing about to fill in the time providing for the debate. In the House, speakers on both sides will be exptected to take up the full fifteen or twenty minutes allocated to them by the standing orders. When they don't, the Whips get into a flap, trying to find additional speakers to keep the program going.

The Whips are not highly paid for their efforts (in 1977 the chief government Whip in the House of Representatives was paid $4250 in addition to his ordinary salary. This was $500 to $3000 more than the other Whips received). Nor does a Whip normally rank highly in the party's hierarchy. The one exception to the rule was created by the Liberals in 1973 when R. V. Garland, as chief Whip while the party was in opposition, sat as a member of the opposition executive. Australian parties do not follow the British practice of allowing the chief Whip to sit as a member of the cabinet. However good Whips can be very useful to the party leadership. They tend to have a better knowledge than other members of how backbenchers feel about particular issues or particular leaders. They are good "numbers" men and ought to be able to estimate fairly accurately how a particular vote will go in a party meeting. The nature of their job means they have to know all the parties members fairly well, know their foibles, how they can be approached to seek a favourable vote—in general, how they can be best cultivated.

In 1967-68 Gorton had the Liberal Whips in both the House and the Senate working on his behalf. While they may not have been the most astute politicians (Gorton rewarded their support by giving them ministerial jobs: neither was a success), they were good at organising numbers which was what the leadership contest was about.

The Liberal experience in 1975 also demonstrated the importance of the Whip. Snedden found himself in the awkward position of having to find someone other than his Whip, Garland, to be his "numbers man" when he was trying to defend his leadership against Fraser. In the period leading up to the crucial ballot, Garland was a supporter of the challenger, Fraser.

Discipline is not exercised entirely through Whips and control of party endorsement. Having won his party's leadership, Fraser set about strengthening his position in the traditional way of Australian politics—by rewarding his supporters. But the 1975 general election which gave Fraser's government control of both houses also created a potentially difficult parliamentary situation for Fraser. With a record majority, most of his backbenchers would be underworked and those with the most vulnerable seats (the oncers) were not likely to be kept in line by the promise of future promotion or even the threat of loss of endorsement. Fraser did not follow the usual sort of advice: to create more and more parliamentary committees to keep the backbenchers busy. Instead he concentrated on establishing close and continuing personal relationships with as many backbenchers as possible. He tried to invite at least half a dozen backbenchers every week to dinner at the Lodge, and even more were invited to drop into his parliamentary office for drinks late on parliamentary sitting evenings. Party committees, rather than parliamentary committees, were used to keep his MPs occupied.

Fraser did not completely ignore the question of parliamentary committees. He handed the problem over to a special parliamentary party committee that was chaired by his Senate Whip, Fred Chaney and that included his former House Whip, Garland. After the 1977 election, which saw most of his oncers turned into twicers, Fraser began to take up some of the Chaney committee recommendations. He also turned to a less conventional source for advice on what to do about keeping his backbench busy and under control—his own public service staffed department. Thus even the bureacracy was brought into the battle to keep the parliamentary party firmly under the control of the government.

6   Parliament at Work

Parliament does not govern; and the legislation it passes is mostly dictated by the government of the day. Yet despite its apparent powerlessness, it does play an important role in the Australian political process. Successful ministers and ambitious backbenchers devote considerable efforts to mastering its procedures and demonstrating their own parliamentary talents. They do not do so because of some self-deluding belief in the power of parliament. They recognise that their actions inside the parliament can result in political advantage or disadvantage for themselves or their party outside the parliament. They appreciate that parliament can be used as a platform to expound or expose, or as a shield to hide, the activities of a government. They also consider that while what happens in the parliament will rarely have any direct affect on the mass electorate, it may have very considerable indirect consequences.

This chapter examines five aspects of the parliament at work to look at the interaction between parliamentary activity and "politics". It aims to illustrate the main rules of the parliamentary game, and the way in which the players may manipulate them to achieve their various ends.

Government under attack: question time and urgency debates

Question time is the most "political" aspect of the daily procedure of the House of Representatives. It is supposedly the time when ministers have to account for their administration to members of parliament. It is parliament's most popular activity, in terms of attendance at least. Ministers who are in Canberra must attend; backbenchers try to be present.

As discussed below, the contest between those who ask the questions and those who answer them is most unevenly weighted in favour of those on the receiving end of the questions. To use a cricketing analogy, only one side has a chance to bat and put any runs on the board. The analogy is not perfect, because both sides share equally in bowling up problems for the batsmen (though the difficult ones come mainly from the opposition). But the important political fact is that only one side can score—the other, to make any impression on the spectators, has to skittle plenty of ministerial wickets and keep the scoring by the government to a minimum.

Most attention is focused on the leaders of the respective teams. The Leader of the Opposition asks the most questions, and the Prime Minister tends to give most of the answers. How well they perform can help determine how long they retain their jobs. Members of the various parliamentary parties constantly judge the performances of their fellows and their leaders in parliament, and at least once every three years they get the opportunity to support or throw out their own party leader. While the voters may take little notice of what happens in parliament, parliamentarians do, and their judgement of their leaders appears to be based largely on parliamentary performance.

The mood of a parliamentary party varies with the performance of its leader in question time. If, over a period of months, the party sees its leader being constantly outwitted and out-performed by the other side, its morale suffers. Changes in the morale of the parliamentary party don't have immediate or direct effects outside the parliament, but it does seem that if there is a deterioration of morale for six months or so, party workers and then the public do become aware of it and are affected by it. This is impossible to quantify but people in parliament believe it and their own actions (such as disposing of the party leader) are sometimes predicated upon their acceptance of the truth of the proposition.

Between 1967 and 1975, four successive leaders of the Liberal Party lost support (and three of them were removed from office) because they did not pay enough attention to performing well in the parliament. In question time, in major no-confidence debates and in the general handling of parliamentary tactics, Whitlam repeatedly demonstrated his parliamentary superiority over Harold Holt, then John Gorton, then William McMahon and finally Billy Snedden. In the first three cases, the political consequences of his demonstrations of superiority were neither immediate nor startling but they could be discerned. The initial effect of Whitlam's parliamentary success was confined to praise for the leader from his parliamentary followers (and to a much lesser degree from a few areas of the press). The Prime Minister who had suffered the drubbing at Whitlam's hands initially tended to lose some respect among his followers. There were moves under way to challenge Holt's leadership at the time he drowned at the end of 1967: these moves were either caused, or encouraged, by his poor performances against Whitlam, mainly in the House.

The most dramatic example of the effect of a demonstration of parliamentary inferiority occurred with Snedden in 1975. Late in 1974, Snedden had survived fairly comfortably a challenge to his leadership by MPs acting on Malcolm Fraser's behalf. Having beaten off this challenge, Snedden should have been safe until the next election. But in 1975 he dismayed his followers by his failure to show leadership at crucial times and, more importantly, by his ineptness in the House. Snedden was caught out by the decision of the N.S.W. Premier, Mr Lewis, to replace Senator Lionel Murphy (who had retired to take up a High Court appointment) with a non-Labor Senator. This was contrary to established practice and while there seemed to be some political advantage for the opposition in such an appointment, there was general unease about breaking the convention. Snedden was apparently against the appointment but he issued a statement in which he said he had no power to intervene in any way. Whitlam used question time in the House for a bitter attack on Snedden's lack of leadership, in a speech prepared well before the House sat. Snedden, listening to Whitlam's denunciation, blurted out a childish and meaningless interjection, "Come on, woof, woof!" His fellow Liberals were astounded. Over the next few weeks Whitlam kept up the pressure on Snedden, to the evident embarrassment of many of Snedden's supporters. For weeks Liberals wandered the parliamentary corridors discussing the weakness of Snedden's parliamentary performances with journalists, and each other.

The parliamentary highlight came after Cope was removed from the Speakership. On the next ordinary sitting day, Snedden moved a no confidence motion in Whitlam. Whitlam, who had anticipated the move, proposed an amendment censuring Snedden and the Country Party Leader, Anthony, for failing to use their influence with their MPs to have them obey standing orders. Whitlam's speech attacked Snedden, claiming that he was only concerned with acting in a way which would help him stave off the next challenge for leadership from Fraser. Whitlam was worried when he left the Chamber that he had gone too far in his speech. He was right to be concerned. The moves against Snedden accelerated and during the next short recess of Parliament, Snedden was forced to call a special meeting of the Parliamentary Liberal Party: Snedden was deposed and replaced by Fraser.

The Prime Minister does not need to be a better parliamentary performer than the Leader of the Opposition to out-perform him in the House. The standing orders and the fact of being in government give the Prime Minister enormous advantages over the Leader of the

Opposition, all other things being equal. A Prime Minister can use question time to berate and belittle his principal opponent; the Leader of the Opposition can do little more than listen to whatever insults the Prime Minister chooses to direct at him. Any retort can only be delivered in the form of an interjection which can be answered by an appeal to standing orders (which will generally be dismissed) or in the form of a further question which will give an adept Prime Minister yet another opportunity to attack his quarry.

In 1976 Whitlam was not able to overcome the natural disadvantages of being in opposition when faced with Fraser as Prime Minister. Fraser showed himself able to use the forms of the House, and willing to do so to Whitlam's discomfiture in much the same way as Whitlam as Prime Minister had used them to attack Snedden, though without quite the devastating result. Yet it did have an effect. Whitlam's detractors within the ALP pointed to his poor showing against Fraser as a reason why he should be displaced from the leadership before the next elections. In May 1977 Hayden failed by only two votes to take over the leadership from Whitlam. But the party which re-elected Whitlam had little faith that he would be able to best Fraser in an election campaign: it went into the 1977 election certain that it would be defeated.

A casual observer would reasonably conclude that the forms of parliament provide an opposition which is doing its job properly with very considerable opportunities to expose and politically damage a government which is failing to perform adequately. During question time, ministers can be put on the spot to answer for the administration of their departments. During urgency debates, two or three times a week, the opposition can choose a topic for debate which will try to highlight a particular deficiency of the government. Together these two activities, which can occupy the first hour and a half of each sitting of the House (and even longer in the Senate) would appear to provide the opposition with great advantages in its parliamentary contest with the government.

The appearances, however, are deceptive. Oppositions rarely succeed in inflicting political damage on the government during question time. The impact of any concerted attack is immediately lessened by the fact that in question time an opposition question is immediately followed by a question from the government benches. (The opposition in the House of Representatives is granted the right to ask a supplementary question without the intervention of the government question very rarely—perhaps once every few years when a Speaker is feeling particularly indulgent.) The question from the government backbench is usually friendly, giving the minister to whom it is directed an opportunity to expound on government policy or to attack the opposition's policies or personalities. Questions from government backbenchers are frequently communicated to ministers before question time, so that answers can be properly prepared. Sometimes the questions are prepared by ministers and handed out to backbenchers to ask—these are referred to as Dorothy Dixers, named after the "Dear Dorothy Dix," advice to the lovelorn newspaper column. So the government can always use question time to attack the opposition—and it usually does.

Opposition members with questions which might provide difficulties for the government have several hurdles to clear before they can achieve their object. First they have to get the Speaker to call them. This is a tedious and frustrating battle, as there is great competition among opposition members for the right to ask questions. Normally an opposition member will be allowed to ask about one question every three weeks depending on the size of the opposition. The Speaker actually keeps a score card on his desk to ensure that everyone gets approximately the same number of questions—if they wish to ask them. These score sheets are regularly provided to the Whips who make them available to all MPs. The Leader and Deputy Leader of the Opposition are exempted from this battle for the right to ask a question: the House has adopted the practice that they get preference over all other opposition members when it is the opposition's turn to ask a question. It is not uncommon for an opposition leader to ask three questions during a question time in which the oopposition would have had the opportunity to ask a total of only eight or nine questions (this is about the average). And the Deputy Leader normally asks at least one question.

The next major hurdle is to get the question approved by the Speaker. The more contentious a question is, the more likely it is to infringe the standing orders which severely limit the content and style of questions. Provocative questions are likely to prompt the Speaker to invoke standing orders either on his own initiative or at the prompting (through the taking of points of order) of ministers or government backbenchers.

The final hurdle is to get an answer from the minister. Ministers can dodge questions in a number of ways. The normal method of evasion is for the minister to answer only part of a question and bring into the answer irrelevencies which involve an attack on the opposition or a strong defence of a praiseworthy government activity—not necessarily the one he has been questioned about. The question can be dismissed in a few words or sentences, or it can be answered with a five-minute harangue. If the minister is really in trouble, he can reply simply by asking the questioner to "put the question on the notice paper".

The ability of ministers to dodge questions is well understood by oppositions which rarely take the trouble to organise concerted campaigns during question time. Perhaps once a year the opposition leadership will decide that the government is particularly vulnerable to a question time attack. It will then organise what questions are to be asked and in what order. Members of the opposition will be instructed not to compete for the speaker's eye during question time: only the questioner who has been chosen by the opposition to put the next question in the series will rise.

Such tactics are not popular with oppositions, however. It is often difficult to persuade all members of the opposition that the attack will bring any benefits because ministers can avoid difficult questions and can use their own questions to damage the opposition. A backbenchers on the opposition side also tends to consider that the interests of his particular electorate are better served with a parochial question relating to its particular problems. Such parochial questions normally constitute more than half the questions in each question time period.

While it would seem that oppositions must inevitably be able to find questions to which the ministers cannot supply answers, in fact the subject matter of questions tends to be fairly predictable and ministers can prepare themselves with answers before they enter the House. Many questions are based on newspaper or radio reports of the day. Most are based on issues which are current. For all these subjects affecting their portfolios, ministers will have briefs prepared by their departments.

Each day before question time, both Whitlam and Fraser devoted half an hour or more to preparing themselves for whatever they might be asked. The procedure has been for the Prime Minister to hold a half-hour briefing session with his staff in his office immediately before the parliament met. By the time that meeting began, he would generally have read briefing notes prepared by his own department and by the department of Foreign Affairs on issues which might be raised by the opposition or by government backbenchers. The briefing session would be attended by the senior staff from the Prime Minister's office (about half a dozen), plus representatives from the Prime Minister's Department (usually including several deputy secretaries) and the Foreign Affairs Department (normally the Public Information Officer). Fraser often included the Federal Director of the Liberal Party, Tony Eggleton, at question time briefings but Whitlam didn't like the idea of outside party officials being present. Those present would suggest questions which might be asked and answers which could be given. Sometimes they would suggest questions it would be useful to have backbenchers ask, and if the Prime Minister approved, these would be drafted and handed out to an appropriate MP. Fraser was more likely than Whitlam to consult or to bring into the briefing ministers who were likely to be in for a tough question time that day.

Other ministers would not normally attempt such detailed preparation (unless they were aware they were to be under a sustained opposition attack). They are normally supplied by their departments with comprehensive notes on every subject in their portfolio which might be queried in parliament. Ministers try to memorise these briefs and/or take them into the House for question time. It is quite common to see a minister fishing around in his folders for an answer as a question is being asked. He then takes it to the main table, lays it on the dispatch box and uses it at his discretion. A minister who reads from it too blatantly can be called on by the opposition to table the document from which he is quoting—but if the document is confidential the minister may decline to do so, and it is up to the minister to say whether or not it is confidential.

While ministers can avoid giving direct answers in question time, they cannot normally opt out of debates on current issues initiated by the opposition as "urgency" debates. Such a debate is formally known as a "discussion of a matter of public importance". Urgency debates are usually initiated by the opposition leadership—though perhaps once in two months the government, through one of its backbenchers, will bring on the discussion on a subject allowing the government to attack opposition policies. Two or sometimes three are permitted each week, with a maximum total time of about two hours every week. The opposition leadership determines the subject for the debate and notifies the government of the topic about an hour before question time begins. After questions and ministerial statements, the Speaker announces that he has received a letter from the Honourable member for (the opposition spokesman leading the debate) stating that he wishes the House to debate a definite matter of public importance, namely (then follows the topic). When he has received a letter from both government and opposition proposing urgency debates, the Speaker then announces which debate he considers the more urgent and important. He calls on those who support the debate to stand. The opposition (or government as the case may be) then stands and provided that more than eight members indicate support, the debate then proceeds. The two principal speakers get fifteen minutes each, and the remainder (generally only one or two more from each side) ten minutes each. The debate concludes when no more speakers rise to catch the eye of the presiding officers or when the government moves successfully that the business of the House be called on. There is no vote on the subject of the matter of public importance.

The opposition chooses its subject matter for these debates to try to highlight those political issues of the day on which it thinks the government is vulnerable. The issues will be well known and the minister responsible will invariably be well briefed on the subject because it will have been something about which he has been concerned. For example, during May 1976, urgency debates in the first two weeks concerned:

- The urgency for the Australian government to use all avenues available to it to bring about a genuine act of self-determination for the people of East Timor.
- The necessity for the government to make a prompt commitment to selective decentralisation.
- The government's failure to honour its election commitments on Medibank.

On all these topics ministers would have needed little, if any, additional preparation for a debate. However on being notified of the opposition's intention to raise the matter as an urgency debate, the ministers would probably have had their staff check with their departments for any additional material which could be used. By the time he went into question time, a minister would have had a reasonable idea of what he would say in the debate. During question time his staff would probably give him even further information, sometimes including actual speech notes and material with which he could attack the opposition. Staff would also supply other government speakers with material they could use in the debate.

The opposition would have had more time to prepare speeches. Subjects for urgency debates are generally determined by the opposition parliamentary executive on a Monday for the coming three days, and sometimes even further ahead. All the opposition speakers would be chosen and have the opportunity to prepare their speeches at least a day in advance, except in circumstances where the topic for the urgency debate arose suddenly as a result of extraordinary political developments.

While urgency debates have the potential to provide a good forum, they rarely arouse much interest. The press tends to disregard them. Reports of them are generally tucked away on the inside parliamentary pages of morning newspapers and are mostly ignored by radio and television unless one of the leading speakers hits on some compelling piece of information or vituperation which he makes sure the press gallery is aware of. If a speaker really wants to get publicity, he does not rely on the one or two reporters who will have sat through the debate to tell their colleagues what he said.

The Senate handles urgency debates somewhat differently from the House. In the upper chamber, urgency debates are initiated by the opposition proposing that the Senate adjourn to some time other than that fixed for the normal time of the next meeting of the Senate, so that a particular matter of urgency might be debated. The mover of such a motion must give notice of it in writing to the President one and a half hours before the Senate sits (so again the government can prepare itself for the debate). He must also be supported by four other Senators (which means that an independent must get the support of four other independents or other party senators to bring on a debate). An important difference between the proceedings in the two houses is that the Senate debate does conclude with a vote, so the government does have to declare its feelings about the motion. Senate urgency debates, which can continue for up to three hours, are far more rare than in the House however.

Question time in the Senate also has a different flavour because so few ministers are located in the Senate. Five or six Senate ministers have to answer questions directed at the whole range of the ministry. As a consequence, it is far more common in the Senate to hear ministers suggesting that questions be put on notice, or saying that the question will be referred to the appropriate minister for an answer. So question time in the Senate is far less significant than in the House unless the opposition can focus its attention on the actions of a minister sitting in the Senate. A Senate minister can get a far worse savaging than a minister in the House: as there are fewer Senators to ask questions, it is far easier for the opposition to organise a quite intensive and prolonged barrage of questions.

Questions on notice are an important non-part of the procedure of the House. Members may submit any number of questions on notice to the Clerk of the House. If they are within the standing orders they are printed in the daily notice paper on every sitting day for the weeks, months and sometimes years it takes for them to be answered. The answering takes place by means of a letter from the Minister to the MP, and the answer is printed in the back of the daily Hansard. In the Senate most of the answers are read out by ministers after questions without notice have been dealt with.

As opposition leader in the 1960s, Whitlam used the device of questions on notice to gather an enormous amount of information on government activities and detailed statistics on everything from transport to urban economics, from northern development to the functioning of interdepartmental committees. The questions were worked up by Whitlam and his staff, and the answers provided generally showed the way to more questions. By the late 1960s, Whitlam was putting dozens of questions on notice every week and the government was beginning to complain at the work load being imposed on departments to find answers. However, this was about the only way the government did have to provide factual information to the parliament. The committees were paying little attention to the functioning of government; questions without notice could not secure the detailed, factual, often statistical information that Whitlam was after. The information he gathered was not only used in the parliament: it was used with damaging effect in by-elections where Whitlam was able to use the government's own statistics to point to deficiencies in government policies in the particular area, and it was used in the formulation of new Labor policies.

The weapon of questions on notice was later used with very great effectiveness against Whitlam when he was Prime Minister. Throughout 1975 the opposition put together a series of questions on the loans affair which dragged the government deeper into difficulties with every answer it provided. The problem for the government was that the opposition was being fed some of its questions by a senior Treasury officer who knew, or could guess, more about the activities of ministers than Whitlam himself knew or was able to find out from them.

The one device that was not used by the opposition over the loans affair (until it was all over) was the censure motion. While theoretically the most devastating weapon of an opposition—if successful such a motion should result in the government's resignation—the censure motion tends to be a squib in its use in the House of Representatives. Governments simply don't take it seriously, frequently limiting its discussion to just two or three speakers a side. As the normal practice is for question time to be abandoned if a censure motion is debated, the censure tends to be unpopular with oppositions as well. An urgency debate will normally be used instead, and while it may not be reported very widely, neither will the censure motion.

The Presiding Officers

The Speaker of the House, though the presiding parliamentary officer, is held in fairly low standing by most Australian parliamentarians. He is not regarded as being an important political figure and his activities are not normally regarded as having political consequences. Ceremonially, historically and theoretically the Speaker of the House and the President of the Senate stand high in the parliamentary pecking order. The official Commonwealth order of precedence ranks them after the Prime Minister but before all his ministers. (It used to rank the President above the Speaker. Whitlam, who wanted to assert the House's authority and status, had the order of precedence changed to provide that precedence went to the presiding officer with the greater seniority—the Speaker is normally elected a few hours before the President.) The presiding officers are on the same high level of salaries and allowances as ministers, and like them are entitled for the rest of their days to be called "The Honourable". Politically, however, they rank with backbenchers. The speakership has been held by an occasional maverick or eccentric who has insisted on upholding what he considered to be the rights of the House against his government. But such clashes have rarely resulted in more than passing embarrassment for the government. But the following dramatic example shows that a government can suffer politically if it installs the wrong man as Speaker.

On 17 February 1975, Mr Speaker Cope was having a bad morning. It was the second anniversary of his uncontested election as Speaker of the House but the mood was far from festive. During the second question of the morning, he had had to deal with repeated points of order, interjections and disruptive conduct as the Labor Minister for Social Security, Bill Hayden, attempted to attack the Liberal opposition's attitude to Medibank. Hayden's answer was so long, provocative and damaging to the opposition that eventually they moved that Hayden be no longer heard. The motion was defeated, but when Hayden finished Prime Minister Whitlam decided that question time had gone on long enough. However the confrontation between government and opposition continued as first the Leader of the Opposition, Billy Snedden, and then Whitlam made personal explanations. Then the Minister for Labour and Immigration, Clyde Cameron, took a personal explanation; he was followed by the opposition shadow minister Michael MacKellar. Then a Liberal backbencher, Dr Jim Forbes, took a point of order accusing Cameron of lying and a heated series of exchanges followed in which Cameron tried to have the allegation withdrawn. Cope failed to deal strongly with the developing situation and Cameron, when brought to order by the Speaker, said, "Look, I don't give a damn what you say. I..." As opposition members called on the Speaker to "name" Cameron, Cope repeatedly asked Cameron to apologise. Whitlam, furious at the disorder and at Cope's handling of the situation, interjected "No" when Cope asked, "Is the Minister going to apologise?" Cope then said, "I name the Minister for Labor and Immigration".

Normally when a Speaker "names" a member of the House in this fashion, the Government's Leader in the House moves that the member be suspended—the suspension is for twenty four hours if it is a first offence for the session, a week if it is the second—but on this occasion the Government did not move for suspension. The opposition's Ian Sinclair then moved suspension and the government members rose to cross to the opposition benches to vote against the proposal. As Whitlam moved to cross the floor he paused by the Speaker's chair and whispered in Cope's ear, "If this motion is defeated, and it will be, you ought to resign". No one in the House heard the comment but towards the end of the division, opposition members drew attention to Whitlam's action in speaking to Cope.

Former Liberal Prime Minister William McMahon said the Prime Minister's conduct was "totally disorderly and appeared to be offensive and threatening". Cope answered that "What the Prime Minister said to me is my own business".

Finally, Cope, to cries of shame from the opposition, announced the result of the division as 55 ayes and 59 noes and added "Gentlemen, I hereby tender my resignation as Speaker of the House of Representatives". To more cries of shame, he called for order and added that he would resign in writing, to the Governor-General. He then called on a deputy Speaker to take the chair and retired to his office. Late in the afternoon he sent his formal letter of resignation to the Administrator (the Governor-General was overseas). That evening the House elected Gordon Scholes as the new Speaker.

Cope need not have resigned. Earlier speakers had suffered reverses at the hands of the government which had put them in the chair, but none had resigned. In the early 1950s the Liberal Speaker Archie Cameron seemed continually at war with Prime Minister Menzies. Cameron suffered three voting defeats when the government turned against him. On one occasion, when Cameron insisted that Menzies withdraw a comment, Menzies refused and moved instead that Cameron's ruling be dissented from. During the division a Labor frontbencher, Eddie Ward, asked Cameron whether he would leave the chair if the motion was carried. The Speaker replied, "It will not have the slightest effect on me." [Hansard, 6.3.1953. p.674].

Cameron was a strong Speaker, Cope was not. Indeed Cope's weakness as Speaker was never so well illustrated as in his acceptance of Whitlam's whispered order that he resign. He could have simply ignored Whitlam or he could have taken the fight into caucus.

When the Labor caucus selected Cope as its nominee for Speaker after the 1972 elections, it was not because it considered that he was the best man for the job. It was, rather, a reward for mustering numbers in the party, and for long service. In 1974 when caucus again chose Cope as its nominee for Speaker, he had already demonstrated his inability to control the House. However, on that occasion caucus had just re-elected all the Labor ministry and was obviously intent on not making changes.

Cope's lack of control of the House enabled the opposition to make political mileage out of the disorder in the House. The government had to resort to using its numbers to force its measures through and to gag its opponents more than was politically acceptable. The constant uproar during question time in particular distracted attention from the very real concessions which Labor made to increasing the opportunities for backbenchers of both sides to speak in adjournment debates and on general business of their own choosing. The government had to accept the odium resulting from the excessive use of numbers to control the House; a reasonable Speaker exercising some authority would have been able to stifle the blatant disruption of the House's proceedings and prevent a situation arising in which either government or opposition had to suffer politically. Certainly the House was far better managed by Cope's successor, Scholes, and the government had far less need to resort to tough tactics in suppressing disruption. The difference between the two was that Scholes knew his standing orders, was prepared to enforce them and was willing to "name" people who deliberately tried to disrupt the proceedings of the House.

The Speaker of the House of Representatives derives his high formal status and salary from the association of his office with that of the Speaker of the House of Commons, who can trace his lineage back to 1377. As his name suggests, the Speaker's original role was speaking to the King on behalf of his fellow members in the House of Commons. It was not always a popular duty—nine early Speakers died violently as a result of holding the office. The Speaker was often likely to be a King's man—as a result, because the Commons did not trust him, they enshrined the practice of having the Speaker vacate the chair whenever they moved into committee. It was not until the eighteenth century that the Speaker ceased to hold other government appointments and became truly independent both of the Crown and the government. British tradition now requires Speakers to be independent, impartial, knowledgeable and learned in the ways of Parliament. A Speaker's rulings cannot be challenged by the House of Commons. Upon his assumption of office, the Speaker retires from partisan politics and he is generally not opposed in his constituency at election time. He continues to hold office as Speaker, irrespective of changes of government, until he retires (generally to be given a viscountcy) or dies.

Australia borrowed the name of the Commons' presiding officer for the House of Representatives. The Speaker of the House of Representatives also borrowed the dignity and ceremony of the British office. Non-Labor Speakers (and Presidents of the Senate) wear the traditional robe and wig of the British Speaker. However the Australian Speaker has not taken over all the characteristics of his British counterpart. The most important difference is that in Australia the office has become a political prize for politicians generally of the second or third rank—though occasionally a politician who has been a minister, or who later becomes one, does take on the office.

It is possible to draw a clear distinction between the British and Australian Speakers in at least four respects: their partiality in the chair; their knowledge and understanding of the standing orders; the status of their rulings from the chair; and their degrees of political independence.

It is unparliamentary behaviour to reflect on the partiality of the Speaker (or President) except in the course of a motion directed against him (which does occur in the House of Representatives whenever the opposition considers it politically appropriate). It is also dangerous for a reporter to make any reflection upon a particular Speaker because he can be dealt with by the Parliament's privileges committees. He can also be dealt with by the Speaker himself who can bar him from the Parliament and from the press gallery (access to which is vital for political as well as parliamentary journalists). It is for this reason that the public rarely hears much about the particular qualities of individual Speakers, except by way of opposition complaints. It is not that Speakers do not often deserve criticism; but they are above criticism in the sense that one cannot criticise them with impunity.

Speakers show partiality in a variety of ways. Essentially the result of their partiality is that the government is treated better than the opposition and that the government rather than the opposition tends to get the advantage of the standing orders. In fact standing orders are written in such a way that even a totally impartial Speaker would appear to favour the government of the day. Most Speakers, however, tend to side with the government even more than the standing orders require and occasionally they produce interpretations of standing orders which considerably advance the government's cause. In 1970, for example, Sir William Aston as Speaker ruled that the government could introduce an amendment to a censure motion moved by the opposition. The amendment allowed the government to rally all its supporters and prevented any direct vote on the opposition motion which had the potential to attract the support of some dissident government backbenchers. Subsequent Speakers have followed his example and allowed the government to turn motions of no-confidence in the government into motions condemning the opposition.

Other opportunities for displays of bias from the chair occur in the handling of ordinary debates: some MPs are allowed more latitude in their use of abusive words, for example, than others; government members are given more opportunities to recover themselves when faced with being "named" for misconduct. More subtly, the Speaker can protect the government at question time by avoiding calling members of the opposition who are known to ask difficult questions, or who are clearly going to embarrass a particular minister. (The Speaker does not however have the same opportunity to discriminate between possible speakers in a debate because he is in effect required to follow a list provided by the party Whips.)

Although Speakers and Presidents of the Australian Parliament would insist that they strive for impartiality, the fact is that governments expect some favourable treatment from the presiding officer they have put into the Chair; oppositions only complain when the partiality becomes too blatant.

Australian Speakers sometimes have a good knowledge of their standing orders, the traditions of the House and those aspects of May's *Parliamentary Practice* which are relevant. (The first standing order of the House of Representatives makes May, which describes procedure in the House of Commons, the ultimate authority for dealing with parliamentary situations which are not dealt with conclusively by the House of Representatives standing orders.) Nevertheless it is common in the Australian Parliament to see the Clerk of the House or the Clerk of the Senate coming to the rescue of his presiding officer during a discussion of standing orders by giving him chapter (and sometimes verse). Most Australian presiding officers have a general rather than a specific knowledge of the standing orders. It is the clerks, the permanent officers of the parliament, who are the guardians of the parliament's standing orders and traditions rather than the presiding officer *pro tem*. A Speaker may certainly produce his own interpretations of the standing orders and possibly influence subsequent Speakers in their interpretations. But presiding officers don't always feel bound to follow the rulings of their predecessors and they are likely to vary even their own rulings if they see fit.

Rulings by the presiding officers in the Australian Parliament also have less force than in Britain because they can be overturned by the House itself in motion of dissent from the Speaker's ruling. Such motions are common. They can represent the opposition's disapproval of a particular ruling by the Speaker or simply be an attempt to prolong or impede a particular debate. It is rare for the government to move dissent from the Speaker's ruling. This is not due to the inherent quality of the rulings but to the fact that they mostly favour the government.

The political relationship between the presiding officer and the government is totally different from that in the House of Commons. In Australia the presiding officer is not expected to retire from the political battlefield upon his election to office. When he is not in the chair he is expected to take an active part in politics, particularly in his own electorate where he will certainly have to defend himself against an opponent at every subsequent election. Speakers and Presidents generally attend the weekly meetings of their parliamentary party and in the case of the Labor Party they take an active part in determining its parliamentary business through voting on the bills proposed by the cabinet.

When there is a close division of government and opposition forces in the House or Senate, the presiding officer is expected to use his vote.

In the Senate he has a deliberative vote and he uses it in ordinary divisions (he does not leave the chair but the tellers mark his name on their lists as having voted). In the House he has a casting vote only, but he can and does vote in committee. It is not unknown for Speakers to participate in debate too. Less publicly, a knowledgeable Speaker can expect to be consulted by his Prime Minister about procedural devices which might be attempted in a tight parliamentary situation. Whitlam certainly consulted Scholes, when he was Speaker, on points of unusual procedure which might be tried in the House for tactical or political reason.

The Australian Speaker is assisted by a chairman of committees and a series of unpaid Deputy Speakers. The Speaker always takes the chair at the start of each day's sitting and presides through question time before handing over to the chairman or one of the half dozen or so Deputies. The Speaker is generally in the Chair whenever a major statement is made, important legislation is introduced or debated, and at the end of the day's proceedings. On average, he will be in the Chair for about nine hours in an average sitting week of twenty three hours.

The rest of his parliamentary time is spent in ceremonial, political and administrative work. The two presiding officers are nominally the equivalent of ministerial heads of the departments responsible for providing administrative services to the chambers—that is, the Department of the House of Representatives and the Department of the Senate. They have joint responsibility over the Joint House Department (which is responsible for the rest of Parliament House) and special responsibilities for Hansard and the Parliamentary Library. They do a lot of entertaining and administer the Canberra branches of the Inter-Parliamentary Union (the international organisation of parliamentarians) and the Commonwealth Parliamentary Association (a body of parliamentarians from the states and other British Commonwealth countries). Through these two organisations they tend to get more overseas trips than the average backbencher, though fewer than the average minister.

While the presiding officers have an important role in administering parliamentary activity, their status even in this respect is not very high in governmental eyes. When the government is drawing up its annual Budget, the presiding officers have no say in cabinet determination of the estimates affecting parliament and are not even permitted to argue their case before the Cabinet. As Speaker, Snedden tried to change this, but without success. In 1976 he had a brush with the Minister for Administrative Services over the funding of a reception he wanted to give in Norway while he was on an official visit. The government's refusal won headlines, and was raised in both the parliament and the Liberal Party room, as was the question of presiding officers' inability to influence or control the monetary vote for the parliament. Snedden lost the battle but he kept trying. And outside the parliament he made speeches trying to emphasise the importance of the role of the presiding officers and the parliament itself.

Snedden was elected as Speaker after he had failed to gain selection in Fraser's ministry at the end of 1975. With his knighthood at the end of 1977, he seemed likely to be entrenched in the position as long as Fraser held power. When Snedden was elected he began a serious campaign to improve the status of the Speaker and of parliament. He had never before demonstrated much interest in parliament as an institution, though he had twice been Leader of the House. His appointment as Speaker prompted him to search among Australian academic works for clues as to how he could put his stamp on the position of Speaker, and promote the interests of parliament. After nine years of wielding ministerial power, he suddenly became a champion of parliamentary supremacy. In the federal parliament the role of parliamentary reformer had previously been limited to backbenchers whose chances of elevation to the ministry appeared minimal. Snedden certainly gave new heart to the reformers, even if his conversion to the cause appeared a little belated.

The Speaker and the President in the Australian Parliament are not highly prestigous personnages despite their high rating in the formal lists of precedence, their comfortable accommodation and their high salaries and perquisites. The job has sufficient status to be attractive to a discarded party Leader like Snedden, but generally it is not a job sought by a man likely to become a minister (though this is not always the case, particularly in the Labor Party). The selection of a Speaker like Cope, a man close to retirement from parliament and with mainly his long service and his sense of humour to recommend him, cannot be regarded as atypical. It was certainly not regarded as particularly unusual in 1973 by the opposition which did not nominate a candidate to oppose him. Yet Cope's term of office demonstrated just how important it can be for a government to have a Speaker who is capable of controlling the House, demonstrating his knowledge of standing orders and willingness to stand by them in the face of opposition harassment. If he can also show a degree of fairness in keeping order he will probably gain respect from the opposition and make his own job easier. A good Speaker or President in the Australian Parliament has these attributes. But no matter how good he is, he will not be able to prevent the opposition from causing chaos from time to time—the rules don't stop that and there are occasions when an opposition can only resort to "bad" behaviour to drive home a political point. But if the Speaker is weak, the House is likely to witness such behaviour more frequently and the government will have to indulge heavily in the use of closures of debate (gags) and other procedural devices to force its measures through, and in so doing create a public impression of intemperateness.

Tactics: standing orders and legislative process

The tactics a government or an opposition employs in the parliament can be of vital political importance. In 1975, for example, it was crucial to Fraser's hopes of forcing the Labor government to a premature election to avoid a vote on the merits of the Hayden Budget. There were two reasons for this. The first was that it was unlikely that Fraser could control his own Senators sufficiently to make them vote against the Budget. Some were prepared to vote for deferral of a vote (and did so on many occasions), but were unwilling to vote "no" on the Budget bills. The second reason was that the Hayden Budget was the only Budget any government would have to work with until a new parliament could be elected. The House of Representatives (controlled by a Labor majority) would not pass any other Budget.

The first reason was clear to everyone in parliament throughout late 1975, and Labor responded to the crisis by trying to devise ways to get the Senate to a "real" vote—away from its procedural moves to defer the Budget vote. The second reason only became important when Fraser was appointed Prime Minister in the run-up to the elections, which could only have happened because the Budget had been passed. The House of Representatives would not have passed a Budget that would have allowed Fraser to govern. It was only the fact that it had long before passed the Hayden Budget that put Fraser in a position to assure the Governor-General that he would have supply during the election period (he could guarantee the passage of the Budget through the Senate).

Tactics might have been exploited to prevent Fraser fulfilling this promise, however. They were not considered, because Whitlam had a blind spot concerning parliament. In his efforts to promote the superiority of the House of Representatives over the Senate, he tended to equate "parliament" with the "House of Representatives", and to ignore the Senate. On 11 November 1975, when faced with his dismissal from the prime ministership, Whitlam concentrated his efforts on finding ways in which the House of Representatives could reverse the Governor-General's verdict. He completely neglected to take the Senate into account, and did not inform his party's Senate leadership of the events which were taking place.

When the Senate met, the Labor leaders were still trying to push the Budget bills through as quickly as possible, and they were somewhat surprised suddenly to find the opposition equally as anxious to have them passed. A more appropriate tactic would have been that which the opposition had been pursuing for two months—delay. Although the opposition had the numbers to pass the bills, there were procedural means open to the government—including just talking—which would have delayed passage of the bills. The most effective tactic, however, would have been to force the Senate to adjourn. This could have been achieved by the simple expedient of creating so complete an uproar that the President (a Labor Senator) would have been justified in adjourning the Senate till the following day. Had this occurred before the Budget was passed, the Governor-General would not have been able to dissolve the parliament, and he would not, for long, have been able to continue to ignore the motion of no-confidence in Fraser's government passed by the House.

The rituals of legislative and other public activity in the House and the Senate are mostly specified in the separate, different standing orders adopted by the two Houses. These standing orders are not unchangeable, but major alterations such as those made in the early 1960s governing the treatment of financial legislation are very rare. Indeed changes of any kind are infrequent. For example, in the ten years from 1965 to 1975, there were only seventeen standing orders changed and only one of these, dealing with time limits to speeches, was of any importance. As each of the Houses is master of its own standing orders, proposals for change are invariably considered by the standing orders committee for each House.

The House committee must contain the Speaker, the Chairman of Committees, the Leader of the House and the Deputy Leader of the Opposition (at the time the standing order was written, the Deputy of the Opposition functioned as the opposite number to the Leader of the House). In 1976 other members of the House Standing Orders Committee included the deputy Prime Minister and the former Labor Speaker, Gordon Scholes. At that time in the Senate the committee contained the President and Chairman of Committees plus the Leader of the Government and Leader of the Opposition, the Leader of the Country Party, one other minister, a former minister and the Government Whip, together with two former Senate Presidents. Overall the committees were more representative of the government and opposition establishments than they were of backbenches. They were unlikely to favour radical changes aimed at improving the lot of backbenchers. They also did not meet very often.

Most of the standing orders are neutral in tone and do not appear to give any particular advantage to government or opposition. However, the standing orders have to be read with the understanding that the government, through its majority in the House, can suspend standing orders at any time to suit its convenience. If the government has a hefty majority it will easily be able to suspend standing orders without giving notice of its intention (it needs an absolute majority for this). If it has difficulty obtaining an absolute majority, it can suspend standing orders with a simple majority after giving a day's notice of its intentions. Governments in fact give contingent notice of motions to suspend standing orders to carry out regular procedures such as moving directly from the second reading of a bill to the completion of the third reading, but they do not need to invoke their numbers to force such suspensions because the opposition grants leave.

The standing orders heavily favour the government in the conduct of question time. They forbid questions to contain arguments, inferences, imputations, epithets, ironical expressions or hypothetical matter; questioners may not ask ministers for an expression of opinion, any announcement of government policy or a legal opinion. In answering, ministers are required to be relevant, but no limit is put on the content or length of their answers or their style of rhetoric. The other main area in which the standing orders distinguish between ministers and other members of the House is in regard to financial legislation. Only ministers may bring in taxation proposals and only ministers may move amendments to increase charges.

Although only the government can hope to suspend standing orders in the House of Representatives, the opposition can move for suspensions of standing orders in order to highlight a grievance, or attract attention to a particular policy area they believe should be debated, or to disrupt the government's legislative or parliamentary timetable. Moving for the suspension of standing orders was a tactic exploited at great length by the opposition in the early 1970s. The tactic wasted a lot of the government's time, as once the opposition MP caught the Speaker's eye, obtained his call, and moved the suspension of standing orders, more than half an hour would pass before the government could get the House back to its scheduled business. (The mover and the seconder both had the right to speak for ten minutes before the government could move the gag on the debate. Even if the government moved to gag both the mover and the seconder, it would be faced with three divisions, each taking about seven minutes. And any attempt to gag the mover and seconder would generally result in the opposition again moving suspension of standing orders next time it obtained the call).

In 1971 the government had the standing orders changed to limit the time the opposition could take up in this way. The mover of the suspension of standing orders was limited to ten minutes, the seconder to five and the leading government speaker to ten. A total period of twenty-five minutes was fixed for the debate, and the motion would then be put without the necessity of a gag. But even this limitation proved insufficient for government purposes so it brought in a temporary sessional order suspending the right of anyone but a minister to move for the suspension of standing orders. This was not a permanent veto against opposition moves to suspend standing orders, but it showed the way to future governments. The same tactic can be invoked if the opposition of the day makes too much use of this procedural device to waste time.

The most common time-wasting device, however, cannot be so easily overcome. This is the division, the counting of those for and against a particular motion. The counting is done by two "tellers" (under normal circumstances, the Whip and Deputy Whip from the Labor Party plus the Liberal Whip and the Country Party Whip, though the Speaker can call on any members to perform the task). Equipped with a roll-call sheet and pencils, the tellers on each side check every member present. One calls out the name, the other marks it off on the roll-call sheet, indicating whether the member is sitting on the side for or against the motion.

Divisions are usually called by those likely to be on the losing side of a vote. The presiding officer puts the question to the House, calling in order for those in favour and those against the question. He then normally says, "The ayes have it" if the government favours the yes vote. If the opposition wishes to force a division, its leading members will dispute the speaker's verdict and say, in this case, "The noes have it". If there is more than one call for a division, the Speaker must order the bells to be rung. The Clerk then operates a button which causes bells to be rung throughout Parliament House, while the Deputy Clerk upends a sand-glass which takes two minutes to empty. (In 1973, when for six months the Prime Minister's office was located at the furthest end of the building on the Senate side, the division time was increased to three minutes.) At the end of two minutes the Speaker orders the doors to be locked, the bells are turned off, and the Speaker then tells those who wish to vote aye to move to his right (the side normally occupied by the government), those voting no to his left. He then appoints the tellers. If the House is fairly evenly divided the count will take about five minutes. If it is particularly lopsided (as it sometimes is in a free vote) the division can take up to ten minutes to count.

Given the party discipline which occurs in the Australian Parliament, the division's main achievement is not to determine which side has won the vote. Voting against one's party is extremely rare and deliberately abstaining from a vote is also very uncommon. A party might have some of its members absent without the leave of the Whips by accident, but votes are mostly quite predictable. The main effect of divisions is to take up time. The introduction of electronic devices to speed up the counting of divisions has been opposed by many parliamentarians on the ground that it is desirable *not* to eliminate this time-wasting device. Five minutes does not seem too long a period to sacrifice in the interests of giving the opposition one respectable parliamentary delaying tactic which avoids uproar. However, the total time taken up in divisions, including the ringing of the bells, is quite formidable. Over a full parliamentary year it is not unusual for the House to spend twenty-three hours in divisions. That is around five per cent of the total time the House meets, a not insignificant proportion.

Governments have organised the proceedings of the House so that divisions which might have political importance are minimised. The case of censure motions has been dealt with above (see page 58). Nor does the government have to face divisions over priorities within the Budget because the opposition is not permitted to move amendments increasing spending or charges. On everyday political questions the government rarely has to record a vote because debates on matters of public importance take place without the benefit of a specific motion being formulated. Governments can even avoid committing themselves in a vote on items brought up by the opposition in general business: they can talk the matter out until the time for the general business item expires and vote against any closure motion the opposition might move in an attempt to force a vote on the issue. The only time a government is forced to vote in the House of Representatives on matters on which it would prefer not to express an opinion is when the opposition moves amendments to bills proposed by the government.

Divisions in the House of Representatives serve an unusual but extremely important political purpose. During a division, members do not necessarily have to sit in their normal seats, and of course when the government votes no in a division, all the members have to move across the chamber and can sit anywhere.

During these divisions it is common for a minister with a particular problem to talk it over with other ministers, or even with the Prime Minister. Ministers and backbenchers, who might at other times have difficulty arranging to see the Prime Minister urgently, can be assured of five minutes with him during a division. Similarly government backbenchers who might have been unable to see a busy minister can secure his attention during a division. Divisions also allow the leading party members to go into huddles to discuss current parliamentary or political tactics.

Divisions can throw out the programming of the Leader of the House. They also tend to disrupt government business being conducted outside the chamber. Many cabinet committees (though generally not the full cabinet) meet while parliament is sitting as do many party committees. Divisions break into all these. They also tend to disrupt a minister's program of meetings in his office with people having business with him or his department, or visitors from interstate or overseas whom he has arranged to meet. A long series of divisions can completely ruin a minister's working schedule for that day and force him to reschedule subsequent working days.

As well as divisions, ministers have to worry about hurrying to the chamber to answer quorum calls. The quorum is the other major weapon available to an opposition which is in the mood to disrupt the government's parliamentary day. Any MP can at any stage (even while another MP is speaking) call the presiding officer's attention to "the state of the House". The Constitution and the standing orders provide for a quorum of one third of the House membership, so once the Speaker's attention is drawn to the state of the House, he (assisted by the clerks) must count the numbers present. The Speaker orders the bells to be rung if less than one third of the members are present (and the quorum call would not be initiated unless this is the case—a quorum called when the House is properly attended can result in the MP calling it being suspended from the House). Unless the required number of MPs enters the Chamber within two minutes, the Speaker is required to adjourn the House. Quorum calls are frequently initiated by a backbencher who thinks he has been badly done by in proceedings in the House, or are undertaken as part of a concerted opposition campaign. They are extremely unpopular with government MPs who have to rush continually to the chamber. Opposition MPs don't answer quorum calls: the ideal result for them is if the government does not fill the House in time and the sitting has to be adjourned—the theory is that it is the government's responsibility to provide quorums, not the opposition's. Although the bells which summon MPs to a division are the same as those used to call a quorum, opposition MPs will know the difference between them either through having been listening on loudspeakers to the proceedings in the House, or through the shouts of the Whips down the opposition corridors warning "quorum, quorum".

A Leader of the House faced with an opposition which is being obstructive has several devices to ensure passage of legislation according to his program. He can resort to use of the "gag" (the motion "that the question be now put") but sometimes literally dozens of such motions might be necessary to get a bill through the House. With more certainty he can apply the "guillotine". This is a device which allows a Minister to declare a bill urgent (by a subsequent vote of the House without debate); the Minister then allocates the time in which the various sections of the bill must be considered (second reading, committee, and the remaining stages of the bill). The House may debate this proposal for twenty minutes before voting on it. Standing orders can be suspended to allow the minister to move one motion to declare a number of bills urgent, and then to allocate the time for various debates in one proceeding. Occasionally the guillotine will be used to guarantee passage of one particular bill, sometimes for several bills at a time, and more rarely, at the end of a session, for a great mass of them. The most extraordinary recent use of the guillotine was in 1977, when the Fraser government had nineteen bills guillotined through the Senate in just over four hours.

The Senate has procedures and arrangements between the parties which parallel, though they do not precisely equate, those of the House. Responsibility for the conduct of government business is in the hands of the Leader of the Government in the Senate (though for two years under Labor a junior Minister was appointed as Manager of Government Business). The Leader of the Opposition in the Senate is responsible for handling the opposition's side of business arrangements in that chamber. They are assisted by a Senate official, the Principal Parliamentary Officer, and since 1972, by a government official, the Parliamentary Liaison Officer. The Senate Whips play an important part in adjusting any arrangements which are made, a function in which the Whips are not involved in the House.

The Senate's smaller numbers mean not only that its members have more time allotted to them for speech-making, but also that there is far less pressure on the government to introduce closures of debate or gags on individuals. Apart from which, the government frequently does not have control of the Senate: in such cases it can rely only on persuasion to have its parliamentary program accepted.

Co-operation between government and opposition is an important element in the running of the parliament. Ultimately, however, both sides are concerned with using parliament for their own political advantage. In this conflict, the government of the day (particularly if it also has a Senate majority) has many elements weighted in its favour. The government gains more assistance than the opposition from the standing orders and the presiding officers. Only the government has direct access to the public service which provides ministers (and sometimes government backbenchers) with material which is used in every phase of parliamentary activity. Even the Parliamentary Liaison Officers, who play a critical role in the evolution of the parliamentary program and in the running of the parliament, are officers of the government, not the parliament. Their task is to provide advice which will improve the partisan political advantage which the government can gain from its performances in parliament.

The general pattern of parliamentary procedure is laid down in standing orders but can usually be varied if a government considers it necessary. Each day begins with prayers (the wording of which is laid down by the standing orders of both Houses); the presentation of petitions; the giving of any notices of motions; and then questions without notice for forty-five minutes to an hour. The House of

Representatives then deals with ministerial statements followed by government business, which consists primarily of legislation. The last half hour of the day is taken up with a generalised adjournment debate. Every second Thursday, an hour and a quarter of general business precedes government business, and every other Thursday the first order of the day for government business is a private members' debate of grievances. Members can also originate an urgency debate on a matter of public importance before the beginning of government business. In the Senate approximately the same timetable is followed, though there are variations to take account of work of Senate committees and different procedural forms for urgency debates, general business and adjournment proceedings.

Within this framework, the Leader of the House of Representatives will try to manipulate business to maximise the government's political advantage. Ministerial statements will be made by ministers when to the government's advantage to publicise a particular issue, either in advance of legislation (e.g. economic policy) or on a subject on which legislation is not to be presented (e.g. foreign affairs). Statements which the government particularly wants to emphasise will probably be inserted into the program later than at the time scheduled in the standing orders. Sir Robert Menzies used to like the 8 p.m. time spot for his announcements; changed viewing and listening habits following the introduction of television have persuaded most subsequent Prime Ministers to try to make their statements at about 5.15 p.m. The timing of legislative debates is mostly arranged according to how much publicity the government wants from the particular bill. A controversial bill which the government believes will win it votes will be programmed at a time when it will gain maximum publicity, and the debate may be spread over several days. Bills which the government sees no merit in emphasising will be sandwiched together and dealt with on a Wednesday, when the proceedings in House are not broadcast.

In the meantime, the opposition will have been planning its parliamentary tactics to maximise the impact it can make. It normally has at its disposal two or three urgency debates a week, on subjects of its own choosing. It can oppose or propose amendments to legislation as it sees fit. It can debate ministerial statements when they are made. (If it delays replying immediately, it takes the risk that government will never provide parliamentary time for the debate.) It can introduce censure or no confidence motions to dramatise the failings of a Minister or of government policy. It can try to obstruct the business of the House.

Nevertheless, most of what happens in the House is predictable and planned. Half an hour before each sitting day begins, the members receive a "blue" paper printed by the House officials but prepared by the Parliamentary Liaison Officer, which lists the business the government expects to complete during the day, and the order in which it will be considered. It also includes the title of any opposition's urgency debate (for the Government insists on getting notice of the subject matter so that relevant ministers and backbenchers can prepare for their side of the debate. House standing orders require that anyone proposing a debate on a matter of public importance notify the Speaker of its subject matter at least one hour before the House is scheduled to meet.) The "blue" also lists the titles of ministerial statements and gives the approximate time at which they will be delivered. The government normally gives the opposition a copy of any ministerial statement two hours before it is read, to allow the opposition time to debate the matter immediately if it so wishes. (Failure by the government to do so can be met by the opposition refusing to give leave for the statement to be made at a time other than that set down for ministerial statements. However, the government can overcome any refusal of leave by using its numbers to suspend the standing orders).

The "blue" lists all the bills that will be dealt with, and states how far it is proposed that the debate should be carried (second reading introduced, second reading concluded, committee stages, third reading, etc.) Details of when bills are to be debated and how many speakers there are to be, would have been discussed earlier by the Leader of the House and his opposition counterpart—this often takes place through the Parliamentary Liaison Officer and sometimes an opposition staff member. They would also have discussed whether debates on ministerial statements will take place immediately, be held over till later in the week or later in the session, or adjourned indefinitely. Frequently, these arrangements need to be varied. Sometimes the Leader and his opposite number meet "behind the [Speaker's] chair"—literally— to inform one another of variations in the agreed program, or to bargain about times and procedures.

Occasionally the opposition will announce to the House that the government has broken its word about various debating arrangements. But only very rarely does the co-operation break down to any damaging extent. It is not in the interests of either the government or the opposition that it should. The government does not want to have to muster its numbers to batter down the opposition at every moment because the process is time consuming and can be made to appear bad in the eyes of the public. The opposition generally can get more time for debating the matters it considers important if it does co-operate with the government. Both sides are aware that life is a lot easier if they work closely together.

This program of proposed business is issued for the general guidance of Members. It is not a formal document and the business listed is subject to change.

Friday - 7 April 1978
10.30 a.m.

Prayers

Petitions - The Clerk to announce petitions lodged for presentation.

Mr Speaker to call on -

    Notices

    Questions without notice

    Presentation of Papers - Ministers
                       (Minister, by leave, to move for
                         authorisation of publication of papers)

    Ministerial statements, by leave - Mr Killen (Minister for Defence)

COMMITTEE OF PRIVILEGES - Mr D.M. Cameron (Chairman - Fadden) to present the following report from the Committee of Privileges, to move for printing, and, by leave, to make statement:

        Report relating to an editorial published in the
        Sunday Observer of 26 February 1978, together with
        minutes of proceedings of the committee.

Mr Sinclair (Leader of the House) to move - That the consideration of the Report be made an order of the day for Wednesday, 12 April 1978.

DISCUSSION OF MATTER OF PUBLIC IMPORTANCE - Mr Hayden (Leader of the Opposition) -

        The misleading statements on Aboriginal welfare
        by the Minister for Aboriginal Affairs.

Requires support of 8 Members; Time limits : Discussion 2 hours; Proposer and Member next speaking 15 minutes; other Members 10 minutes.

Government Business

ORDERS OF THE DAY

No. 1 - Australian Apple and Pear Corporation Amendment Bill - Resumption of debate on second reading; second reading; committee; adoption of report; third reading, by leave.

No. 2 - Public broadcasting planning - Ministerial statement and paper - Motion to take note of papers - Resumption of debate.

No. 3 - "Croatian Embassy" - Ministerial statement - Motion to take note of paper - Resumption of debate.

ADJOURNMENT.

                        J.A. PETTIFER
             Clerk of the House of Representatives

Fig. 6.1 The "blue", the unofficial program issued each day for the House of Representatives. It provides a good, but not infallible guide to the day's proceedings. One event not mentioned on this program for 7 April 1978 was the presentation of a Bill by the Treasurer, Mr Howard, aimed at reducing tax evasion.

Standing orders require that on the day before a bill is introduced into the House, notice is given of its full title which is also printed in the next day's notice paper. The following day when the notice is called on (by number: The Clerk reads out, "Notice Number x"), the minister says, "I present a bill for...," and gives its short title. The Clerk is then given a copy of the bill and he reads the short title, prefacing it with the words, "First reading. A bill for..."). The minister then says, "I move that the bill be read a second time." And he then begins the second reading speech which supposedly explains the Bill and its purpose. The speech will have been prepared for him by his department. He may (though he probably will not) have had it rewritten or amended. While he is making his speech, copies of the bill will be issued to all MPs sitting in the House, and a short time later they will be made available to journalists and others through the Bills and Papers Office. At the end of the minister's speech, the opposition frontbencher handling the bill will move for and obtain the adjournment of the debate. The adjournment is generally for a minimum of a week.

During the adjournment period the Opposition spokesman shadowing the minister who introduced the bill will consult colleagues inside the parliament and experts outside it on the virtues and vices of the legislation. He will probably take it before a meeting of the party committee which covers the area affected by the legislation before going to the opposition executive with a recommendation. The executive recommendation will then be put to the party meeting, either for information and discussion in the case of a Liberal Party opposition, or for debate and decision if the Labor Party is in opposition.

The decision as to whether the party will support the bill, not oppose it, try to amend it, or try to defeat it, is generally announced to the press after the party's weekly meeting. Sometimes the merits of particular amendments will be expressed to the media while at other times the opposition will disguise the nature of its amendments because it hopes to catch the Government out and embarrass it on the day.

The debate is resumed at a time convenient to both government and opposition and the second reading stage is generally concluded on the same day. The House then bypasses the committee stage (with the consent of the opposition) and agrees to the third reading of the bill without any debate. Bills that are particularly complex or significant, on which the opposition wishes to move amendments in detail, may be taken into committee in the House, but frequently the amendments are not brought forward until the bill reaches the Senate. At the second reading stage the principal speaker for the opposition may propose an amendment of substance on the principles of the bill if the opposition feels sufficiently strongly about it. He may then require a committee debate in order to make a further point of the opposition's objections to the bill. An individual member of the government or opposition who feels he has not been able to speak during the second reading stage and feels badly done by can refuse leave for the committee stage to be omitted and insist on his right to speak to a particular clause. An opposition member who does so against the wishes of his leader is unlikely to be popular as the leader will probably have given assurances to the Leader of the House that the bill will be allowed through without difficulties.

After its passage through the three readings in the House, the bill then goes to the Senate. It is formally presented and read a first time. When the second reading is taken (sometimes the same day, sometimes the next), the Minister in charge of the bill reads a speech prepared by the Department responsible for the bill. This speech is generally in precisely the same terms as the one delivered by the minister in the House on the second reading there. Occasionally there may be changes in the speech to take account of political developments that occurred while the bill was in the House; very rarely the Senate minister may wish to amend the text given to him. Although the Senate will be aware of the bill and its contents, an adjournment is again taken by the Leader of the Opposition or the Senator who will take charge of it for the opposition. When the debate is resumed, however, Senators generally do take account of what was said when the Bill was debated in the House, and argument tends to develop beyond what was said there. There is a greater tendency for Senators to interject on one another with debating points, and to answer such interjections. The Senators have much more time at their disposal (each may speak for one hour on Tuesday or Thursday, and for half an hour on Wednesday when the Senate is being broadcast. In the House, second reading speeches are limited to twenty minutes).

At the end of the second reading in the Senate, the bill generally goes into committee where amendments which were not considered when the bill was before the House are frequently discussed. Debate is much freer of party pressure at this stage and the minister in charge of the bill will frequently consult with the departmental officials sitting beside him to provide answers to the debating arguments used in favour of amendments. If the minister becomes convinced that there is some merit in an amendment being proposed, or if he is persuaded by government Senators that they see merit in it, the minister may seek postponement of further consideration of that particular clause until he has time to consult with the minister from the House of Representatives whose Bill it is. If the Minister from the House persists in opposing an amendment, in the case of a Labor government he would be supported by all Labor Senators. Liberal and Country Party ministers cannot be so sure of the complete support of their party Senators at this stage of the legislative process however.

After the committee stage, the Senate votes on accepting the report of the committee and then on the third reading of the Bill. If there are any amendments, the bill is returned to the House of Representatives which goes into committee to consider them. The minister responsible for the bill will have discussed the amendments with the Senate minister who handled the bill and with his Department. He will probably consult the Prime Minister or other senior ministers before determining what action to take (unless of course the amendments were sponsored by the government in the Senate to clarify points of detail or correct errors which the Department and/or the minister had become aware of).

In committee, the Minister informs the House of his intentions and the government party (or parties) provide him with the numbers to either accept or reject the amendments as he proposes. The opposition, however, can use this period to further advance its arguments. If the amendments are rejected, a message is sent back to the senate informing it (generally in one sentence) of the reasons for declining its amendments. The amendments will then be reconsidered by the Senate, in committee. Depending on the relative strength of the parties, and the strength and determination of the majority which sought the amendment, the bill can then shuffle backwards and forwards between the two Houses indefinitely. There is no other settlement machinery less than a double dissolution of the parliament. What happens depends on the will and political aims of the protagonists. An opposition may back down, or allow some of its members to back down, if it considers that the government is determined not to have the Bill passed rather than have it passed with the amendment. Another reason for a capitulation is if the Opposition considers that it would suffer political damage by being seen to have prevented the legislation from coming into effect.

For example, at the end of 1973 the opposition was steadfastly refusing to pass the Whitlam government's legislation to establish an Australian Schools Commission which would make grants to government and private schools throughout Australia. Eventually the Country Party opened negotiations with the acting Minister for Education, Lionel Bowen, for some concessions, having decided that it could not afford to reject the legislation outright given the electoral popularity of the measure. The Liberal Party remained opposed to it, despite the Country Party action, but Labor needed only Country Party support to ensure passage of the legislation through the Senate.

Confrontation can also end with the government deciding it would rather have amended legislation than none at all. This occurred over the Interstate Commission Bill in 1975. Rather than have the bill rejected and added to the pile of prospective double dissolution bills which might never be enacted, Whitlam decided to make major concessions to the opposition in order to have the bill passed by the Senate. The bill was not then put into operation however, as the Labor government was dismissed a few days after the legislation was passed.

Occasionally the government will agree to its legislation being amended because although it considers it will eventually win the day, it recognises that continued conflict will be more damaging politically than any concession it might make. This appeared to be the case in 1976 when the Fraser government conceded changes to social welfare legislation which had proposed, among other things, the abolition of funeral benefits. It was faced by an opposition reinforced on this issue by six government backbenchers. While some of them could have been forced into line and the bill passed as originally proposed, the Prime Minister decided the fight was not worth continuing, in view of the comparatively small financial outlay involved and the great damage the conflict appeared to be doing to the N.S.W. Liberal Party which was then contesting a state election (which it subsequently lost narrowly).

Finally the government can continue to insist on a bill, the opposition can continue to refuse, and the legislation can be defeated and reintroduced three months later as a possible double dissolution bill.

After a bill has passed both Houses it is sent to the Governor-General for his signature, and his assent is then announced in the House where the bill originated. The Act, as it has now become, does not necessarily take effect immediately. It will contain a clause stating when its provisions should commence to have the effect of law. Sometimes that is when the bill is signed, sometimes on a date specified in the legislation, and sometimes on a date to be proclaimed by the government. In many cases the operation of the Act will depend on the formulation and proclamation of regulations by the Government department administering it. The legislation is supposed to spell out the principles of the law, while details consistent with the principles are detailed in regulations. The operation of the legislation are reviewed by the department and any necessary amendments are suggested to the minister for discussion in cabinet and the drafting of amending legislation.

Every May and November, as the Federal Parliament prepares for a two or three month recess, the government of the day foreshadows longer sitting hours and additional sittings. The pace of legislation through the House of Representatives increases dramatically. Invariably there is a debate about the changes to the sitting hours and the first or second speaker for the opposition bitterly denounces the government's proposals for "legislation by exhaustion". Everyone smiles at the phrase, it is so hackneyed. It is also a poor description of what occurs, unless the government keeps the House sitting long after ,nidnight (which is rare). For the most part, the opposition continues to co-operate as bills are pushed through the House with less time for debate than previously (clearly there is no exhaustion if the only effect of the procedure is to reduce the time available for debate).

Opposition members are generally as anxious to end the parliamentary sittings as government members. And everyone knows that no matter what is said, it is unlikely that the legislation will be in any way affected. End of session pressure effectively strips away much of the pretence of legislative debate. At this time the parliamentary rubber stamp machine is seen operating in full public view, for the most part endorsing the proposals submitted by the government.

Financial Legislation

Considerable technical and constitutional importance is attached to parliamentary control of finance. Historically it was through its power to grant or refuse money to the King that the British Parliament built up its power first as a legislature, then as the watchdog over the King's ministers and finally as the provider of the ministers. The power to refuse to grant finance remains the parliament's ultimate weapon against the executive, and it can still be a deadly one, as the Whitlam government discovered in 1975. Through 1974 and 1975 the Senate has emasculated the Whitlam government's legislation, twice rejecting twenty one bills, but it was only when it considered deferring financial legislation that the government's life was threatened, and eventually ended.

For over sixty years the Australian Parliament copied, not always perfectly, the House of Commons' highly complex, ornate and mostly meaningless forms of procedure when it considered financial matters. At various times during these proceedings the House called itself a committee of ways and means, a committee of supply, and a money committee, though the committee in each case was the whole House. In 1962 the House of Representatives finally amended its standing orders to provide that financial matters should be treated in much the same way as other legislation. The Senate also changed its procedures to allow it to consider the details of annual budgets at the same time as the House. In 1971 the Senate made further changes to give five newly created estimates committees the ability to make very detailed studies of government expenditure proposals.

Financial legislation includes all bills which raise money through loans, taxes, tariffs and excise, and all bills which spend it by annual

1977

THE PARLIAMENT OF THE COMMONWEALTH OF AUSTRALIA

HOUSE OF REPRESENTATIVES

Presented and read a first time, 16 August 1977

(*Treasurer*)

A BILL

FOR

AN ACT

To appropriate certain sums out of the Consolidated
Revenue Fund for the service of the year ending
on 30 June 1978.

BE IT ENACTED by the Queen, and the Senate and House of
Representatives of the Commonwealth of Australia, as follows:

1. This Act may be cited as the *Appropriation Act* (*No.* 1) 1977–78.   Short title

2. This Act shall come into operation on the day on which it receives   Commence-
the Royal Assent.   ment

3. The Treasurer may issue out of the Consolidated Revenue Fund   Issue and
and apply for the services specified in Schedule 2, in respect of the year   application
ending on 30 June 1978, the sum of $4,553,792,000.   of
$4,553,792,000

4. The sums authorized by section 3 of the *Supply Act* (*No.* 1) 1977–78   Appropria-
and by section 3 of this Act to be issued out of the Consolidated Revenue   tion of
Fund, amounting, as appears by Schedule 1, in the aggregate to the sum $8,066,055,000
of $8,066,055,000 are appropriated, and shall be deemed to have been
appropriated as from 1 July 1977, for the services expressed in Schedule 2
in respect of the financial year that commenced on that date.

5. (1) In addition to the sum referred to in section 4, the Treasurer   Additional
·may issue out of the Consolidated Revenue Fund for the service of the   appropria-
year ending on 30 June 1978 amounts not exceeding such amounts as   tion in
he determines in accordance with sub-section (2).   respect of
increases in
salaries

6.038/11.8.1977—12781/77   MR

Fig. 6.2 Appropriation Bill (No.1), the first of the Budget Bills presented by
the then Treasurer, Mr Lynch, on 16 August 1977. Schedule 2, which contains
the details of proposed expenditure on departments and services, runs to 128
pages. Appropriation Bill No. 2, which covered capital works and services,
covered the spending of $584 million.

appropriation, special appropriation, grants and bounties. The most important and vital financial bills are those which make up the annual Budget (normally introduced after the financial year has begun), those which provide additional appropriations towards the end of the financial year, and those which provide a government with "carry-on" finance between the beginning of the financial year and the passage of the annual budget.

The Budget is normally brought down by the Treasurer in mid-August, on the day parliament resumes after its winter recess. At 8 p.m. he presents the Appropriation Bill No. 1 and delivers his Budget speech as the second reading speech for that bill. When he finishes, and the debate is adjourned, he presents the other bills associated with the Budget, in particular Appropriation Bill No. 2 plus any sales tax and charges bills which are necessary. Appropriation Bill No. 1 deals with such matters as salaries, administrative expenses and other services which are the responsibility of government departments. Appropriation Bill No. 2 deals with capital works and services, payments to or for the states and other services to be paid for as a result of new government policies which are not dealt with in special legislation.

While the Treasurer is presenting his Budget speech in the House, the Leader of the Government in the Senate tables the Budget papers there and reads out the Treasurer's speech. The debate in both Houses is adjourned for a week and is resumed by the Leader of the Opposition who generally proposes an amendment critical of the government's economic or other policies. This amendment used to take the traditional and meaningless form of a proposal to reduce one of the estimates by £1. Now the amendment is proposed to the second reading of the bill and can specify the policy objection which the opposition has to the Budget or to the government's policies generally.

The debate generally proceeds for two or three weeks, and while much of it focuses on general economic policy, MPs are allowed to range as widely as they like. A similar debate takes place in the Senate. When the second reading debate is concluded, the House then goes into a committee to discuss the individual estimates for each Department. This allows a series of debates limited to the specific policy areas. When the Senate reaches the estimates stage, it divides itself into five committees. Generally only two of the committees meet at any one time, allowing Senators to look in on the work of committees other than the particular one to which they have assigned themselves.

When the Budget bills are finally cleared by the House of Representatives and are introduced into the Senate they generally are allowed to pass with little or no further debate.

Additional estimates are generally introduced about April. They provide for additional expenditure by Departments to take account of wage or price increases (Appropriation Bill No. 3) and new policy decisions which require expenditure for capital works (Appropriation Bill No. 4). The Treasurer's speech on this occasion is mainly explanatory of the additional amounts required. The debate can be general again, but both it and the estimates debate in committee are much briefer than at Budget time. The Senate does not consider these bills until they have been passed by the House, but it again divides into its estimates committees after a general debate on the second readings of the bills.

In April or May the Government also introduces its Supply Bills which are designed to appropriate money for the first five months of the next financial year (which runs from July to June). It is assumed that the Budget will pass before the end of November in the next financial year. The Supply Bills normally provide for expenditures which are 5/12ths of those in the then current financial year (i.e. five months *pro rata*); they can also contain additional amounts to take account of spending decisions already reached by the government and of any foreseeable contingencies which will have to be met. The Supply Bills are sometimes debated in conjunction with the additional estimates (Appropriations Bills 3 and 4). But when they are introduced later, they generally provoke only a short general debate—unless a government is facing an opposition-controlled Senate in which case they can be a vehicle for governmental discomfiture and possibly the forcing of an election.

Other financial bills are dealt with much as ordinary legislation, with debate limited to the subject matter of the bills. There are a few technical requirements, however, which distinguish them from ordinary bills. First, finance bills can be introduced only into the House of Representatives (Constitution, section 53). Second, any Bill appropriating money must be accompanied by a message from the Governor-General recommending the appropriation (this symbolises the importance of the government in the process and is a requirement of section 56 of the Constitution. The message is normally read after the second reading has been agreed to). Third, revenue-raising measures may be introduced without notice and no member other than a minister can move an amendment seeking to increase the proposed charge or broaden its effect (House standing order 293). Fourth, the Senate may not amend bills imposing taxes or appropriating revenue or monies for the ordinary annual services of the government, and it may not amend a bill to increase any proposed burden or charge (section 53 of the Constitution). However the Senate may make requests to the House for amendments though it cannot itself make the amendments. The requests are made and replies received from the

House before the third reading of the bill is passed by the Senate so that the Senate can determine whether or not to approve the legislation. Fifth, bills appropriating money for the annual services of government cannot contain any other matters; a bill imposing taxes can deal only with taxes and with one subject of taxation only; customs bills can deal only with customs; and excise bills only with excise duties (sections 54 and 55 of the Constitution). This prohibition of "tacking" (as it is called) is designed to prevent the House of Representatives from including extraneous matters in a bill which the Senate is not permitted to amend. Tariff measures come into effect on being announced by the government (usually when the Parliament is sitting, but not always). Tariffs are then collected in anticipation of authorising legislation being subsequently passed. The High Court has upheld this procedure, which is designed to protect the revenue.

Financial legislation provides the parliament with an opportunity to discuss the whole range of government policies at least two or three times a year (Budget, Supplementary Estimates, Supply, Loan Bills) both in general terms and in specifics (second reading and committee stages of the estimates). In the Senate, general debate is possible also on the first reading of any money bill (which the Senate cannot amend).

The Constitution and the provisions of standing orders make it difficult for members of either House to propose effective amendments to the details of financial legislation. However it is not beyond the powers of the Senate to propose amendments in the form of requests which it might be difficult for a government to resist. If the Senate does ever exercise this power (and some of its members were contemplating doing so early in 1978) a new field of legislative endeavour would open up in the Senate, and government control of the Senate would become even more imperative than it presently is.

Committees

The sudden growth of the committee system in the Senate in the late 1960s and early 1970s occurred at the time when Lionel Murphy (later Mr Justice Murphy of the High Court) was Leader of the ALP in the Senate. It was no mere coincidence.

Murphy was elected to the Senate in 1961 and took his place in July 1962. Before the end of his first six-year term of office he had become Leader of the Opposition in the Senate (in February 1967). His rapid rise was due in part to his energy, his obvious ability (he was a Q.C. and also had a science degree) and his youth in a chamber where the Labor Party had placed few young and talented men or women. Murphy was identified with the left wing of the Labor Party which made life rather difficult for him, because his continuance in the Senate depended on his pre-selection by the right-wing controlled N.S.W. branch of the ALP. His general strategy in trying to retain pre-selection would not dare refuse him pre-selection. His first target was to become leader of his party in the Senate, his second was to make that position more important by making the Senate seem more important.

That second task appeared to be the more difficult. The Labor Party had written a plank for abolition of the Senate into its platform more than fifty years earlier. The party regarded it as a blot on democracy that a government elected through the House of Representatives could have its measures altered or rejected by an upper house. Labor's suspicions of the Senate were hardened by the experience of the Depression years when its Scullin-led government was eventually forced out of office in part because of its inability to get legislation through the Senate. In the late 1940s, when it did control the Senate, the then Labor government had passed legislation altering the method of electing the Senate, introducing a proportional representation system which incorporated preferential voting. It was thought that such a system would help Labor retain control of the Senate even if it lost control of the House of Representatives. Labor's control was shortlived, however, as Menzies forced a double dissolution little more than a year after he had won control of the House. The double dissolution left the Liberal–Country Party Government in control of both Houses, a situation which persisted until 1967. At that point, control of the Senate shifted away from the government and the balance of power was left in the hands of a series of independent and Democratic Labor Party Senators throughout the next eight years (1967–75).

Thus Murphy came to the opposition leadership in the Senate at a time when the government was losing its absolute control of a Senate majority. Over the previous decade a number of Liberal Party Senators (Wright and Wood most notably) had demonstrated their preparedness to buck the party line and vote against their government if they felt strongly enough about an issue. Murphy set about cultivating the friendship of some of these occasional rebels as well as appealing to the political self-interest of the independents and the DLP Senators. He sought to enhance the self-esteem of these and other Senators by suggesting important committee work that the Senate might undertake. The government of the day appreciated the dangers of Murphy's strategy and tried to match it by also proposing the establishment of a number of committees.

In the first sixty five years of the Senate, a total of twenty-eight select committees had been established, some to inquire into individual grievances, some into proposed legislation, and some into more generalised subjects such as the development of Canberra, road safety or the encouragement of Australian productions for television. In the three years following Murphy's accession to opposition leadership in the Senate, a further eight select committees were appointed, half of them at the instigation of the opposition or government backbenchers. The government tried to keep Senators busy with interesting but non-political subjects such as the container method of handling cargoes, the metric system of weights and measures, air pollution and water pollution. The opposition proposed inquiries into subjects such as medical and hospital costs, an inquiry which ran in competition with an inquiry headed by a judge appointed by the Gorton government on the same subject.

Murphy's aggrandisement of Senate committee inquiries had received Whitlam's blessing at the end of 1967, when an election was held for the Senate; Whitlam attempted to produce a policy speech relevant to the Senate as well as to the general political situation. Murphy went further, however, in attempting to use the Senate to embarrass the government in such instances as the VIP aircraft affair, rejection of increased postal charges and other quite political exercises. By mid-1969, the Senate's anti-government role had been so enhanced that the Labor Party seriously considered dropping its anti-Senate policy plank (the party conference in effect suspended the policy until the 1971 Federal Conference, when it was restored).

Gorton's elevation from Liberal Senate leadership to Prime Ministership had a marked affect on the perception of Murphy's possible ambitions. He was seen as a possible future rival for Whitlam for the party leadership, though Labor Party rules would have prevented the kind of transition to the lower House leadership which Gorton had managed in the Liberal Party. Murphy fuelled these rumours with his continued efforts to boost Labor policy through the Senate, and to boost the Senate's status. In early 1970 he was responsible for proposing the formation of a Senate Select Committee into Securities and Exchange, later known as the Rae Committee, which held a devastating inquiry into the manipulation of the share market in Australia.

From mid-1969 Murphy had been considering proposals to formulate a US congressional-style committee system in the Senate, with permanent committees established to look at particular areas of government policy and administration. He privately sought briefing from the research service of the Parliamentary Library, while more publicly he raised the question of standing committees in the standing orders committee of the Senate. Murphy persuaded the committee to have the clerk of the Senate, Mr Jim Odgers, prepare a report on a possible committee system. Murphy and Odgers had had frequent

Public servants tend to be wary of the PAC without fearing it. It is the Auditor-General they have more reason to fear.

One of the disabilities the PAC suffers from, in its watchdog capacity, is that its chairman is a member of the government party or parties (as is the case with all parliamentary committees in Australia). In Britain the equivalent committee is chaired by an opposition MP and its activities are seen to be less quiescent.

Nevertheless the PAC proved more impressive than the Public Works Committee, whose main function seemed to be providing committee members with opportunities to have trips throughout the nation. It rarely caused the Departments to change any of their plans and gave little evidence that it saved the taxpayers any money in its review of all public works over a minimum figure (from 1973, $2 million). When the Menzies government in 1957 decided to revive the construction of Canberra as the national capital, it excluded the responsible authority (the National Capital Development Commission) from the requirement that its plans should be examined by the Public Works Committee.

Probably the most effective continuing committee was established by the Senate in 1932, the Regulations and Ordinances Committee. It examines all subordinate legislation (legislation in the form of regulations and ordinances approved by the Governor-General) to see that it conforms with various principles which the committee established. The committee, which mostly works in a non-partisan way, ensures that subordinate legislation:
a)   is in accordance with the legislation which authorised it;
b)   does not trepass unduly on personal rights and liberties;
c)   does not make personal rights and liberties dependent on administrative instead of judicial decisions; and
d)   is concerned with administrative detail and does not amount to substantive legislation involving matters of principle which should be approved by parliament.

The committee can enforce its standards through votes of the Senate as a whole: under the Acts Interpretation Act the Senate can nullify any regulation or ordinance with fifteen sitting days of its approval by the Governor-General. The committee's non-partisan reputation helps ensure that it normally receives voting support from both government and opposition. In fact the committee's reputation is such that once it has made a recommendation against an ordinance or regulation, the Department concerned usually withdraws the ordinance or regulation and redrafts it in accordance with the committee's wishes—without the necessity of a formal Senate vote.

The Regulations and Ordinances Committee is not the only committee on which members of all parties usually work in a non-partisan manner. Indeed this approach is the norm on committees of the Australian Parliament. Occasionally there are complaints that members of a particular party on a committee have "caucussed" to come to a common view, but this is rare. The Labor Party does not have a policy to commit its members of parliamentary committees to present a united party view: indeed in one Senate committee in 1975, Labor Senators unanimously agreed to recommend the withdrawal of a Labor government bill (on the introduction of a national compensation scheme).

In 1973, soon after coming to government, the Labor Party approved the establishment of a Committee on Committees. This was to be a joint committee of both Houses of Parliament with the aim of developing a rational system of parliamentary committees, combining the work of both Houses. At that time there was no "system" of committees at all. They had grown to meet needs and pressures and, in the case of the new Senate committees, ambitions.

Because of disagreements between the parties and the Houses, the Committee on Committees did not get underway until September 1974, more than a year after it was proposed. It attracted evidence from such notable politicians as Whitlam and Fraser and brought down an interim report late in 1975. It was reformed, with a Liberal–National Country Party majority, in 1976, and after a few months brought down its final report in much the same terms as its interim, Labor-controlled predecessor had in 1975.

Before its final report, however, the new Prime Minister, Fraser, had decided to implement his own version of a new committee system. In 1975, as Leader of the Opposition, Fraser had told the Committee he thought there should be an expenditure committee established, based on a similarly named committee of the House of Commons, to see that money was spent in accordance with parliament's directions and to see that the taxpayer got the best value for money within the framework of established government policy. Clearly the philosophy was different from that behind the establishment of Senate committees, which could be critical of government policy if they saw fit. Fraser's expenditure committee, however, would accept the goals of government policy, and try to ensure that the policy was carried out in the best (value-for-money) way. This was a parliamentary committee which no government, of whatever colour, could really object to, performing a worthwhile sort of job.

At the time of writing (early 1978), the committee had completed only two investigations. One was on accommodation for married servicemen, the other on Australia's overseas representation. But as the committee complained in a report summarising its first year's work ("A Year's Experience"), its recommendations had not prompted any government action—or even response—despite a prime ministerial promise that responsible ministers would promptly table government responses. This pointed criticism by the committee suggested a bipartisan determination by its members to make its presence felt.

The establishment of the Expenditure Committee did not meet with the approval of the Committee on Committees which preferred a general re-arrangement of committee functions in both the House and the Senate. This was partly to ease the burden on Senators, and partly to better reflect the idea that the House of Representatives should have prime responsibility for the supervision of financial matters that come before the parliament. The recommendation was for the abolition of the committee structure as it then stood, and its replacement with a more logical arrangement of standing committees specialising in subject areas, joint committees and select committees. The committee gave some indication of its own assessment of the value of its work when it titled its final report "A New Parliamentary Committee System".

Fraser's reaction was to ignore its recommendation about financial committees and to refer the whole report to a party committee headed by his Senate Whip for yet another report.

Though it made no public report, that government party committee did favour the creation of a network of legislation committees, one of the more important recommendations of the Committee on Committees. The legislation committees would take over the often non-committees stages of the examination of bills by the House, dealing with them out of the public spotlight in what was hoped to be a non-partisan way. During 1977 cabinet considered aspects of this proposal several times and considered bringing it into operation on a trial basis before the end of 1978.

Independents and minor party Senators

The emergence of Don Chipp and his Australian Democrat Party in 1977 made it inevitable that the House of Representatives elected in 1975 would have only a two-year term. The possibility that the Australian Democrats could attract a substantial number of votes persuaded both major parties that the Senate election due to be held between July 1977 and June 1978 had to be accompanied by an election for the House of Representatives.

There was no doubt that an election held separately for the Senate would magnify the vote for the Democrats and any other independant or small party group. Senate elections held in conjunction with House of Representatives elections are supposed to reduce "protest" votes against the major parties and concentrate the minds of voters on the major issue of which party should form the government.

With public opinion polls showing that the public disapproved of the leadership of both the government and the opposition, and showing that support for the Democrats was anything between 8 and 20 per cent, it was thus a foregone conclusion that the Senate election would be held in conjunction with the House of Representatives election. Despite this handicap, and the fact that the party was less than a year old, the Democrats managed to win over 10 per cent of the national vote, and to capture two Senate seats, one for Mr Chipp in Victoria, and one for Mr Mason in New South Wales. They joined a select group of independents and minor party members who have been elected to the Senate.

A change in the voting system for the Senate which came into operation in 1949 paved the way for an increase in independents and representatives of small parties. It also made it likely that these Senators would often be in a position to determine whether government or opposition prevailed in the Senate. The new system was proportional representation. Coupled with an increase in the size of the Senate, it meant that any individual who gained almost 17 per cent of the vote in a state would be elected as a Senator. In a double dissolution a candidate would need just a little more than 9 per cent of the vote to gain election. The new system was similar to the one that had been used in the Tasmanian Lower House.

The Constitution laid down a system of overlapping terms for Senators. Each Senator was to be elected for a six-year term, but half the Senators would retire every three years. Any Senator who died or retired would be replaced by a Senator appointed by the parliament of the state he represented and such appointees would have to face the electorate at the time of the next election—whether it be for the House of Representatives or the Senate (though this was changed by the 1977 referendum). The changes introduced in legislation passed in 1948 meant that each state would have ten Senators. At each Senate election (normally but not necessarily held in conjunction with House of Representatives elections) five Senators would be elected. Using a system of proportional representation a party would gain one senator for every 16.67 votes it accumulated in a state at the Senate election. Normally the ALP would be certain of two places, the Liberal--Country Parties of two, and the remaining seat would go to whichever of the two polled the better, overall, in that State.

Until 1954 only one independent had ever been elected to the Senate (in 1904). But from 1954 to 1978 another sixteen men were elected or appointed as independents or members of minor parties. From 1967 to 1975, the members of this group were generally in the position of

SEATING PLAN

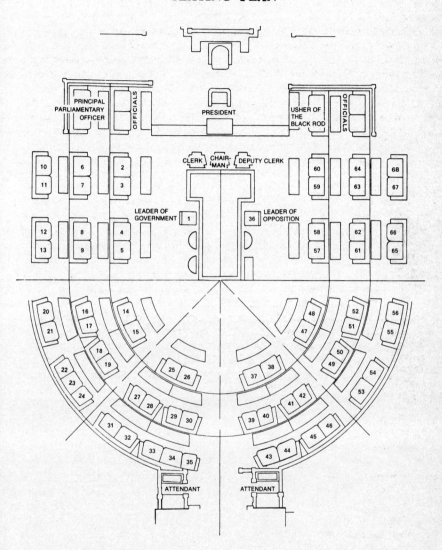

Fig. 6.3 Seating plan in the Senate. Ministers occupy seats 1-5, and 14. Independent and minor party Senators take up the seats nearest to the centre aisle, at the rear (43, 44, 39. 40).

deciding whether Labor or Liberal–National Country party legislative policies would prevail: they held what is commonly referred to as the "balance of power".

The group which benefitted most from the new voting system was the Democratic Labor Party. Formed in 1955 by groups which broke away from the Australian Labor Party, the DLP had its greatest strength in Victoria, Queensland and Tasmania. While it was never able to muster the 50 per cent needed to elect an MP in a House of Representatives electorate, the 20 per cent support it sometimes obtained in Victoria and Queensland was sufficient to allow it to elect a Senator at an ordinary (choosing five Senators) Senate election. The DLP (or "Australian Labor Party—Anti-Communist", as it first called itself) gained its first parliamentary representatives by defection from ALP ranks: Senator George Cole had been elected an ALP Senator from Tasmania in 1951 and he changed to the DLP during the split. Unlike his colleages in the Lower House who joined the DLP's ranks, Cole was able to get himself re-elected in his own right as a DLP Senator at subsequent elections. He remained in the Senate until 1965. Frank McManus was elected as a DLP Senator to represent Victoria in 1955. He held the position for one term (until 1962) and then was elected again in 1964 and re-elected in 1970. Vince Gair, a former Queensland Labor Premier, was elected by his state in 1964 and 1970 and became leader of the two-man group in 1965 when he and McManus took up their positions. In the next Senate elections (in 1967) two more DLP Senators were elected, Byrne (an ALP Senator in the 1950s who left the ALP with Gair) from Queensland and Little from Victoria.

The 1970 Senate elections which were not held in conjunction with Lower House elections returned a record number of Senators from outside the major parties. As well as the three DLP Senators, two independents (Negus from Western Australia and Townley from Tasmania) were elected. This surge of new blood was caused by a massive turning away from the major established parties by the Australian voters in the 1970 elections: 20 per cent of the total Australian vote went to independents and minor parties, compared with less than 5 per cent to these groups in Senate elections held between 1949 and 1955 and about 11 per cent in elections after that date. There was a return to a more normal pattern in the 1974 double dissolution when only 9 per cent of the votes were for independents and minor parties. In 1974 the DLP lost all its representation in the Senate, but the independent Townley retained his seat and Steele Hall, a former Liberal Premier of South Australia won a seat as Leader of the breakaway Liberal Movement.

The DLP's success from 1955 through to its defeat in 1974 could be largely attributed to its ideological appeal to an identifiable group in the community, though in some elections and in some states this was supplemented by the popularity and personal campaigning of some of its leaders (Cole in Tasmania, Gair in Queensland, McManus in Victoria).

Tasmanians have shown an unusual willingness to elect independents and minor party candidates. This can be attributed partly to the very small electorate, which allows candidates to become better known than is possible in the larger states. The state electoral system, which is almost the same as the Senate system, encourages the political parties to concentrate their campaigns around individuals, and Tasmanians have become accustomed to picking and choosing among lists of candidates put up to them by the major parties. People with political identities in Tasmania tend to do well in either federal or state elections there. Turnbull owed his success in the 1961 and 1967 elections to having been a minister in a Labor Government (Treasurer and Minister for Health) and for having been a well-known medical practitioner in Launceston. Townley possessed a name long associated with Tasmanian politics.

The victory of Negus in Western Australia was the result of a long campaign he had mounted on a particular issue—abolition of death duties—which hit the hip-pocket nerve. He gained personal support of those interested in the cause, amassing over 100000 signatures on petitions. In South Australia, Hall's success could be attributed both to his personal popularity and the appeal of his party which was a breakaway group formed from the Liberal Country League.

The strategic position occupied by all these independents and minor party Senators between 1967 and 1975 can be seen from Table 6.1:

Governments and oppositions recognised the importance of these men in the middle and did their best to cultivate them and secure their votes. They were also courted by lobbyists, who normally pay little attention to individual backbenchers. On a crucial issue the independent and minor party Senators could expect to receive a barrage of mail and calls from their associates "back home", that the groups most affected would try to interview them in Canberra to lobby for their support, and that both government and opposition Senators would seek to influence them through personal contact.

The way in which governments may seek to influence the votes of independents and minor party Senators can be seen in a number of actions which affected the status of the DLP and other Senators. The DLP was given the rights of a "minor" party in the Senate when it contained two members. Its Leader had a special allowance and later additional staff and improved office accommodation were provided. When it became a five man group, even its Whip was given additional

TABLE 6.1   *Senators' Party Affiliations, 1967–75*

	Liberal-(National) Country Party	Demo-cratic Labor Party	Indepen-dent	Liberal Move-ment	Australian Labor Party
November 1963–June 1965	31	1	1		27
July 1965–October 1966 (Senators elected at 1964 Senate elections join those elected 1961.)	30	2	1		27
February 1967–October 1967 (ALP Senator elected at 1966 House election to replace Liberal Senator. Hannaford resigns from Libs and becomes independent.)	28	2	2		28
November 1967–June 1968 (Senator Hannaford dies and is replaced by Liberal)	29	2	1		28
July 1968–December 1969 (Senators elected at 1967 Senate election join those elected 1964)	28	4	1		27
February 1970–June 1971 (Liberal Senator replaced by ALP at 1969 House election)	27	4	1		28
July 1971–April 1974 (Senators elected at 1970 Senate election join those elected 1967.)	26	5	3		26
July 1974–November 1974 (Senators all elected at double dissolution 1974)	28	—	1	1	30
February 1975–June 1975 (Retired ALP Senator replaced by appointed Independent)	28	—	2	1	29
September 1975–November 1975 (Deceased ALP Senator replaced by appointed Independent)	28	—	3	1	28

NOTE: Vote required to carry resolution in the Senate during this period: 31

privileges. Senator Turnbull had a brief association in 1969-70 with the Australia Party as its leader and sole parliamentary member, but was unable to persuade the government to give him any special privileges. However the Liberal–Country Party government was happy about giving him overseas trips—long ones. In both 1970 and 1971 he was chosen to join the Australian delegation at the United Nations, a move which seemed to owe more to the government's desire to have him out of the Senate (he was more inclined to vote with Labor than with the government on crucial issues) than to any high regard for his diplomatic abilities. Between 1970 and 1972, DLP Senators also received many overseas trips as members of parliamentary delegations and as delegates to the Inter-Parliamentary Union. The government normally could afford to allow one or two DLP Senators to be absent without affecting its ability to control the Senate if the remaining DLP members supported it—as they mostly did. Naturally there were no arrangements for "pairs" while these independent and DLP Senators were overseas.

Under Labor, similar approaches were adopted. Senator Hall, like Senator Turnbull before him, was leader of just a one-man parliamentary party. But the Labor Government was sympathetic to him and thought it would benefit from giving Hall additional status as a leader, which meant he had additional staff, accommodation and transport facilities at his disposal. Senator Townley, who could be counted on to vote against the government on most occasions, also was given a trip away—during the time the Senate was sitting.

There was nothing improper about these activities by various governments, it was just a question of exploring the way the system could be used to benefit friends! If these were any improprieties, they never surfaced and it is unlikely that they would have been associated with governments. Steele Hall was once approached by a Liberal backbencher who suggested that he had some friends who might make available $100 000 to the Liberal Movement (the backbencher claimed the funds had previously been directed to the DLP). The money didn't materialise.

Getting sufficient money to run a full campaign can be seen as one of the greatest problems facing these men. Hall raised about $150 000 in four years and his party organisation raised a similar amount. The DLP spent even larger amounts on television advertising. But none of the smaller parties could raise anything approaching the vast sums spent by the major parties. In the 1977 elections the Democrats' constant complaint was their lack of money and campaign facilities.

Another problem faced by these men (but not by the average backbencher) was that they actually had to make decisions on how they would vote on issues before the parliament sat. The average backbencher simply does what his party tells him to do. The DLP Senators mostly voted together as a party and decided jointly on policy stances. But for the independent who wanted to demonstrate his independence, matters were not quite so simple. Each tended to vote with a particular party on unimportant issues (Hall and Townley with the Liberals, Turnbull with Labor) but then had to decide when to break away. Hall did this more frequently than Townley. Turnbull was more likely to abstain. On important issues the independents would sometimes be influenced by other Senators, sometimes by associates from their home states, sometimes by lobbyists. Hall was more ready than most of his colleagues to call on the parliamentary library to prepare an appreciation of a particular problem. Frequently the independents would talk matters over among themselves, aware that if they voted together they would increase their influence and probably determine the outcome of a particular measure. Hall certainly worked hard on persuading Townley to vote with him in supporting vital clauses in the Labor Government's Restrictive Trade Practices legislation, one of the few occasions when Townley did not vote with the Liberals.

The independents and smaller party Senators could exercise power over motions, bills and procedural matters which either government or oppositions initiated. But they had very little power themselves to initiate anything. The standing orders precluded them from bringing on an urgency debate unless they could get the support of four other members of the Senate. (In 1971, the DLP was able to propose its own urgency debates without the support of other Senators; however getting anything carried still required the support of other Labor or Liberal–Country Party Senators.) Their lack of power in this regard matched that of backbenchers on both sides of the parliament and the comparatively meek acceptance of this position can be seen in the rarity of private member's bills in the Australian Parliament. Few are introduced and it is rare for one to be passed through both Houses.

In the House of Representatives, the standing orders are weighted against private member's legislation, which normally can only be discussed during general business that occupies about one and a half hours every fortnight. Unless a bill is disposed of within that period, and that means it will not be debated at all adequately, it will not be discussed again. Once adjourned, a general business motion goes to the bottom of the list of general business items and its chances of ever being revived are very dim. In the Senate the prospects for the private member are somewhat better, partly because more time is available for general business and there tend to be fewer items of general business, and partly because there is a more sympathetic approach by Senators to such matters. But even if a bill does clear the Senate it has little prospect of clearing the obstacles placed before it by the House standing orders and government control of the House.

Through the late 1960s and early 1970s, the ALP in opposition made use of private member's bills to highlight sensitive political issues where the government could be damaged. Murphy introduced into the Senate a private member's bill to introduce votes for eighteen-year-olds. It passed the Senate, but not the House. He also obtained Senate approval for a bill to abolish capital punishment for federal crimes and in the Territories, but this too failed to get through the House. But bills from government backbenchers, the DLP or the independents were rare. The DLP introduced a bill to provide for *per capita* grants for private schools; Senator Negus introduced a bill to abolish death duties; but neither succeeded. The main private member's bill to pass the parliament in recent years was introduced by Murphy when he was Attorney-General. This was his Family Law Bill. It was dealt with as a private member's bill because both the government and the opposition decided it should be treated as a conscience issue, with all MPs and Senators having a free vote. But it obtained special treatment not normally given to private member's legislation. It was debated in time specially allocated for it in both chambers and in the House of Representatives additional sitting days were set aside to consider it.

Another successful private member's bill was introduced by Senator Wright. It dealt with the site for the proposed new parliament house. Only two other private member's bills have ever passed the parliament—in 1909 (dealing with arbitration) and 1924 (making voting at elections compulsory). An overwhelming majority of private member's bills introduced in both Houses have been officially sponsored by the opposition. The Senate has generally been preferred as the House of origin of these bills because of the better prospects of their passing one of the two houses, and attracting publicity.

The 1975 double dissolution brought to at least a temporary end the powerful influence of men like Senator Hall. In 1976 the Liberal–National Country Party coalition had a clear majority in the Senate as well as in the House. It was in no immediate danger of losing its majority in the Senate, and unless it had exceptional losses through deaths or resignations, it was going to keep its majority through the next election also. Senator Hall was one of two Senators elected in 1975 who did not belong to one of the major parties. The other was a Tasmanian, Senator Harradine, who had split from the ALP in contesting his seat. Neither was able to exercise any power in the Senate, however, and neither was able to generate worthwhile publicity. As if in recognition of the reduced status of independence in such circumstances, Senator Hall had rejoined the Liberal Party by the end of the first sittings of the new parliament. He later announced he would not seek pre-selection for another term in the Senate and narrowly failed to gain election to a South Australian seat in the House of Representatives in the 1977 election.

The two Australian Democrat Senators elected in 1977 found themselves very much in the same position as Hall and Harradine in 1976–77 (Harradine continued in the Senate, not facing an election until 1980–81). While they were free to vote for or against measures as they saw fit, and to initiate their own proposals for legislation, inquiries or debates, they had no power. The government, with a majority in the Senate as well as the House, had no need to rely on them at all or to take any notice of them, except insofar as they might attempt to encourage dissent and revolt among the ranks of government Senators.

7 Parliamentarians: Work and Worth

Australia's national parliamentarians are paid to be full-time members of parliament. The various commissions and tribunals which governments have had inquire into parliamentary salaries have all recommended salary scales based on the proposition that being a member of the Australian Parliament entails work which generally does not permit the earning of a supplementary salary. As Mr Justice (later Sir John) Kerr reported on his 1971 inquiry into *Salaries and Allowances of Members of the Commonwealth Parliament,*

> Members of parliament are occupied full-time in their parliamentary duties. Previous Commonwealth committees have come to the same conclusion. This is true for almost all members, if one takes parliamentary duties to include their work not only in the parliament but also in their electorates where they are required to move amongst the electors, be in a position to represent their views and help them with their problems in the parliament and in other places. A few members seek to continue the practice of their professions on a very limited scale. This may be possible in the case of some lawyers. Doctors find it much more difficult to do part-time professional work. Members who were previously salaried employees find it impossible to carry on employment. Some members endeavour to some extent to continue previous occupations, for example, in rural production. This is done mainly in the limited amount of spare time available and generally with additional help. It is clear that what may be done by relatively few members cannot be their main pre-occupation because parliamentary duties press upon them and are most demanding on members' time.
>
> It must be remembered that members have to spend much of their time in Canberra and this in itself, apart from the constant nature of their parliamentary and electoral duties, makes it almost impossible to carry on most occupations even on a limited basis.

Despite previous statements by committees of inquiry that the work is full-time work many people do not know or believe this to be, as it is, the case.

Members work long hours both in the parliament, on associated activities such as parliamentary committee work and in their electorates attending to the demands and problems of their constituents, or in accepting social and other engagements which fall to their lot because of their positions as parliamentarians. These engagements are not to be thought of as mere pleasurable activities in a parliamentarian's leisure time. Attendance is necessary politically and the ear of the parliamentarian is constantly sought at these functions for various representational purposes. The suggestion was made that members should be discouraged from placing so much emphasis on such aspects of their activities in the electorate, or should have an agent to take the burden of most of it. However, members appear to believe that most of this work is politically necessary and it will certainly continue in the foreseeable future at the present level. (pp 29-30)

The Constitution makes the parliament itself responsible for determining the salaries and allowances of members and ministers, but most governments have regarded the task as invidious. They have preferred to seek outside advice on salary levels rather than be seen as assessing their own worth. The McMahon government, which commissioned the Kerr study, also sought from Kerr a permanent answer to the problem of how salaries should be set. The unstated premise was that the government wanted a system that would allow a regular review of salaries while in some way reducing the odium associated with the idea that the politicians were setting their own salaries. Kerr recommended the establishment of a Salaries Tribunal to make regular reviews and then make recommendations. The idea was taken further by the Whitlam government which proposed legislation (that was accepted by the Parliament) for a Remuneration Tribunal which would not only make regular reviews but actually make determinations about various salaries and allowances which would become operative unless either House disallowed them. As well as examining parliamentary salaries and allowances, the Tribunal was also to be responsible for determining the salaries and allowances of first division public servants and other public office holders and for reporting on salaries and allowances which should be paid to federal judges. As an attempt to remove the question of parliamentary salaries from the area of politics this legislation was not successful. The very first determinations and recommendations of the Tribunal were disapproved by the parliament following a dispute between the opposition and the government. The same fate befell the Tribunal's third determinations and recommendations. The second report of the

Tribunal, which was adopted, repeated the terms of the first. But in the fourth report (in 1976), the Tribunal decided not to repeat what it had suggested in its third report. The Tribunal said:

> Our Reports and Determinations at this time have been influenced, to some extent, by what we consider to be the extent of the increase in the level of the remuneration package for Senators and Members which either House of the Parliament might not disapprove as being unreasonable in the present economic climate....
>
> In the present economic climate where wage restraint is stated by the Government to be an essential ingredient of its economic policy, this Tribunal feels unable to give full salary justice now to all persons within its jurisdiction when its determinations are subject to disapproval by the Parliament. (pp. 11, 12)

Thus, bringing the salaries of judges and most senior public servants within the orbit of the Tribunal determining politicians' salaries did not have the effect as had been hoped, of freeing the salaries of politicians from political constraints, but rather introduced those constraints into the determinations of the salaries of the judges and senior public servants.

At a time when governments were trying to combat a high rate of inflation in Australia and politicians were being challenged to provide a lead in steadying the rate of increase in wages and salaries, it was inevitable that there would be some deterioration in the comparative level of parliamentary salaries. In the late 1960s the parliamentarians had managed to reach near-equality with the lowest level of the second division of the Commonwealth Public Service.* The 1974 review

---

* Commonwealth public servants are divided into four divisions. The first divisions consists of the permanent heads of Departments (in June 1977, just twenty eight men). The second division (in which there are six levels) contains about 1300 people who form the top management, policy advising and administrative group in the public service. The third division, of about 67 000 people includes specialist, administrative and clerical staff—the largest group being in the clerical–administrative area. There are ten classes in the third division, ranging from a base grade clerk through to a class 11. Examinations for entry to the third division are based on end of secondary school educational standards. The fourth division includes trades and support staff, typists and clerical assistants.

In mid-1977, the basic salary for first division officers was $38 000 plus an allowance of $2 500. Heads of some of the "top" Departments (e.g. Treasury, Prime Minister's) were paid slightly more. Second division salaries ranged between $25 108 (level one) and $36 931 (level six). In the third division a newly promoted class 11 (at the top of the division) would receive $20 770, a class 8 (attained by a graduate after five or six years in the service) $16 699; a class 6 (to which a graduate would be quickly promoted) $13 744; and a base grade clerk (i.e. basic entry into the third division, at class 1) $7 838.

would have put MPs half way up the second division scale, but the 1976 report by the Remuneration Tribunal left parliamentarians well below the lowest level in the second division with their base salary of $21 250 compared with $22 902 for public servants. And this was only slightly higher than the salaries paid to state politicians who would appear to have lower workloads and lesser responsibilities than the federal parliamentarians. Nevertheless, the salary paid to MPs and Senators was substantial (almost two and a half times average male weekly earnings). Table 7.1 shows recent salary proposals for federal parliamentarians, including those which were rejected by the parliament.

TABLE 7.1   *Basic Salary Recommendations for Senators and Members, 1952–76*

1952	1956	1959	1964	1968	1971 not accepted	1973	1974 not accepted	1975	1975 not accepted	1976	1977
3500	4700	5500	7000	9500	13000	14500	20000	20000	20720	21250	24369

Source: Reports of the Remuneration Tribunal

Table 7.2 compares salaries paid to federal MPs and Senators in 1977 with salaries paid to state parliamentarians.

TABLE 7.2   *Salaries paid to Australian Parliamentarians, June 1977*

	Common-wealth	N.S.W.	Victoria	Queens-land	South Australia	Western Australia	Tasmania
Basic Salary	24369	20660	20750	21840	19770	19611	18975
Date of last increase	1.6.77	1.1.77	1.6.76	1.7.76	1.1.77	1.12.76	1.7.76

Source: Remuneration Tribunal 1977

All parliamentarians, federal and state, are also paid special electorate allowances, which are supposed to cover expenses of office. These allowances do not have to be accounted for in any way (except to the taxation office). The allowances have not increased as rapidly as

salaries and their rate of increase fell behind salaries particularly
during the late 1960s and early 1970s. The Remuneration Tribunal
restored their relativity to salaries (about 30 per cent) in 1976 when it
found that 70 per cent of state parliamentarians received higher
allowances than their federal counterparts although, as the Tribunal
pointed out, most federal electorates embraced more than one (and up
to twelve) state electorates. The Tribunal also decided to reintroduce
differential rates of electorate allowances which varied with the size of
the electorates. The electorate allowances were further increased in
1977.

TABLE 7.3   *Allowances paid to Parliamentarians, June 1977*

	Common-wealth	N.S.W.	Victoria	Queens-land	South Australia	Western Australia	Tasmania
City MPs	6000	6300	5225	3620	2960	4200	2087
Country MPs	7500	9900	7035	8830	6800	9000	6461

NOTE: Senators are paid at the rate of city MPs.
Source: Remuneration Tribunal 1977

In addition to electorate allowances, MPs and Senators receive a
vast range of other payments, allowances and entitlements. These are
also now largely determined by the Remuneration Tribunal, though
the Tribunal has to take into account changes in government policy
involving the introduction of new or different entitlements. For
example, the Labor government decided to allow all MPs to hire a
research assistant though the Tribunal had not favoured such wide-
scale use of these assistants. After the proposal was adopted, the
Tribunal added it to the list of entitlements for MPs. In 1977 it
recommended that MPs be allowed another research assistant when
office accommodation became available in Parliament House.

In 1977 all MPs and Senators received a basic stamp allowance of
$1000; they were also entitled to 1000 postage-free envelopes (to be
used only from Parliament House) a month—this facility was worth
$2160 a year). Senators and members were paid an allowance of $37 a
day while they were in Canberra and $45 a day elsewhere in Australia
when their stay was caused primarily by a meeting of the parliament,
or a committee, or attendance at official functions. As from 1976,
shadow ministers were entitled to be paid travelling allowances for up
to twenty overnight stays a year when performing their duties as
shadow ministers. All federal parliamentarians were entitled to free
first-class air travel inside Australia on official business except between
Melbourne–Canberra–Sydney), including electorate business, or first

class travel on rail or other scheduled transport operations. They could use official cars when travelling to and from parliament, and they could be paid for use of their own cars at public service rates. MPs from the eight electorates bigger than 200000 square kilometres could use charter aircraft to a value of $4000 a year for electorate work, while the fourteen MPs with electorates of between 30000 square kilometres and 200000 square kilometres could spend up to $2000 on charter aircraft. The two Northern Territory Senators were also given this right to use charter aircraft.

All parliamentarians were provided with free telephones in their private homes, though from 1976 they were expected to make a small contribution for private calls. They were all issued with credit cards entitling them to make free long-distance calls and send free telegrams anywhere in Australia, on political business. Each MP and Senator was provided with an electorate office and could hire an electorate secretary and an additional staff member who could be located in the electorate or in Canberra and who could serve as a research officer. This research officer position could be pooled with other MPs (thus increasing the salary the employee could be paid) or several could be employed on a part-time basis.

Every MP and Senator was entitled to fly his spouse or nominee to Canberra at government expense six times a year and interstate once a year, as well as to all official functions for which an invitation was issued (such as the opening of Parliament, or a reception for Royalty).

Parliamentarians who served more than one term in the parliament became eligible to one free, first-class, round-the-world air ticket for every subsequent parliament they served in. This was to be used only for fares for "overseas study travel" but could be used to pay fares of the parliamentarian's spouse. A "credit" for the trip in one parliament could be carried over and used with the credit in the next. This system of providing for overseas travel was introduced in 1976 and replaced a complex series of arrangements which entitled MPs and Senators to flights to Australian territories and to New Zealand.

Some parliamentarians were entitled to additional salaries, allowances and facilities because of their positions as "office holders" in the parliament. These included the Leader of the Opposition, the presiding officers and their deputies, and the various Whips in the two chambers, together with chairmen of parliamentary committees. The Leader of the Opposition in 1977 was paid an additional salary of $11750 and an allowance of $6600. The two presiding officers each received $10500 a year salary and an allowance of $5500. These salaries and allowances equated them with senior ministers and ministers, respectively. The salaries and allowances of other office holders as at June 1976 are listed in Table 7.4.

TABLE 7.4 *Additional Salaries and Allowances* Paid to Office Holders, 1 June 1977*

Office	Rate per annum of additional salary $	Rate per annum of special allowance $	Travelling allowance per overnight stay	
			Canberra $	Elsewhere $
Leader of the Opposition ‡	11750	6600		
President of the Senate ‡ / Speaker of the House of Representatives ‡	10500	5500	37	57
Deputy Leader of the Opposition ‡ / Leader of the Opposition in the Senate ‡	8500	5250		
Chairman of Committees in the Senate / Chairman of Committees in the House of Representatives	4500	1100	37	57
Deputy Leader of the Opposition in the Senate ‡	4250			
Government Whip in the House of Representatives ‡	4250	Nil		
Opposition Whip in the House of Representatives ‡	3750	Nil		
Government Whip in the Senate ‡ / Opposition Whip in the Senate ‡	3500	Nil		
Third Party Whip in the House of Representatives	2500	Nil	As for a Senator or member ($37 in Canberra; $45 elsewhere)	

Deputy Government Whip in the House of Representatives	1250	Nil	
Chairman of the Joint Parliamentary Committee of Public Accounts			
Chairman of the Parliamentary Standing Committee on Public Works	1000	Nil	
Third Party Whip in the Senate			
Deputy Government Whip in the Senate			
Deputy Opposition Whip in the Senate			
Deputy Opposition Whip in the House of Representatives	600	Nil	As for a Senator or member
Chairman of a Parliamentary Committee other than Public Accounts or Public Works			

‡ *Denotes that the holder, in addition to the stamp allowance which he receives as a senator or member, shall be provided with unlimited postage in relation to the duties of his office.*

Source: Remuneration Tribunal 1977

In addition to the pay and allowance they received as MPs, ministers received pay and allowances which recognise their additional duties. Salaries and allowances were increased in 1976, allowances only in 1977.

Ministers received a higher rate of travelling allowance ($57 a day) than ordinary MPs ($45) when they were outside Canberra, but the same ($37) when in Canberra. However they would be expected to do

TABLE 7.5   *Minister's Salaries and Allowances, 1977*

	Salary per year $	Allowance per year $
Prime Minister	28 250	13 200
Deputy Prime Minister	14 250	6 600
Treasurer	13 250	6 600
Leader of the Government in the House/Senate	11 750	6 600
Minister in Cabinet	11 750	5 500
Minister not in Cabinet	10 500	5 500

Source: Remuneration Tribunal 1977

considerably more travelling than backbenchers and were entitled to claim whenever they travelled on "official business as a minister". The Prime Minister received no travel allowance but all his accommodation and sustenance while he was on official business were to be provided at government expense, provided he was not at his home base. Ministers had an unlimited stamp allowance for their official business, they had cars allocated to them in Canberra and at their home offices on virtually a permanent basis, and they had access to official cars and other facilities wherever they travelled in Australia (or abroad).

All these facilities, pay and privileges were available to MPs, Senators, office holders and ministers whether they earned them or not. They appeared to be calculated to meet the needs and deserts of the politicians who work hardest. Thus the salary for all MPs and Senators is supposed to include an element which takes account of increased parliamentary activity in recent years as well as the abolition of special sitting fees for committee work. Not all MPs or Senators sit on committees, however, and the workload is spread very unevenly among those who do. The electorate allowance takes account of the many expenses which an ordinary MP has to undertake within his electorate (donations to charities, travel, etc.) but there is no compulsion on MPs to spend *all* the allowance on electorate expenses. There are other elements of the allowances and other facilities which are also open to abuse. It was not unknown, for example, for an MP to turn his stamps into cash (the Remuneration Tribunal took this into account when it had franking machines introduced into the offices of MPs. The stamp allowance was thus available only through use of the franking machine and the letters posted from Parliament House). Some MPs find it financially rewarding to drive their cars long distances for the parliamentary sessions, as the cost this way can be considerably less than the first-class air fare with which they are reimbursed for their efforts.

Ministers are in an even better position to take advantage of their allowances because they get so many more. Ministerial cars, for example, are frequently used for other than official business. They have been used for taking the minister's wife (or staff) shopping, for ferrying children to and from school or for going to the theatre or to a non-official dinner. Regular drivers tend to be used as additional office staff, as batmen, and as escorts for the minister's family. Travel facilities are used to transport a minister anywhere in Australia for any purpose: it is easy enough for any minister to introduce an "official business" element into a journey. On overseas trips, where ministers are paid their expenses in advance, not all bother to do an accurate accounting, though most of their meals and travel expenses will be paid for by others, and on occasions their accommodation will be supplied entirely by the government of the country which they are visiting or by the Australian Embassy.

Perhaps the greatest potential source of additional income for MPs and ministers is provided through their basic travelling allowances, both in Canberra and elsewhere in Australia. While some MPs and ministers live in hotels and have to pay out at least as much as they receive in travelling allowance, many manage to make arrangements (particularly while they are in Canberra—which accounts for the lower allowance paid while they are there) which net them a profit on their allowance. Some MPs have clubbed together to buy houses or flats and then devoted their travelling allowance to paying off these assets. Others board cheaply and simply pocket the difference. While in Canberra, MPs have the advantage of being able to eat very cheaply at Parliament House in the dining room which is heavily subsidised by taxpayers, and which extends very long-term credit.

Generalising about the way in which these various perquisites are used is difficult. It is probably fair to say that those MPs who work hard in their electorate, particularly those with fairly borderline seats who cannot be sure that they will be returned to parliament in the next election, or the one after that, don't make much money out of their parliamentary office. They have to spend all their allowances in order to live in the manner which they think their constituents believe is fitting for a parliamentary representative. It is probable that an MP who loses his seat after one or two elections will not have received adequate financial compensation for the disruption to his way of living and his occupation entailed by his parliamentary experience. Perversely, all the privileges and benefits of parliamentary life are adjusted to suit those who stay longest in the parliament.

This is illustrated in the way in which special travel benefits are made available to former parliamentarians. Those who have served twenty years in the parliament (or who have been ministers or senior office holders for six years or Prime Minister for one) are entitled to a "life gold pass" which entitles them and their spouse to free air, rail and other transport in Australia. Those who serve less than this time can get some free travel, for themselves and not their spouses, at a rapidly decreasing rate: those who have served for three parliaments get two years free travel, those who were in two parliaments get one year and those who were in only one parliament get six months free travel.

The same principle applies in the determination of retiring allowances. All MPs and Senators pay 11.5 per cent of their salary into a compulsory retiring allowances scheme. MPs and Senators who serve in fewer than three parliaments and who are then defeated at an election are entitled only to the return of their contributions plus a Commonwealth contribution (double what they paid in). Those who pass the three parliament (or eight year) barrier, or those who retire voluntarily after being in parliament for twelve years, qualify for the allowance proper. The allowance varies with service, those who have been in the parliament for eight years getting 50 per cent of the parliamentary allowance (which is adjusted to keep it equal to current parliamentary salaries). For every additional year of service, the retiring member gets an additional two per cent of the allowance, which reaches a maximum of 75 per cent of the current parliamentary salary when a member has served twenty years or more.

The various tribunals which have looked at parliamentary salaries and allowances have resiled from conducting "work value" studies on parliamentarians to see just what they are worth. The view has been that they should be paid not so much for the work they do as for the position they hold in society. In 1971, Mr Justice Kerr said:

> Each Member makes his individual contribution to national affairs and satisfies his electors periodically as to his fitness for the task of being their parliamentary representative. He is accountable to his electors for the value of his work, in most cases through the operation of the party system. Ordinary work-value concepts, though relevant, provide an inadequate approach both to the assessment of the importance and prestige of the national Parliament and its Members and to the determination of parliamentary salaries.
>
> Parliament is a central institution established by the Constitution. For the operation of Australian political democracy, the adoption of national policies, their embodiment in legislation and the debate of great national issues, Parliament and Members of Parliament are a constitutional and political necessity. I take it for granted that their work and activities are of a multi-skilled kind of

great importance and that they are central to the process of government in Australia. . . .

To fix a salary for Members, however, is a much more complex task than fixing a salary for any group of employees, however exalted the latter may be. It is not a question merely of putting a money value on their work. If value were the sole criterion it could lead to the fixing of a salary at a level which could distort the representational quality of Parliament. It is argued by some that the work is so important and so demanding in relation to ability that it should be as highly rewarded at least as is the work of the most senior public servants. Those of this view appear to believe that only essentially political persons would seek a political career even if the salaries were very high. (page 25)

Kerr rejected that view. Like all his predecessors and successors who have made recommendations on parliamentary salaries, Kerr tried to draw a line between setting a salary which was so high that it would attract everyone to want to be an MP and setting it so low that it would have the effect of keeping out of the parliament too many people who could not make the necessary financial sacrifices. The 1974 Remuneration Tribunal was of the opinion

that members of parliament should be able to provide for their families a standard of living not inferior to that available to many persons occupying positions substantially below the heads of government departments and instrumentalities and private enterprise concerns. (page 8).

This Tribunal accepted that it was not appropriate to make a work value judgment, noting that "a parliamentarian's occupation possesses qualities which are unique and there are no strictly comparable occupations for salary determination purposes". (page 6). Nevertheless it made a work judgment of sorts when it said it was satisfied

that the workload of Members has increased over the last three years. This is reflected in the number of sitting days in both the Senate and the House of Representatives in recent years (allowances being made for election years) and in the increased volume of legislation. It is reflected also in the increased volume and diversity of committee work both at parliamentary and party levels. (page 7).

Tables of sitting days and legislation provide an indication of how much the parliament produces, and what time it spends producing it. Tables 7.6 and 7.7 list sitting days of both Houses, and the Acts passed by the parliament since federation.

However these tables do not say much about the work of individual parliamentarians, or even the average parliamentarian, apart from suggesting that the parliamentarian of the 1970s devotes far less time to

TABLE 7.6   Commonwealth Parliament: Sitting Days

Year	Senate	H. of R.	Year	Senate	H. of R.
1901............	85	113	1939............	33	51
1902............	93	107	1940............	34	43
1903............	62	78	1941............	38	50
1904............	64	122	1942............	36	45
1905............	66	90	1943............	36	48
1906............	57	70	1944............	43	57
1907............	65	97	1945............	51	90
1908............	84	91	1946............	42	65
1909............	71	98	1947............	38	92
1910............	65	83	1948............	39	90
1911............	46	61	1949............	32	80
1912............	60	105	1950............	66	83
1913............	34	74	1951............	40	56
1914............	53	61	1952............	39	74
1915............	57	72	1953............	40	61
1916............	33	32	1954............	35	48
1917............	48	52	1955............	36	52
1918............	68	86	1956............	58	79
1919............	39	51	1957............	54	63
1920............	76	114	1958............	37	48
1921............	79	93	1959............	71	71
1922............	44	53	1960............	71	74
1923............	35	52	1961............	52	55
1924............	64	83	1962............	65	66
1925............	31	36	1963............	42	53
1926............	61	84	1964............	62	65
1927............	44	59	1965............	63	76
1928............	43	62	1966............	46	55
1929............	43	54	1967............	65	62
1930............	64	98	1968............	68	67
1931............	76	94	1969............	53	51
1932............	53	73	1970............	73	73
1933............	49	67	1971............	73	74
1934............	22	35	1972............	63	60
1935............	37	55	1973............	80	81
1936............	49	71	1974............	64	62
1937............	27	29	1975............	72	69
1938............	46	66	1976............	79	79
			1977............	68	72

TABLE 7.7   *Commonwealth Parliament: Bills Enacted*

	Where initiated				Where initiated		
Year	Senate	House of Represent- atives	Total	Year	Senate	House of Represent- atives	Total
1901.....	5	12	17	1939.....	11	76	87
1902.....	3	18	21	1940.....	7	92	99
1903.....	4	17	21	1941.....	1	69	70
1904.....	3	12	15	1942.....	3	55	58
1905.....	4	22	26	1943.....	2	56	58
1906.....	3	20	23	1944.....	6	40	46
1907.....	4	8	12	1945.....	3	56	59
1908.....	2	25	27	1946.....	2	79	81
1909.....	8	21	29	1947.....	13	80	93
1910.....	6	35	41	1948.....	13	80	93
1911.....	5	24	29	1949.....	14	73	87
1912.....	8	35	43	1950.....	7	73	80
1913.....	1	23	24	1951.....	5	77	82
1914.....	1	35	36	1952.....	5	104	109
1915.....	6	47	53	1953.....	18	78	96
1916.....	11	30	41	1954.....	11	72	83
1917.....	3	37	40	1955.....	10	61	71
1918.....	10	37	47	1956.....	14	99	113
1919.....	4	28	32	1957.....	17	86	103
1920.....	12	44	56	1958.....	20	63	83
1921.....	4	39	43	1959.....	7	97	104
1922.....	10	32	42	1960.....	10	101	111
1923.....	1	35	36	1961.....	6	92	98
1924.....	8	53	61	1962.....	4	104	108
1925.....	6	26	32	1963.....	10	93	103
1926.....	7	45	52	1964.....	7	123	130
1927.....	3	35	38	1965.....	11	145	156
1928.....	9	39	48	1966.....	3	90	93
1929.....	—	35	35	1967.....	6	118	124
1930.....	4	74	78	1968.....	13	144	157
1931.....	2	54	56	1969.....	—	102	102
1932.....	14	62	76	1970.....	6	121	127
1933.....	7	67	74	1971.....	5	133	138
1934.....	6	61	67	1972.....	5	134	139
1935.....	10	63	73	1973.....	17	204	221
1936.....	8	86	94	1974.....	13	153	166
1937.....	4	43	47	1975.....	8	123	131
1938.....	3	75	78	1976.....	12	197	209
				1977.....	10	147	157

each bill he considers than his forebears did (particularly in view of the fact that the parliament was increased in size in 1949). Getting relevant and worthwhile statistical information on the work of parliamentarians is particularly difficult. The Remuneration Tribunal made an attempt to do this in 1976, when it circulated a questionnaire to MPs and Senators in which it sought information on time spent in parliament house and elsewhere on parliamentary work, time spent travelling on parliamentary business, time spent overseas and time spent on non-parliamentary work. The Tribunal did not publish the results of its survey, which appeared to be directed primarily at discovering electorate and other expenses of MPs and Senators, and when approached, it declined to make the statistical data available. When it undertook a similar survey in preparation for its 1977 review of salaries and allowances, the Tribunal warned MPs that some of the statistical information collected might be made available for publication. Again, however, the Tribunal refused to release the information.

On international standards, the Australian MPs were quite reasonably paid, on the same level as MPs in Denmark, Italy and France, and getting about double what their counterparts in New Zealand and Great Britain were getting. However they received less than half what US or West German parliamentarians were paid, and about two-thirds of what Japanese, Belgian and Dutch politicians received.

In looking at the salaries and allowances paid to MPs and Senators, all inquiries have noted that some parliamentarians will not be as well paid in parliament as they would have been had they remained in their previous occupations. Parliament certainly appears to attract a large range of professional men—particularly from the profession of law— and there appears to have been a steady rise in the qualifications of members in recent years. Tables 7.8 and 7.9, prepared by the parliamentary library, lists the qualifications and previous occupations of MPs and Senators in the parliament in 1976.

One of the problems in assessing the work of parliamentarians is that no two MPs work in the same way, or make the same contributions to legislative, committee or other parliamentary work, and no two MPs work their electorates in the same way. However it is possible to look at the different types of activity which an MP engages in to give some indication of the extent to which any particular MP will concern himself with it.

Making parliamentary speeches is among the least of a backbencher's occupations. It is unlikely that he will speak to more than four or five bills during a year. Sometimes considerable preparation will be involved, as when he speaks to the Appropriation Bills and can

TABLE 7.8 *Higher Academic Qualifications of Members and Senators of the Thirtieth Parliament, 10 June 1976*

Qualifications	House of Representatives			Senate			Parliament			
	LIB.	N.C.P.	A.L.P.	LIB.	N.C.P.	A.L.P.	LIB.	N.C.P.	A.L.P.	Total
Master of Administration				1			1			1
Bachelor of Arts	11	1	5	4	1	5	15	2	10	27
Master of Arts	5		1	1		1	6		2	8
Master of Business Administration										—
Bachelor of Civil Law	1			1			2			2
Bachelor of Commerce	7		2				7		2	9
Master of Commerce	1						1			1
Bachelor of Dental Surgery										—
Bachelor of Economics	6			1		1	7		1	8
Bachelor of Education	1					2	1		2	3
Bachelor of Engineering	1			1			2			2
Bachelor of Laws	20	1	3	7	1	2	27	2	5	34
Master of Laws										—
Bachelor of Medicine	1		2		1	1	1	1	3	5
Bachelor of Surgery	1		3	1		1	2		4	6
Doctor of Medicine	1					1	1		1	2
Bachelor of Science		2						2		2
Master of Science										—
Bachelor of Science (Agriculture)	1						1			1
Master of Rural Science										—
Diploma of Agriculture	1	1			1		1	2		3
Diploma of Business Studies	1		1			1	1		2	3
Diploma of Education										—
Diploma of Public Administration	1				1		1	1		2
Doctor of Philosophy	1					2	1		2	3
Accountancy Qualification (as recognised by the Society of Accountants or the Australian Institute of Chartered Accountants)	9	3		4	1	1	13	4	1	18
Management Qualifications	4			1			5			5
Optometry (as recognised by a State Board of Optical Registration or similar authority)										—
Pharmaceutical qualifications, e.g. Ph.C.			1						1	1
Secretarial (Associateship of the Chartered Institute of Secretaries)	1		1	1	1		2	1	1	4
Number of Individual Members and with one or more of the qualifications listed	76	5	31	25	5	13	101	10	44	155

TABLE 7.9 *Occupations of Members and Senators of the Thirtieth Parliament, 10 June 1976*

The statistics in this table are based on one occupation only being designated for each Senator or MP. Where a Senator or MP has two or more occupations, the choice made was based on the principal occupation in which each individual was engaged prior to his or her entry to Federal Parliament.

Occupation	House of Representatives			Senate				Parliament				Total
	LIB.	N.C.P.	A.L.P.	LIB.	N.C.P.	A.L.P.	IND.	LIB.	N.C.P.	A.L.P.	Other	
Accountant, Secretary	5	1	3	4				9	1	3		13
Agents, etc.[1]				2				2				2
Armed Services		1	1						1	1		2
Clerical	1		1		1			1	1	1		3
Company Director	12							12				12
Consultant	8							8				8
Economist	2							2				2
Engineer	2		2					2		2		4
Journalist						1				1		1
Lecturer or Tutor[2]			2	1		1		1		3		4
Legal[3]	18		3	7	1	3		25	1	6		32
Medical Practitioner	1		3	1	1	1		2	1	4		7
Member of State Parliament	3				2	1		3	2	1		6
Minister of Religion	1	1						1	1			2
Party Official			1	2		1		2		2		4
Pharmacist	2							2				2
Policeman			2							2		2
Primary Producer	7	11	2	6	4	1		13	15	3		31
Public Servant[4]	2	1	3	1		2		3	1	5		9
Retailer or Wholesaler[5]	1	1			1	3		1	2	3		6
Teacher	1		1			2		1		3		4
Tradesman			2	1		2		1		4		5
Union Official			6			5	1			11	1	12
Other incl. unspecified	2	5	6	2	1	3		4	6	9		19
Total	68	23	36	28	8	27	1	95	32	63	1	191

[1] Agents, auctioneers, real estate and travel agents.
[2] At tertiary level.
[3] Solicitor or barrister.
[4] Commonwealth, state or local government officer.
[5] Including hotel keepers and caterers.

choose his own subject. At other times he will have only a few hours or a few days notice of the subject on which he is to speak, and he will not be expected to make any original contribution to the debate. Sometimes he will be speaking on a subject about which he is knowledgeable and he may not need more than a few minutes preparation. He might also speak in an adjournment debate or grievance debate half a dozen times during the year, and generally this will involve some research about the particular problem he is airing—often it will be a recitation of correspondence to and from a particular minister over a problem raised by a constituent. He might also ask half a dozen questions during the year, some of which may have been suggested to him by other people.

Senators will generally have had a busier time in parliament than Members of the House of Representatives—with half the House's membership, the Senate still has to deal with the same number of bills and sits for only slightly fewer hours than the House.

Frontbench members on both the government and the opposition sides will have done considerably more in the House than most backbenchers. They will have been required to speak to far more legislation, providing a lead for the debate. They would have been prominent in urgency debates (normally the first two speakers on either side in an urgency debate will be shadow ministers and ministers—and often the debate ends after they have spoken). They will have asked (on the opposition side) more questions than backbenchers. And they will have been rostered to be in the House more frequently than backbenchers to supervise the conduct of their own side of the House. Some ministers and shadow ministers will have done little compared with their colleagues, little even compared with some backbenchers, but generally the front-benchers are required to be the more active. The forty or so members of the opposing frontbenches predominate in the work of the 127-member House. In the Senate the frontbench is kept busy, but the difference between the work of an individual frontbencher and of an average backbencher is not as great as in the Lower House.

In 1976 the officers of both chambers took out figures relating to question time performances in the Houses, in response to questions on notice. Tables 7.10 and 7.11 show the very uneven spread of questions in the House and the more equal spread of work in the Senate. In the House each question plus answer averaged 2 minutes 36 seconds, while in the Senate each question plus answer averaged 1 minute 47 seconds.

Parliamentary committees, (not including domestic committees such as Library, House, Privileges, Standing Orders, Disputed Returns and Printing which meet irregularly, infrequently, and usually on sitting days) can occupy a considerable amount of a parliamentarian's time

TABLE 7.10 *Questions without Notice in the House of Representatives, 17 August–18 November 1976*

Minister or Minister representing	No. of questions directed to	Answers given (including supplementary oral answers)
Aboriginal Affairs	10	10
* Administrative Services	1	1
Attorney-General	23	23
Business and Consumer Affairs	20	20
Capital Territory	4	4
Construction	9	9
Defence	23	23
* Education	6	6
Employment and Industrial Relations	35	37
Environment, Housing and Community Development	17	17
Foreign Affairs	37	36
Health	32	32
Immigration and Ethnic Affairs	16	16
* Industry and Commerce	—	—
National Resources and Overseas Trade	13	13
Northern Territory	2	3
Post and Telecommunications	32	32
Primary Industry	34	36
Prime Minister	133	133
Productivity	1	1
* Repatriation/Veterans Affairs	3	3
* Science	—	—
* Social Security	3	3
Transport	40	43
Treasurer	94	94
Leader of the House	1	1
TOTAL	589	596

* Indicates Minister in the Senate

Source: House of Representatives Hansard, p.3679, 9.12.76

TABLE 7.11   *Questions without Notice in the Senate,*
August–October 1976

Minister	No. of answers given
Cotton	101
Webster	64
Withers	135
Guilfoyle	164
Durack	68
Carrick	201

Source: Information in Senate Hansard, p.1695, 4.11.76

NOTE: During the period for which the statistics refer, the ministers in the Senate represented (and would have answered question on behalf of) the following Departments of Ministers in the House:

Cotton:	Overseas Trade, Treasury, Primary Industry
Webster:	Northern Territory, Construction, Capital Territory
Withers:	Prime Minister, Foreign Affairs, Defence, National Resources
Guilfoyle:	Health, Immigration and Ethnic Affairs, Aboriginal Affairs
Durack:	Employment and Industrial Relations, Attorney-General, Business and Consumer Affairs
Carrick:	Federal Affairs, Transport, Posts and Telecommunications, Environment, Housing and Community Development

and effort—more than his appearances in the chamber. However not all parliamentarians participate in committee work and not all of those who are members of committees contribute much to their effectiveness. In 1976, thirty-six Senators were members of the six Senate estimates committees, which met to consider both the supplementary estimates (in April–May) and the full Budget estimates (in August–September). These committees supplemented the work of the Senate, but did not add to what would otherwise have been normal sitting hours of the Senate. The normal practice was for the Senate to adjourn during what would have been regular sitting times to allow a brace of these six committees to sit at any one time. While the arrangement meant that more work was done, the Senators involved had to contribute little extra in the way of time, while those not involved had more time to themselves.

The other wide ranging set of Senate committees was the legislative and general purpose standing committees of the Senate. These contained forty-two Senators. Only five Senators on estimates committees were not also members of legislative and general purpose standing committees. These committees met outside regular Senate hours, generally in non-sitting weeks or on Mondays and Fridays of sitting weeks. As at December 1976, they had the following matters before them.

CONSTITUTIONAL AND LEGAL AFFAIRS:
The Evidence (Australian Capital Territory) Bill 1972
The preservation of the constitutional right of the Senate to amend proposed laws appropriating revenue or moneys for expenditure on matters other than the ordinary annual services of the Government
The alterations of the law made by the Australian Capital Territory Misrepresentation and Manufacturers Warranties Ordinances
Compulsory retirement age for judges of Commonwealth Courts

EDUCATION AND THE ARTS:
All aspects of television and broadcasting, including Australian content of television programs
The means of overcoming the educational problems of "isolated school children"
Employment of musicians by the Australian Broadcasting Commission

FOREIGN AFFAIRS AND DEFENCE:
Vietnamese refugees
Australia and the Indian Ocean region
The implications for Australia's foreign policy and national security of proposals for a new international economic order
The need for an increased Australian commitment in the South Pacific

SOCIAL WELFARE:
Introduction of a National Superannuation Scheme
Relevant aspects of Report of Select Committee on Drug Trafficking and Drug Abuse
Evaluation of the adequacy of Australian health and welfare services

TRADE AND COMMERCE:
The promotion of trade and commerce with other countries, the operation of Australia's international trade agreements, and the development of trading relations
The economic consequences of the introduction of a thirty-five hour working week
The effect of the container method of handling cargo on the stevedoring industry and shipping
The effect on the wine making and grape growing industries of variations in the tax structure

NATIONAL RESOURCES:
  Solar Energy
  The Commonwealth's role in the assessment, planning, development and management of Australia's water resources
SCIENCE AND THE ENVIRONMENT:
  Continuing oversight of the problems of pollution
  The effects of the development in Australia of large new inland cities upon inland waters
  The impact on the Australian environment of the current wood-chip industry program
  Australian Science Policy

There were two other important Senate committees: the Regulations and Ordinance committee, which contained seven Senators, five of whom also had places on other standing and estimates committees of the Senate, and the Select Committee on Aborigines and Torres Strait Islanders, all six of whose members also served on other committees of the Senate.

The amount of committee work in the House of Representatives was pitched at a far lower level. As at December 1976 it had the following standing and select committees (excluding domestic committees): Aboriginal Affairs; Environment and Conservation; Expenditure; Road Safety; and Tourism. All were made up of eight MPs except the Expenditure committee which had twelve members. The forty-four positions on these committees were filled by thirty-nine MPs (i.e., five sat on two committees each).

When joint committees were included, members of the House of Representatives still averaged less than one committee assignment for each backbencher—there were eighty-three positions available among about 104 backbenchers whereas in the Senate there were 111 positions available for fifty-two backbenchers. Almost one in every two members of the House had no committee assignment at all, while only one backbench Senator did not have a committee position. One in every three Senate backbenchers had three committee assignments or more. Party committees add considerably to this committee work.

Attendance at committee meetings is not as regular as attendance at meetings of the parliament itself. As suggested below, the work of each committee tends to fall on two or three members who, with the full-time secretariat, determine the direction of the committee's investigations and the nature of its report. The dominating committee members are not always the chairman and the government nominees. The Senate Select Committee on Securities and Exchange was known as the Rae Committee after Tasmanian Liberal Peter Rae even after the Labor Party took control of the committee following the 1972 elections. Indeed Rae dominated it even before he was its chairman.

The House of Representatives provides a different sort of example: in the first six months of the expenditure committee the dominating figures, in terms of work, direction and ideas, were the chairman, Liberal Vic Garland, together with a former Treasurer, Labor's Frank Crean, and another former Labor minister, Frank Stewart, who had been minister assisting the Labor Treasurers from 1972 to 1975.

Party committees also command a considerable amount of the time of MPs and Senators—though unlike most of the parliamentary committees, party committees mostly meet on parliamentary sitting days, generally during meal breaks, in the morning, or late at night. During sessions, these committees meet at least once a week. While parliamentary committees work towards the production of a final report with recommendations which the government may or may not adopt, party committees have a continuing role in the evolution of party policies which, if the party is in government, will be most likely to be adopted by the government. This applies to both Liberal and Labor Parties. A policy recommended by a Labor Party committee is most likely to be adopted by the caucus as a whole as those who formulate the particular policy are likely to lead the debate, and the votes, in the caucus. The Labor cabinet, or the particular minister, is going to be bound by caucus policy, and will be greatly influenced by a committee's policies. Indeed much of a Labor minister's energy will be devoted to keeping his committee informed and onside.

Liberal party committees do not have as much direct power over government policy but they do have considerable influence. No Liberal minister wants to be offside with the party committee which looks at his policy areas, and he will try to direct its policies in the direction he wants. When there is a conflict he will probably give way, if the pressure from the committee is very strong. In 1976, for example, the Minister for Posts and Telecommunications, Eric Robinson, was forced to redraft his own bill on broadcasting to take account of the strong feelings of a meeting of the Committee on Communications and Administrative Services, a meeting which was attended by over fifty government backbenchers. It is only when such massive turnouts of backbenchers occur, and when such large turnabouts in policy are made apparent, that it is possible to get an inkling of the influence of the coalition committees. In each case the minister realised that unless he gave way, there would be a revolt by some of his party supporters in the parliament itself.

Conflicts between the Labor caucus and a Labor government are made obvious by the recording of votes on all issues that come before the caucus. Every piece of legislation has to be voted upon by the caucus, any amendment proposed by a backbencher has to be voted on, and any policy proposal brought up for discussion has to be terminated with a vote. The Labor party meetings are normally held every Wednesday morning when parliament is in session from 10.30 until 1 p.m. The Labor caucus also meets at 11 a.m. on the day preceding the autumn and Budget sittings of the parliament. Each meeting begins with the reading and confirmation of the minutes. Then follow reports and recommendations of the executive and of committees, announcements by Whips, questions to the Leader and other members of the executive, notices of motion, business of which notice has previously been given, and general business. Most of the time of caucus meetings is taken up with discussion of legislation— whether the party is in government or opposition. The minister or shadow minister reports on the recommendations of the cabinet (if in government) or the executive and proposes the adoption of the recommendation. The matter is then open for debate and amendments can be moved. The final vote of the caucus determines the party's attitude. Labor's caucus voting system produced only three major rebuffs for cabinet during three years of government between 1972 and 1975.

In the Liberal and National Country Party meetings, also generally held at 10.30 on Wednesday mornings, votes are rarely taken. When party matters such as leadership challenges or organisational matters do need to be resolved, these are settled in votes at separate meetings of the coalition partners. The joint party meeting, particularly when the coalition is in government, provides an opportunity for the backbench to express views on all current legislation and policy problems, but does not include taking votes. There are no formal standing orders controlling the meeting which deals first with government business and then with general business. The Liberal Leader can arrange and rearrange the agenda to suit his own purposes. Ministers have to make their own assessment, by the variety and range of the speakers on any issue, as to the backbench feeling and as to whether any change of course might need to be taken to assuage party feeling. In the Fraser government's first year in office, ministers made changes to several major policy items to take account of discontent expressed either in party committees (the broadcasting bill) or overtly in the Senate (funeral benefits for pensioners), and many minor ones.

While all ALP parliamentarians are required to attend caucus meetings, many Liberal MPs and Senators are irregular attenders at coalition party meetings. In all parties it is possible to distinguish among MPs who do a lot of talking in the party room (not always those who talk the most in the parliament) and those who mostly observe. Party meetings tend to provide members and leaders with a better opportunity to assess the views and abilities of other party members than does parliament, partly because views are expressed more freely in the party room.

Parliamentary work and attendance at party meetings take two to four hours of the average backbencher's day while the parliament is sitting. The remaining eleven or twelve hours he normally spends in Parliament House will be occupied in an infinite variety of ways, but most of the time he will probably be in his office which is equipped with a loud speaker that relays the proceedings of his chamber. The volume is adjustable, and although most members are not interested in the particular debates taking place in the chamber, they tend to keep it turned on at a low volume, to pick up any disturbance which could result in the bells being rung to summon them to a division or to help make up a quorum.

In his office, the parliamentarian will have many jobs waiting for him, ranging from preparing a speech to answering correspondence. Most members keep in daily touch with their electorate secretary and are aware of the problems she is sorting out for constituents. Sometimes these require the personal intervention of the MP who will write to a minister, phone a public servant, or call into a minister's office to get him or his secretaries personally involved in settling the matter.

Backbenchers frequently have to meet constituents who are visiting Parliament House. Some constituents seek out the politician to lobby him on a particular problem. They might be part of a group of teachers or pensioners or conservationists who have undertaken a one-day campaign to lobby as many MPs and Senators as possible about an issue which concerns them. Others could be visiting Canberra with a business problem they want to sort out with a government department and decide that a politician's introduction or influence could help them. Mostly however, the constituents are simply holiday visitors to the national capital who want the chance to meet their MP whom they might have seen on social occasions in the electorate. MPs also find themselves meeting large groups of school children from their electorate and conducting them around the parliament—sometimes providing them with soft drinks and sandwiches. Some MPs sponsor competitions among school children which include a trip to Canberra as the MP's guest. Except at question time and during party meetings, most MPs and Senators feel obliged to drop whatever else they might be doing to answer any call to have a chat with these always unheralded constituency visitors. That the Parliament is in Canberra keeps the MP or Senator away from his constituents most of the time, so constituents who take the trouble to make contact with their MP while they are in Canberra feel the least he can do is meet them and spend a little time with them.

Backbenchers spend a great deal of time reading. The number one priority is the press. The Parliamentary Library has on display every major and minor newspaper produced in Australia, ranging from metropolitan dailies through to country weeklies. Interstate papers are air-freighted so that every member has his local paper available to him within a day or so of its publication. Members can read papers going back a month or two to check on the development of any controversy, or catch up on news they might have missed. Newspapers are supplemented by a full range of magazines and journals. As well as a substantial range of books of value in almost every field the politician is likely to be interested, the library also has available a large range of fiction—and many MPs are avid borrowers. The daily reading schedule of most backbenchers would include not only their local newspapers but also the political news in most of the major daily newspapers published in Sydney and Melbourne.

Backbenchers also have a vast amount of parliamentary and party material to read. Hundreds of reports are tabled each year in the parliament, ranging from brief financial accounts required under various Acts of Parliament, to multi-volumed recommendations and transcripts from committees of inquiry. A consciencious MP with an interest in just a few major policy areas will have to read thousands of pages of reports a year, just to keep in touch with developments. If he is to try to get ahead of the field, and gets the library to provide him with extracts of all new articles in his area of interest, plus research on specific topics, he will have to spend hours a day digesting the material. To prepare for parliamentary or party committee work, the parliamentarian will also have to read pages of proposals prepared by fellow MPs and pages of transcripts. No backbenchers can expect to read all the material issued in the parliament.

Another major parliamentary occupation is talking. The MP will spend hours each day talking with his colleagues, gossiping with MPs from other parties, exchanging news and views with journalists and letting anyone who cares to ask him know what his opinion is about almost any political topic. Talking centres around current politics, about the strengths and weaknesses of his leaders and of those in other parties, as well as about policies. It occurs in the corridors, in Kings Hall, in bars and in his room. A lot of it also takes place in the two chambers, while speeches are being made.

Younger parliamentarians tend to take great advantage of the recreational facilities provided around Parliament House. It is not unusual to come across MPs and Senators in the corridors on the lower ground floor of the parliament dressed in white shorts and sandshoes and heading for either the tennis courts on the north-eastern side of Parliament House or the squash courts to the south-west. There are also bowling greens (which attendants use more than the MPs) billiard tables, and of course, the bars. Some MPs drink a lot, a few spend more time drinking than anything else, some use the bar facilities sparingly, some not at all. Many prefer to drink in their rooms, and a few hold parties at night if those they share with are companionable. Ministers tend to hold more parties than back-benchers, partly because they have bigger rooms, partly because they have bigger expense accounts—though attending parties is generally on a "bring your own grog" basis. Drinking to excess is an occasional problem—parliamentary receptions for visiting dignitaries are fre-quently followed by rowdy scenes in the House.

Wherever he goes in Parliament House, a backbencher is likely to be pursued by people trying to contact him on electorate, party or parliamentary business. Until 1976, the loudspeakers in corridors were constantly alive with the names of parliamentarians being paged by the telephone switchboard operators. In 1976 a technical revolution reached Canberra when MPs and Senators were issued with small paging units which buzzed when the telephonist was seeking its rightful owner, who then had only to telephone the switch to be connected with whoever was seeking him. The system had the advantage of operating in places like the library, and committee and party rooms which the loudspeaker system had been banned from. But it took getting used to. Some MPs thought they could take anyone's paging unit. It was quickly discovered that the system had bureaucratic uses which reduced the backbenchers' freedom—when an MP left the building he was supposed to leave the unit in a rack by the door for "recharging". However when placed in the rack, the machine set off an indicator in the office of the Whip, who was thus able to tell which of his backbenchers were absent from the building.

In looking after their constituents, MPs generally find themselves obliged to act as lobbyists for manufacturers who have factories in their districts. Any change in the fortunes of such manufacturers is likely to affect employment in the member's district, and the manufacturers take advantage of this to have backbench MPs and ministers press their particular claims in parliament (through questions and speeches), in the party room and in contacts with relevant ministers.

Parliament House provides the focus for the parliamentarian's work, but he is only there for a quarter to a fifth of each year. Most of his time is spent in his electorate, in more mundane surroundings, involved with even less apparently satisfying work than occupies him in Parliament House. With his electorate secretary, the MP will deal with the hundreds, sometimes many thousands, of complaints from constituents which he can expect to receive each year. The average backbencher will have at least 100 inquiries from constituents each week. In a three-year term, a backbencher in a marginal electorate can expect to have dealt with problems from 10 000 of his constituents. Many of the problems concern state or local governments and they can be passed on to the state parliamentarian for the district, or the local council. Federal matters could involve him in having a call made to a Department, writing a letter to a Department, or making representations to a minister. These chores are referred to by most parliamentarians as their "ombudsman" work, but it is a poor—indeed a misleading—description. They make representation on behalf of their constitutents. They don't investigate to see whether their client is right or wrong except to assess their prospects of success and the level at which the complaint needs to be pushed. They simply don't have time to research these problems. If an MP gets 150 problems a week (not an extraordinary number in a marginal electorate) and he and his secretary spend only twenty minutes handling each complaint—interviewing the complainant, contacting the Department by telephone, following this up with a letter to the Department or the minister, conveying the response to the complainant—then fifty hours of their combined working time has been taken up. Many MPs complain that they cannot get the filing and routine work done in their offices without additional assistance. Some spend additional money from their own or party sources to hire extra help. Others organise rosters of volunteer party workers to help in office work. Still others use their research workers to do basic secretarial work.

After the office work has been dealt with, the parliamentarian will have to spend a great deal of time attending meetings of various kinds, opening flower shows and fetes, attending school concerts and speech nights, going to the local show and openings of new buildings. He will have from fifty to two hundred of these functions every year. In addition he will have meetings of his political party branches to attend—scores every year—meetings with local councillors, progress associations, the chamber of commerce, charity organisations and dozens of other community groups.

One Labor MP prepared a diary of his activities for March 1974 for a submission to the Remuneration Tribunal. Table 7.12 shows his activities—normal for an MP in a marginal electorate.

If he is particularly conscientious, he will also be making work for himself. One Labor MP who survived the 1975 landslide against Labor attributed his success to the work he had put into pushing local projects and getting money out of various government departments for developmental work under such schemes as the Regional Employment and Development Schemes (REDS), the local area improvement scheme, and sewerage, health and other works programs. Most of the

TABLE 7.12   *Activities of a Member of Parliament for one month*

March
1   Agricultural Show, Branch meeting at night.
2   Two School Fetes. Dinner function.
3   Interviews/ Art Exhibition.
4   In office Parliament House; 3 appointments, 2 caucus committee meetings, function at night.
5   **Parliament** 1 Standing Committee and 2 caucus committee meetings.
6   **Parliament** Caucus working lunch and dinner meetings; 2 caucus committee meetings.
7   **Parliament** 2 caucus committee meetings; 1 Standing Committee meeting.
8   Interviews all day on Tablelands.
9   Agricultural Show; School Fete; Flat presentation; Dinner.
10   Interviews; visit Repatriation Hospital.
11   Visit to 1 home, 2 factories, 1 school.
12   **Parliament** 2 caucus committee meetings; 1 Standing Committee meeting.
13   **Parliament** Caucus meeting; 2 Committee meetings.
14   **Parliament** 1 Standing Committee meeting; 2 caucus committee meetings.
15   Campbelltown Office; dinner at night.
16   Open 2 Fetes; function at night.
17   Visiting constituents in Bowral area.
18   Campbelltown Office; Branch meeting at night.
19   **Parliament** 1 Standing Committee meeting; 1 caucus committee meeting.
20   **Parliament** Caucus; 1 caucus committee meeting, working dinner; official lunch.
21   **Parliament** 1 Standing Committee meeting; 2 caucus committee meetings.
22   Quarry opening; working lunch and dinner.
23   Aged Person's Home opening; Legacy Dinner.
24   A.G.M. Macarthur F.E.C.; daughter christened.
25   Interviews on Coast; working dinner; Branch meeting.
26   Standing Committee in Melbourne.
27   Tour of electorate with Minister Wriedt.
28   Standing Committee in Melbourne; Working lunch/dinner.
29   Standing Committee in Melbourne.
30   Methodist Breakfast; Agricultural Show; Picnic Races; R.S.L. Opening; A.G.M.
31   Morning off. Lunch and visit Club in afternoon.

proposals originated in talks with local groups, but in each case the MP took over lobbying for the groups in Canberra, making regular weekly calls on all the responsible ministers to see whether they had yet approved his proposal. His electorate got more than its fair share of this money, and he won votes as a result.

Most MPs believe that their electorate work wins them votes—or at least allows them to hold on to some votes they might otherwise lose in a swing against the party. They accept that generally the seats of all MPs will depend on the overall performance of the party, but they believe that they themselves are in a slightly better position because of the work they do in their electorates. Most of them certainly behave as if they were firmly convinced that their future was dependent on the contribution they make to the condition of their electorates and its residents, rather than anything they might do in the parliament.

An essential part of the member's job is communicating his successes through the local media to the electorate. Even in large cities there are suburban newspapers which will devote space to the work of the local members if they provide the material to publish. Some members rely on using ministerial press releases, and inserting their own names as announcing some local project. Others devote time and effort to producing original material, disseminating speeches they have made and questions they have asked in parliament to the media as well as to their local party officials and supporters.

An MP in a marginal electorate is forever worrying about campaigning, and often he will be involved as campaign manager for his party in elections for local councils or for the state parliament. This helps him keep his organisation in a condition to fight his own campaign whenever a federal election is called. As part of this task, he will be concerned about raising campaign finance. By the mid-1970s, a candidate in a marginal electorate could expect to have to spend between $10 000 and $20 000 in a federal election on local publicity, stationery, mailing and posters. This would be in addition to money spent by his party on national and state-wide campaigning.

Opposition frontbench MPs have to spend a substantial amount of time away from their home bases making speeches about their particular specialisations and taking part in activities which help shape their party's policy—through discussions with experts in the field and in committee meetings of their party at a state and/or federal level. Backbench MPs are not as involved in this kind of activity unless they have a reputation for expertise about a particular subject or are trying to establish that reputation with a view to future promotion through the party ranks.

Ministers have less time for constituency work than backbenchers and greater facilities in their offices (and through their ministerial positions) to satisfy the wants of their constituents. They have to spend far more time travelling, making speeches and keeping in touch with their party, and are involved in office work coping with the administration and policy development of their portfolios. Nevertheless, there are few ministers who ignore the apparent needs of their electorates. When parliament and cabinet are not sitting, ministers are more likely than not to be back in their home cities, rather than with their Departments. At home they are able to spend time attending public, political and party functions in their electorates. If they hold marginal seats they also may have to spend time working in their electorate offices, interviewing constituents the way backbenchers do.

The electorate considerably influences the development of MPs who find after dealing with hundreds of cases that they develop a certain amount of at least superficial expertise about subjects such as pensions, old people's homes, migration, employment and health, where constituents are likely to find themselves at odds with the system. MPs representing rural electorates are soon able to talk knowledgeably about all the primary industries in their area, as well as about the costs and inadequacies of postal, telecommunication and broadcasting services. Inner suburban electorates produce MPs who have to become specialists on the problems of migrants. Those from outer suburban areas learn about the problems of people living in "pioneering" suburbs which lack amenities common in older parts of the cities.

Acquiring and keeping abreast of this type of knowledge leaves an MP capable of talking at a minute's notice on dozens of topics in parliament or in the electorate. But it leaves him comparatively little time for the other subjects in which he may have been expert before entering parliament (as a doctor, a union organiser, a teacher or a lawyer) or the areas in which he feels he should become expert if he is to make progress to ministerial ranks. As well as looking after the everyday problems of their electorates, members have to familiarise themselves with the topics of current politics. These tend to change like fashions. Foreign Affairs (Vietnam, Russians in the Indian Ocean) may be the in thing one year, migration the next. All MPs must be able to mutter at least a few words about the economy all the time, but few devote much time to the topic. When an MP has gained better than average knowledge about a subject, his expertise is rapidly recognised by his fellows on both sides of the house.

Most newly-elected backbenchers are disconcerted to discover the amount of electorate work that awaits them and the lack of opportunity they have to make a "worthwhile" contribution to the progress of the nation in the parliament. The idealism generally wears off before the end of their first term as they come to accept that they have to perform in the electorate if they are to retain pre-selection and (in the case of marginal electorates) retain their seat. Many come round to praising the way concentration on electorate matters keeps the MP in touch with the way people really think and provides the citizen with a personal link with a distant administrative and political structure which is several times removed from their immediate neighbourhood.

Very rarely, a group of new backbenchers, all with the same feeling that parliament is not what it should be, will help to force changes. The most important such group in recent years was the new Labor intake of 1969. They constituted a third of Labor's representation in the House of Representatives between 1969 and 1972. They were different from the traditional picture of a Labor MP—they included doctors, pharmacists, accountants, diplomats and senior public servants. As was pointed out earlier, six months after their arrival, most of them held a secret meeting with some Liberal MPs to discuss the prospects for parliamentary reform. They supported Murphy in his efforts to bring in a structured committee system in the Senate, and hoped to use that breakthrough to force the adoption of a similar system in the House of Representatives. They moved also to reform the Labor caucus system, inaugurating standing committees. The reforms helped them have a say in Labor's policies while it was in government, but most of them did not gain election to the cabinet in the 1972–75 period.

Despite the apparently heavy workloads and the seemingly never-ending nature of the work of MPs and ministers, all seem to find it comparatively easy to make arrangements which free them for overseas travel from time to time. Ministers are able to indulge in this activity far more than their backbench colleagues. Some ministers, such as the Prime Minister, Foreign Minister, Defence Minister and Treasurer, can generally find reasons for making several overseas trips a year on ministerial business. Others have annual conferences (in the case of the Minister for Labour, it is the meeting of the International Labour Organisation) which require their attendance. All ministers can find some excuse for overseas travel, and most governments permit at least half the ministers to undertake at least one visit each year.

Backbenchers have to make do with fewer overseas trips, and generally have to travel in company with other backbenchers. Each year two or three "fact-finding" delegations will be organised which will visit several countries. These missions, generally headed by a minister, can contain up to a dozen MPs and Senators. Conferences of the Inter-Parliamentary Union and the Commonwealth Parliamentary Association attract small Australian Parliamentary delegations. The annual meeting of the United Nations provides an excuse for several MPs and Senators to visit New York. So each year at least one minister in every two will get an overseas trip and one backbencher in eight or nine will go abroad—all at government expense. This is in addition to the overseas visits provided for by the Remuneration Tribunal.

The various tribunals which have looked at parliamentary salaries have not felt it necessary to be concerned about the possibility of corruption. Mr Justice Kerr remarked in his 1971 report:

> There is little need to discuss the fixing of a salary which would keep the national parliament above any taint of corruption. Happily this is something from which it appears to have been free, even at times when parliamentary salaries have been relatively meagre. Nevertheless, it is clearly sensible to ensure that the salary paid to a politician is not so low that he must inevitably seek to supplement his income.

Most of whatever corruption there is in Australian politics at a national level probably occurs through party organisations rather than through individual parliamentarians. Donations on a large scale are offered or made to party campaign funds and rewards sometimes appear to be given to the donors. Whether these would have occurred any way is always problematical. Parliamentarians can expect free meals, occasional free overseas travel (or travel at a highly subsidised rate), entertainment and accommodation provided by an overseas host country and other "public relations gestures" ranging from a carton or two of beer at Christmas time to parcels of thousands of shares in rich multinational companies at face value. Most parliamentarians, and most of those who work in Parliament House who might also be offered such prizes, avoid entanglements which will require them to provide return favours. Undoubtedly gifts are offered and received, but this occurs without much real prospect of influence being achieved. An occasional minor scandal—such as the receipt by a minister's wife of a substantial gift of jewellery to mark the launching of a ship—will revive interest in the general subject and result in the adoption of new standards of public conduct. In 1974 the Whitlam government established a joint parliamentary committee to inquire into the pecuniary interests of members of parliament and others (such as public servants, ministerial staff and journalists) involved in national politics. The committee recommended the creation of a semi-public register of the pecuniary interests of members and others, but the Whitlam government was unable to pass such legislation and the Fraser government was not interested in doing so.

Prime Ministers have required their ministers to give undertakings about their pecuniary interests; in 1972 the Whitlam government accepted a code of conduct for its ministers in its cabinet decision No. 2. This laid down that:

Ministers holding directorships in public companies should resign them;

Directorships in private companies which are principally family companies may be retained but directorships in private companies which may be akin to public companies in their operations should be given up;

Ministers are not precluded from making investments on the stock markets but they should not operate as traders and should exercise careful personal judgment and discretion in respect of transactions and, for example, should not purchase or hold shares where this could expose them to challenge.

Following the report of the committee on pecuniary interests, and despite the government's inability to enact legislation, Whitlam required all ministerial staff to make declarations of their pecuniary interests in letters to be safeguarded by his personal private secretary. The Fraser government continued the practice of requiring ministers and staff to make declarations. It also decided that ministers and their wives were no longer entitled to keep gifts above a "nominal" amount of about $100. Gifts valued above that amount could be retained only if the minister concerned paid an amount equal to the valuation into consolidated revenue. Fraser set the procedure in operation by paying into consolidated revenue the value of a camera he was given during a visit to Japan early in 1975. It was a gesture towards propriety.

Fraser's government also rejected attempts by the Labor Party to have rules brought in requiring the disclosure of the sources of party funds. It was seen that compulsory disclosure of the sources of party funds was likely to do more damage to the Liberal Party's funding than the Labor Party's. (The Labor Party raises less than the Liberal Party and much of it is already identified as coming from trade unions.) The Labor Party's proposals for disclosure were therefore rejected on the grounds that they were politically motivated and were not based on any fears that undue influence or corruption could result from secret donations. Arguments about the latter point have not got far because they have always been obscured by the argument about political advantage.

The potential dangers of a secretive approach to the questions of ministerial pecuniary interests and party fund raising were illustrated in the Lynch affair at the end of 1977. Lynch, Treasurer and Deputy Leader of the Liberal Party, was accused of involvement in a Victorian land deal at a time when land dealings of the Victorian Housing Commission were under judicial investigation. Part of the problem concerned the fact that a man who had raised money for the Liberal Party in Lynch's electorate had profited in the land deals. At Fraser's insistence, to try to bury the issue during the campaign, Lynch resigned as Treasurer, while insisting that he had declared his pecuniary interests to Fraser, as was required of him. Lynch gained a deal of sympathy within the Liberal Party over what was regarded as a high-handed action by Fraser, and after the election Lynch easily retained his deputy leadership of the party by a four to one margin. However he did not regain the Treasury portfolio and was instead shuffled off into comparative insignificance within the government.

8 Parliamentary Staff and Public Servants

In the ten years from 1966 to 1975, there was an extraordinary increase in the number of people employed in Parliament House. The size of the staff of the House of Representatives quadrupled, and the staff in the Senate increased by five times. The Parliamentary Library underwent a nine-fold expansion. The expansion was due in part to an increased volume of work. Legislation in the last ten years of the Menzies' rule (1956–1965) had averaged 102 bills a year. In the next ten years it averaged 142 Bills. Committee work increased dramatically in both Houses, though especially in the Senate. There was also a small increase in the number of ministers and ministerial staff more than doubled. The press gallery, despite limits imposed by space and the presiding officers, increased in size by at least 50 per cent as radio and television networks decided to take a meaningful all-year-round interest in national politics.

Within Parliament House this considerable and comparatively sudden staffing increase seemed associated with an increase in the pace of politics. There were always new people to be seen around Parliament House, and it wasn't always appreciated that many of them were in newly created positions. Jobs which previously had been done part-time by an individual, became so involved that three and four people were necessary to carry them out properly. While much of the staffing increase was attributable simply to the need to provide services (whether in handling additional numbers of bills or meat pies), much was caused by the changing functions that ministers, backbenchers and the parliament all experienced.

There are five "departments" containing staff of the Australian Parliament: the Department of the Senate, the Department of the House of Representatives, the Joint House Department, the Parliamentary Library and the Parliamentary Reporting Staff. Parliamen-

tary employees are not like ordinary public servants. They are
supposed to give no special loyalty to the government of the day—
rather they are to serve all the current members of the parliament.
They also can be thought of as serving the "institution" of parliament
(or their particular house), rather than serving the public. These
distinctions are reflected to some extent in the separation of the
parliamentary staff from the Public Service. Unlike public servants,
those recruited by the parliamentary service are not subject to the
authority of the Public Service Board and to the normal competitive
processes which apply to other public servants. Nor do they have to
concern themselves about appeals against any promotions they might
be given inside the parliamentary service—there is no outside authority
to ensure, for example, that "ordinary" public servants who apply for
jobs in the parliamentary service can appeal against those who are
already in it. However those who are in the parliamentary service can
apply for jobs in the regular public service—and can appeal through
the normal processes if they are not promoted. The appointment,
promotion, pay and conditions of members of the parliamentary staff
are controlled by the Governor-General, acting on the advice of the
presiding officers, and are subject to financial limitations imposed by
the government (and parliament itself) in the Budget. The presiding
officers generally obtain and act upon advice from the Public Service
Board on matters such as organisation, pay, employment conditions
and industrial matters and the classification of employees.

The two chambers rarely debate the merits of their parliamentary
servants. During discussions of the estimates for the parliament, a few
MPs and Senators normally discuss parliamentary reform and
occasionally reference is made to poor working conditions of the staff.
At the end of the year the leaders of the parties ritualistically make
speeches saying what fine service they have had from the clerks, and
their staff, from the Hansard people and the parliamentary library, and
from the cooks, bottlewashers, drivers and attendants. However
parliamentarians don't normally become involved in discussions about
just how many people are needed to service the parliament. The staff
growth in the 1960s and 1970s certainly did not result from any staffing
decisions by the parliament, though it is largely attributable to
decisions the two chambers were taking about committee work. Just
what effect the increase in parliamentary committee work had on
staffing can be seen in Table 8.1.

The most obvious and notable increase was in committee staff. It
was not until 1969 that the parliament accepted that there should be a
separate category of staff under this heading, working full-time at
committee work. In 1968 only the Regulations and Ordinances
Committee, the Public Works Committee and the Public Accounts

TABLE 8.1 *Parliament House Departments: 1965-66 to 1976-77*

	1965-66	1966-67	1967-68	1968-69	1969-70	1970-71	1971-72	1972-73	1973-74	1974-75	1975-76	1976-77
HOUSE OF REPRESENTATIVES												
Clerk, Chamber officers, Parliamentary officers	10	10	11	11	15	19	21	22	27	29	28	29
Committee secretariat	..	..	..	..	4	10	14	14	23	27	26	25
Office, typing staff, attendants	28	32	39	44	55	58	62	68	90	94	93	92
Total House	38	42	50	55	74	87	97	104	140	150	147	146
SENATE												
Clerk, Chamber officers, Parliamentary officers	9	9	10	11	12	14	17	17	19	20	24	24
Committee secretariat	..	..	..	2	10	16	21	28	31	34	44	43
Office, typing staff, attendants	16	16	19	22	29	41	47	49	57	61	68	69
Total Senate	25	25	29	35	51	71	85	94	107	115	136	136
LIBRARY												
Administrative staff	16	36	17	18	10	11	12	12	12	13	17	24
Legislative Reference		..	31	27	43	44	55	64	69	70	69	70
Legislative Research	..	6	6	11	24	25	38	41	51	51	48	45
Total Library	16	42	54	56	77	80	105	117	132	134	134	139
JOINT HOUSE												
Administration, housekeeping engineering, gardens, refreshment rooms	51	51	119	116	120	138	146	158	185	207	187	208
HANSARD												
Administration, reporters, technical	29	29	39	40	43	44	52	54	58	71	75	109

Source: Budget documents in Parliamentary Papers 1966-77 inclusive

Committee had the assistance of specialist staff—a lawyer acted part-time for the Senate Committee, and staff operated through the Joint House Department of the Parliament for the two joint statutory committees. Almost all other committees were staffed on a part-time basis by officers of the Department of the House of Representatives or the Department of the Senate, who were assigned to these duties by the Serjeant-at-Arms and the Usher of the Black Rod respectively.

The expansion of committee activity in the Senate in the late 1960s with the formation of select committees into such topics as Off-shore Petroleum Resources, Water Pollution, Medical and Hospital Costs, Drug Trafficking and Drug Abuse, and Securities and Exchange (to mention just those current in 1970) required the hiring of additional staff who were employed full-time servicing these committees. Some committees, such as the Securities and Exchange Committee, hired expert staff from outside the parliament as consultants, sometimes for the duration of the committee's work, sometimes on a *per diem* rate if the committee required them for a briefer time.

These new staffing arrangements tended to change the nature of the operations of select committees. While in most cases the staff were hired as generalists, and were not usually expert in the field the committee was investigating, they were able to devote themselves full-time to acquiring familiarity with all the available published material on the subject and to obtaining sufficient information to be able to plan the work of the committee. They briefed committee members on the type of information likely to be supplied by each witness, and planned the questions which committee members should ask. As the committee proceeded, the staff wrote up the committee report that was circulated to committee members for ratification. The work of most committees tended to be carried out by one or two interested members of the committee (usually including the committee chairman, but not always) plus the senior staff. The committee secretary tended to be a third division officer in the Public Service of about class 10* and he would often have a class 7 and a class 5 officer helping him, along with a steno-secretary. In most cases, the committee and staff consisted of laymen and they aimed to produce a layman's, not an expert's, report. Agreement between MPs and Senators from opposite parties was mostly possible because reports were written on the basis of evidence supplied at committee hearings. Specialists were hired to work for the committees only when specialist investigations were thought to be needed, as with the Senate Select Committee on Securities and Exchange, or the House of Representatives Select Committee on Specific Learning Difficulties.

---

* See footnote (p.99) for details of Public Service salary grades.

The Senate's creation of a full-time Committee secretariat followed the substantial increase in Senate committee work—it was a response to a situation in which the work load was increasing at a great rate. The same cannot be said for the creation of the Committee secretariat in the House of Representatives. There simply was not a great increase in committee work in the House, though House officers wanted to match the Senate's work and its staffing.

Important though the committees were to staff expansion, those who staffed committees were seen as occupying far less important positions within the Parliament House bureaucracy as those working as parliamentary officers. Work on committees was seen as part of the normal training for an officer of the service, and certainly not an end in itself. The end was to be on public view in the chamber, as Clerk, or one of his assistants. And work in the chamber was seen as more intimately involved with "politics" than working on committees. Committee work was seen as technical; chamber work as directly affecting the outcome of politics. Advice on how the standing orders or procedures might be used could result in an advantage to one side or the other in the parliament. Of course such advice was available to both sides. But each staff member tends to develop special relationships with particular "client" MPs or Senators, who learn to regard the particular official as reliable and trustworthy and his advice as useful—and the "clients" will be from both sides of the House. Young MPs or Senators single out young staff members to approach for advice or aid and develop a relationship with them over their stay in parliament. The ties tend to increase and become more significant as both the MP and his parliamentary officer climb the rungs of their respective careers.

Most of this advice is sought and given in the privacy of the parliamentary officer's room, or over the telephone, in the corridors, in a bar or at a social occasion. It is not uncommon to see members and Senators also approaching the Clerks sitting at the table in the House of Representatives or the Senate to seek technical advice about some point of procedure. Here the parliamentarian is normally limited to approaching the Clerk sitting on his particular side of the Table—if he goes to the other side he might be overheard by politicians on that side. Sitting on the right-hand side (the government side) of the Speaker is the Clerk, while his Deputy sits on the left (though in each chamber about seven clerk assistants of various levels may share the jobs during a long day). The Clerks, as well as providing advice, look after the distribution of bills and other papers in the chamber, and prepare documents such as the votes and proceedings or journals, and the notice papers.

The presiding officer relies on the more senior Clerk, sitting on his right, for advice during the sitting. Mostly communication between the two is at the request of the presiding officer (who has a button on his chair which turns on a light, which only the Clerk normally sees, to signal him). However in the event of a problem developing the Clerk will, if he sees the need, pass a note to the presiding officer, or present him with a relevant standing order. The Clerk of the Senate, James Odgers, through long service, the authority of his *Australian Senate Practice,* and his unceasing attempts to enlarge the power of the Senate, is a powerful parliamentary servant. He can be a little more brusque with his President than is the case in the House. He sometimes gets up from his chair, goes to the President's side and talks to him at length, even while a Senator might be taking a point of order—a proceeding which is generally not appreciated by the protesting Senator.

The separation of the parliamentary officers into different parliamentary departments fosters rivalry between the staffs of the chambers which matches the rivalry betweeen politicians of the two chambers. Camaraderie in the Senate is far stronger than in the House (both on the staff level and among the politicians) probably because of the Senate's smaller size and (till recently) its aggressively defensive feelings about its parliamentary significance. This *espirit de corps* in the Senate is strengthened by social gatherings. Parties in the Senate Records office are a regular feature late on Thrusday nights sitting weeks, particularly towards the end of a session. There is plenty of singing and dancing, drinking and arguing among those who attend, including government and opposition Senators, parliamentary officers and attendants, ministerial staff, journalists, and Hansard reporters.

Such semi-public demonstrations of togetherness are not indulged in by the House staff, but this should not be taken as meaning that the people on the House side don't have their pride. Early in the 1970s, for example, the government was anxious to change the quorum of the House from one-third of the total number of members to one-fifth. While there were some protests, there was no doubt the government could have had its way had it pressed the matter. However the Constitution states that the quorum provision can only be changed by parliament, which means the passage of a bill through both houses, and not just a change in standing orders. House staff eventually talked the government out of proceeding with the bill, arguing that it simply wasn't right for the Senate to have a say in a domestic matter affecting only the House.

The Library

Until 1960, the Parliamentary Library also served as Australia's national library. It provided a comfortable lounge and a wide range of reading material for parliamentarians and gradually acquired a large stock of books. Librarians tended to be more interested in its national than its parliamentary functions however, as they encouraged the accumulation of a unique collection of manuscripts, pictures and books on Australia and the Pacific. In the 1960s the two institutions were gradually separated physically with the construction of a separate National Library building and in 1968 the split became complete with the appointment of separate librarians.

The creation of a separate Parliamentary Library corresponded with a developing interest among MPs, particularly Labor MPs, in the provision of more than just reading facilities by the library. Having been out of government for more than a decade by that time, some Labor MPs (particularly some on the backbench) were fretting at being cut off from government sources of information. They contrasted the way ministers and government backbenchers were able to prepare themselves for parliamentary and political tasks with the aid of the public service, with the way they had to rely on their own completely inadequate resources. (The Labor Party had no Canberra secretariat until the mid-1960s, and even when it was created it was unable to provide any assistance to federal MPs). Through the early 1960s, the Library Committee (consisting of the Library Committees of the two houses) considered a number of schemes for the establishment of legislative research services based on the legislative research service provided to American legislators by the Library of Congress. A beginning was made with the provision of a statistical service by the Library through the secondment of an officer from the Bureau of Census and Statistics. Eventually in 1966 the research service was established, staffed by graduates who were not necessarily trained librarians.

By 1968 the library staff was expanding rapidly to cope with the problems of providing its own administration and establishing two distinct services for parliamentarians—a legislative reference service and a legislative research service. The former was staffed primarily by trained graduate librarians. As well as traditional library reference functions, it also provided a current information service. This, by the mid-1970s, had inaugurated a wide variety of service functions. It maintained a filing system under more than 4000 headings (including the names of all current Australian political figures) which *inter alia* contained clippings from all the major newspapers and magazines published in Australia. It provided daily summaries of all national current affairs radio and television programs, and, by using automatic recording devices, was able to provide transcripts of all items on current affairs programs that were broadcast or telecast in Canberra. An ALERT service regularly provided parliamentarians with a summary of articles, books, journals and other material in subject areas in which they had indicated an interest (in a personal interview). These summaries enabled the recipient to obtain copies of journal or magazine articles and to borrow any relevant books.

Running in parallel to the reference service (and often using its facilities) was a legislative research service. This was organised into groups based on the following subject headings: defence, science and technology; education and welfare; finance, industries, trade and development; foreign affairs; law and government; and statistics. The service was to provide MPs and Senators with answers to direct questions, generally by means of short papers which analysed available material. Members sought information from the research service for speeches and to provide the basis of questions to the government. Some groups, of their own initiative, also drafted position papers on subjects they thought would be of general interest to MPs. As well as written advice, the sections would also, through interviews, give personal assistance to MPs in the form of information and even suggested policy lines.

Shadow ministers who did not have the staff available to government ministers, commonly used the research services to help them develop important party policies. Contacts with shadow ministers were often so satisfactory that when in government, ministers continued to get advice from their library contacts. This happened with both Liberal and Labor MPs.

As well as traditional library resources, members of the research service used their own expertise and informal contact with public servants and academics to obtain the information on which their written reports were based. On sensitive issues, however, Departments were likely to be less helpful, realising that the material they might supply to the Library could then be used against the interest of their minister and themselves.

Much of the work of the research service was directly political, oriented mainly towards the needs of opposition MPs and Senators. And while those responsible for the service were aware of the dangers of it appearing partisan, the service inevitably attracted young politically-active graduates many of whom had political biases which they found difficult to conceal. Many developed close ties with the parliamentarians who used the service. Natural client relationships developed as MPs and Senators tended to turn to the same individuals in the area in which they were most interested. Written answers to questions maintained a reasonable standard of impartiality. But some officers of the research and reference services developed contact with parliamentarians outside the Library and in the privacy of members' rooms or more publicly in bars and at parliamentary parties, they offered their political advice to the politicians whose politics they most sympathised with. There were remarkably few rumblings about these contacts (which were mainly with Labor politicians) in the late 1960s and early 1970s, and the Library expanded its staff and its services without apparent government complaint.

The only rumblings were over the public involvement of senior staff in matters of political controversy—for example, the activities of Mr Jim Dunn, head of the research service of defence and foreign affairs. Dunn, before joining the Library, had been a foreign affairs officer, and had served as Australian consul in Timor. From 1975 to 1977 he was publicly identified as an opponent of the Indonesian take-over of Timor. In his public statements, including an appearance before a US congressional committee, he was careful to state that he was acting as a private individual. Nevertheless both Liberal and Labor governments were embarrassed by his association with the parliament. The fact that nothing was done to prevent him from continuing to embarrass the government probably strengthened the standing of the Library research services as independent groups.

It was natural enough that Labor, in opposition when the research services were being developed, should at that time make more use of them than Liberal and N–CP MPs. What was unexpected, however, was that when Labor went into government its parliamentarians continued to make good use of the Library while the then opposition parties were hesitant to take full advantage of it. Some Labor ministers even used the library services to provide them with information which they could use to attack proposals fellow ministers were raising in cabinet or caucus. On all sides politicians used the service to help write speeches which were used outside the parliamentary chambers: some used them in the party room, some used them in speeches in their electorates. The research services also found themselves being used increasingly to provide assistance to parliamentary committees.

Hansard

The rate of growth of the Parliamentary reporting staff in the 1960s and 1970s failed to match that of other parliamentary departments. This was partly due to the fact that Hansard underwent major expansions earlier—in particular in the mid-1950s when a daily Hansard began to be published. The additional hours of work of the recent parliaments and the additional legislation had little effect on Hansard's staffing. But additional committee work did force it to change its techniques and double its staff.

The parliamentary debates of the Australian Parliament had always been recorded by official reporters employed by the parliament who sat at the main tables in the two chambers. Their shorthand notes were dictated to typists, and checked by supervisors. A copy was sent to the Member or Senator whose speech had been reported, who had a limited time (up to an hour) in which to make any necessary corrections before the material was sent (by underground pneumatic tubes) to the Government Printing Office where (since 1975) it was set by a computer photo-composition method and printed the next morning in the daily Hansard. A revised edition of the week's proceedings appeared about a month later, and each year bound copies which included indexes prepared by the Hansard staff were printed for parliamentarians, libraries and approved purchasers. Committee proceedings were mostly recorded on tape, and transcribed by typists. Copies of the typescript were made available immediately to committee members and staff but whether the full record of the committee's proceedings was published and in what form depended on the committee—daily Hansards were produced of Senate estimates committees, while many select committees did not publish their proceedings in printed form.

Hansard does not produce an exact verbatim report of the proceedings of the parliament. It tries to follow the formula established by British practice that Hansard should present a substantially verbatim report with repetitions and redundancies omitted and other obvious mistakes corrected but which leaves out nothing that adds to the meaning of the speech or illustrates the argument. Members and Senators are supposed to be able to make corrections but they are not supposed to be permitted to alter the sense of what they have said or to introduce new matter. The first corrections and alterations are provided by the reporter and his supervisor. They are concerned mainly with the literacy of the report, correcting grammar and sentence construction and even style. After they finish, there should be little left for the politician to do. However many MPs and Senators do make substantial corrections, sometimes to change a word which the reporter may not have properly understood (a technical word, or a quotation in a foreign language), but sometimes to correct a mistake the member himself made in his speech.

Some ministers have been notorious for producing figures in an apparently knowledgeable fashion in question time and then relying on their staff to look up the true figures later and put the corrections into the Hansard proof. While corrections of this sort are not supposed to be made, they are not uncommon. In recent years, however, ministers have found it more difficult to indulge in this type of practice without detection. In the 1970s it became common for journalists working in the press gallery to seek access to ministers' greens (as the copies supplied by Hansard to members of the House of Representatives are called: in the Senate they are called pinks) and to photocopy them. If these copies were made after the minister had made his alterations, the journalists were able to determine the significance of these changes. Occasionally members have objected to such alterations and the Speaker or President has had to listen to a tape recording (made automatically of all the proceedings) by Hansard to determine what was said and whether changes made were acceptable.

Another problem area is the recording of interjections. These normally are not included in Hansard unless they are answered by the speaker. It requires skill on the part of a member to decide on hearing an interjection whether he should respond to it in order to get it on the record, or whether he should ignore it and force it to be expunged from the record. The Hansard reporter will normally try to record as many interjections as he can in case they are responded to. He is normally assisted in this task by a supervisor sitting beside him in the chamber.

Most members spend time and trouble making sure that Hansard contains an improved version of what they have said in the chamber. As a result, Hansard reads a lot better than parliament sounds.

Ministerial Staff

Junie Morosi, Peter Wilenski, Jim Spigelman, Philip Cairns, Elizabeth Reid—these are just some of the people who helped focus attention on the activities and functions of ministerial staff during the Whitlam government. Comparatively little had been heard about ministerial staff before Labor came to power in 1972, though over the previous decade there had been a transformation in the importance of the people who constituted the staff of Liberal and Country Party ministers.

Under the Liberal governments of Menzies, Holt, Gorton and McMahon, ministerial staffing had more than doubled. In 1960 only a few ministers were entitled to employ press secretaries, by 1970 every minister could have one. At the beginning of the sixties most staff came either from the minister's electorate (and handled electorate–political relations) or they came from the Commonwealth Departments for which the minister was temporarily responsible. A minister in 1960 would have a staff consisting of a private secretary, an assistant private secretary and a typist or two—unless he was a very senior Cabinet minister. By 1970 a minister could expect to have a press secretary, a private secretary, a departmental liaison officer, an assistant private secretary and several typists.

The post-Menzies ministerial officers were not all anonymous. Tony Eggleton became the very model of a prime ministerial press secretary. Ainslie Gotto ran Gorton's prime ministerial office as his private secretary before women's lib. became a well-known phenomenon.

These two were accepted as political advisers rather than shufflers of paper. In most ministerial offices, press secretaries functioned as political intelligence operatives for their ministers, as well as handling press releases (most of which would have been prepared in the department by departmental journalists). By 1972 it was accepted in Parliament House (though not perhaps outside it) that a minister's staff would frequently provide political and policy advice as well as servicing his departmental needs.

A number of factors contributed to a major expansion of the ministerial staff when Labor was elected in 1972. These included, not necessarily in order of importance,

(a) a desire to change the system to allow Labor to implement its programs as quickly as possible;

(b) a distrust of the public service establishment;

(c) an acceptance that ministers would need more help in their own offices to offset their lack of government experience;

(d) the desire to have the ministerial office inhabited by people with sympathetic political views who could help the minister achieve his program;

(e) a way of employing experts from outside the public service who had either contributed to policy making or who would play an important part in implementing policy;

(f) rewards for old friends, relations or political associates;

(g) providing the minister with sources of advice from outside the public service;

(h) removing the need for ministers to rely on their departments to do purely political work, a complaint which had been made about some senior Liberal and Country Party ministers; and

(i) providing the minister with a party contact who could report to him on factional problems he might have to deal with.

Different ministers had different reasons for wanting to appoint staff and some did not think it necessary to appoint as many as their colleagues. But in general the ministers appointed more staff than the average minister in the previous L–CP government had been able to appoint.

Different ministers required their staffs to perform different functions. While individual ministerial officers served their ministers in many ways, they were used for such purposes as:

(a) carrying out research for the minister in specific policy areas relating to his portfolio;

(b) providing advice after researching cabinet submissions from his own department, or from other ministers;

(c) conducting departmental or other meetings on the minister's behalf;

(d) providing the minister with general political intelligence gleaned from other ministerial staff, press sources or party sources;

(e) helping organise the minister's work load in terms of engagements, correspondence, research and meetings;

(f) writing speeches and press material;

(g) providing the minister with press liaison;

(h) providing liaison with his department;

(i) providing liaison with members of parliament;

(j) searching for people outside the established political framework who might be experts in matters coming before the minister;

(k) providing the minister with assistance in fulfilling his parliamentary duties, including providing question time briefing, checking speech notes, ensuring his attendance when required;

(l) helping to protect the minister from enemies, friends and sometimes himself.

Which particular function a staff member might perform would depend on the attitude of the minister towards his staff and the functions he thought they should serve, the type of department for which he was responsible, the capacity of the staff member, the workload of staff and minister, and relationships with other ministers, staffs and departments.

While the above list concentrates on matters with a strong political flavour, many senior ministerial staff did little political work at all. Usually only one or two members of a minister's staff were concerned with overtly political material; most were involved in routine office and departmental work. Between one-half and one-third of the 227 ministerial staff at the end of 1974 were in positions which involved them essentially in typing, telephone answering, filing and other clerical work. Staff above the rank of assistant private secretary totalled 107 at this time compared with fifty-three in the last year of the McMahon Government (1972). A survey of these senior staff suggested that almost half came directly from the public service into their jobs, on secondment from the department the new minister controlled. More than a third of the total senior staff appeared to be involved in political work to a noticeable degree, and about half of those so involved were permanent public servants.

Labor ministers appointed their staff without the benefit of any firm guidelines. It was not until Labor had been in office for more than eighteen months that firm controls were set and implemented; it was not until towards the end of its term that the Prime Minister was able to impose some controls over the choice of individuals to fill senior positions on ministers' staffs. The finally agreed establishment for ministerial staff under Labor was: four ministerial officers, one of whom could be designated as a press secretary, two assistant private secretaries, one secretary-typist and one steno-secretary. The ranking of the ministerial officers depended on the ranking of the minister but they ranged from the equivalent of a grade 6 public servant clerk (the rank reached normally by a graduate with several years service) to the middle of the second division. Only the Prime Minister and the Deputy Prime Minister were entitled to appoint second division officers. Ten years earlier, an average minister's sole private secretary was likely to be at about the class 6 level.

While there was a great deal of political criticism about these new arrangements, they were essentially maintained by the Fraser government except that most ministers were not permitted to appoint press secretaries. Fraser also specifically encouraged his ministers to appoint public servants to their personal staffs, rather than employing outside "political" experts from universities or party circles. Public servants were thought to make better ministerial officers for two reasons: first because of their style, second because of the quality of their advice. "Style" included the way they behaved around Parliament House, the certainty that they would indulge less in public activity, the probability that they would mix less with the press and be less likely to involve themselves in internal (among ministers) political machinations. Their advice was thought to be of a type which would incline to keep ministers out of trouble, with an essential quality of conservatism which might not be found in non-public servants employed only on a temporary basis. These were the main lessons the Liberals learnt from what they saw as Labor's "excesses" in the appointment of ministerial staff.

Ministerial staff are employed under the Public Service Act but with special provisions applying to them. They can be hired and fired at a minister's will (permanent public servants dispensed with by their ministers return to their departments) and they owe their allegiance to the minister and not to his department. Departmental officers transferred onto a minister's staff are not supposed to accept directions from the departmental head, or to make reports to him except under their minister's direction, though there have been examples of individual public servants reversing this order of preference—no doubt being aware that their future career prospects would be more influenced by the permanent head's view of them than by any favour they might find with their minister.

Although ministerial staff apparently undertook less political roles in the Fraser government than staff had in the Whitlam Government, the fact that Fraser was unable to drastically reduce their numbers suggests that ministers no longer believed they could cope with their workloads assisted only by a few typists and a secretary to look after their paperwork.

Public Servants

Members of the staff of the parliament and members of the staff of ministers work under special conditions different from the rest of the Public Service. Whether this is to insulate them or the rest of the Public Service isn't quite clear (and was not settled by the Coombs Royal Commission on Australian Government Administration).

The arrangement, however, does seem to imply that those public servants who are intimately involved with politics need to be in some way separated from the remainder of the public service. However the fact is that many hundreds of senior public servants are involved in politics, with parliamentarians and others, and make decisions and recommendations primarily in a political context. Some of these public servants, very largely in the first and second divisions, are frequently visitors to Parliament House, calling on ministers, facing up to parliamentary committees, talking with party committees and individual MPs. Their work probably has more important political effects than the work of parliamentary and ministerial staffs.

In recent years journalists have been freer to talk about these public servants, to mention their names and attribute views to them. Inside Parliament House, and to a lesser extent outside it, there has been recognition of which public servants are politically powerful, and often what their particular policies are (as opposed to the policies of the government which, theory would have it, the public servants are there only to implement). These senior public servants have taken on a more public face as they have had to answer questions directed at them before parliamentary committees. Contact between parliamentarians and public servants has increased to the extent that in 1976 the Fraser government issued guidelines (see p.151) to show the public servants how they should behave in dealing with individual MPs and Senators, and with party committees.

There are no written rules governing relationships between the most senior public servants and their ministers, however. And it is these relationships that require public servants to take on roles which can be highly political. Ministers rely on the advice they receive from their departments. Because most ministers don't involve themselves in administrative matters, such advice tends to be about policy, rather than administration—though most of the time there is no sense in trying to maintain any distinction between those two concepts. What is important is that the views that departments put to ministers invariably have political implications. And while it is true that ministers don't have to accept the advice they receive from their departments, most rely on that advice to help in formulating their own views, and frequently they fully accept the departmental view.

Ministers often receive advice from their departments on the plans of other ministers. Cabinet submissions circulated by a minister are as likely as not to result in briefs being prepared by many other departments for their ministers on the implications of the particular policy proposal. These submissions will not deal explicitly with the political arguments for or against a policy proposal, but they are all prepared with the understanding that they are concerned about influencing political decisions. In the case where a minister invariably accepts his permanent head's advice, it is the permanent head who is exercising political power, not the minister. But even when a minister always treats his department's views with caution, the department can and will influence his decision in its choice of the information which it provides to him. Senior public servants in Canberra recognise the political nature of their work and suggest that they avoid overstepping the political mark through their "professionalism" and experience. But there is no doubting the potential political power of very senior public servants and the actual power that many of them exercise.

When Labor was elected in 1972, some of its ministers demanded the right to have permanent heads who were in sympathy with their policies or their politics. Clyde Cameron disapproved of the then head of his department because he had clashed with him as shadow minister. Whitlam disapproved of the policies of the Department of Foreign Affairs and of the "unreconstructed" views of many of its senior officers. He appointed a Secretary he thought would be more sympathetic with his foreign policy ideas. Sir Lenox Hewitt was brought into Minerals and Energy by Connor because Connor felt he could trust him and his advice (Gorton had made Hewitt Secretary of the Prime Minister's Department for the same reason). Ministers who made such appointments wanted men as secretaries of their departments with whom they could talk freely and from whom they could expect advice which they believed would seek to advance policy towards an accepted goal.

Whitlam, who was happy enough to appoint his own man as secretary of Foreign Affairs because there was a tradition that the head of that department had only a three or four year tenure, resisted advice that he should change the head of the Prime Minister's Department. He did not want to upset the traditionalists in the public service—and at that time he appeared to share their view that permanent heads should not be changed unduly. After two years in government, however, he did move to appoint his own man as secretary of his department—and the appointee had been his private secretary for several years when he was Opposition Leader. Later (in an article published by *The Age* on 5 January 1977 reviewing Harold Wilson's book *The Governance of Britain*), Whitlam was to comment on the appointment:

> The departmental system works well in Australia, provided always that the Prime Minister can choose the head of his department and work closely with him on terms of intimate understanding and absolute trust.
>
> When I chose an "outsider" to head my own department in 1974 I had in mind that a Prime Minister needs a permanent head whom he knows well and whose department can be relied upon to act as a virtual instrument of the Government of the day. No doubt Mr Fraser's choice of a permanent head reflects the same desire.
>
> I do not see any derogation in this system from the principles of cabinet government or Ministerial responsibility. It seems to me that democracy is best served when the Government's policies are implemented and co-ordinated through a departmental head who enjoys the absolute confidence of the Government which the people have chosen.

The argument applies equally well to other departmental heads, and perhaps to other senior public servants in each department who have responsibilities concerning policy and advice which are essentially political.

Fraser recognised the political nature of the role of the Secretary of the Prime Minister's Department when he eventually acted to remove Whitlam's appointee and install his own. Fraser had earlier allowed other Whitlam appointees in the first division of the public service to be removed by other ministers, and had chosen his own man to head the Australian Broadcasting Commission.

In 1976 Fraser introduced legislation to regularise the position of political appointees who take up positions as heads of department, and to try to systematise the means by which all permanent heads are appointed. The new Act provided that the Chairman of the Public Service Board appoint a three-man board (from among permanent heads and himself) after consultation with the Prime Minister of the day, to prepare lists of suitable appointees as permanent heads. Where an appointment is made outside the list from the nomination of a minister or the Prime Minister, the tenure of the new permanent head is limited to five years (with the right to re-appointment). Such appointees can be removed at any time on the recommendation of a Prime Minister of a different political party to the appointing minister. Appointments are made by the Governor-General on the recommendation of the Prime Minister.

The main effect of the legislation appears to be to confirm that political appointments may be made. It divides permanent heads into two classes, those who have the approval of the Public Service Board or the chairman's committee, and those whose appointment is due solely to political patronage. One real difference between the new system and the old is the limitation on the rights of political appointees—until the legislation was passed a political appointee could only be dismissed from the public service (as opposed to being removed from the particular department) after a six-month delay. Another important change is the power put into the hands of the Chairman of the Public Service Board and the Prime Minister. The former may give any possible appointee, even from outside the public service ranks, "established" status and hence full public service tenure. The latter now has the power to appoint permanent heads, a power formerly in the hands of cabinet and the responsible minister.

Much of the contact between ministers and their permanent heads takes place in private. There are no outside witnesses to the seeking and provision of partisan political advice. Whitlam used to acknowledge that his public service advisers should not have to comment on wholly political matters, but he still welcomed their comments when they made them, and he regularly provided the opportunity for them to do so.

The opportunity to give evidence to the Royal Commission on Australian Government Administration allowed a few permanent heads to comment publicly on the political nature of their work. Mr Maurice Timbs, secretary of the then Department of Property and Services, said in his submission to the RCAGA, "the relationship between the permanent head and his minister is a close personal relationship and the permanent head is inevitably drawn into the political spectrum for advice and consultation". The Department of Urban and Regional Development (as it was called) said there were areas of "policy advice to ministers in which a party political flavour cannot be avoided. It would be unrealistic to suggest that the concept of an a-political public service implies unawareness of political constraints". The Department also made the point that "by definition government employees service governments. They do not serve the parliament nor do they serve 'the people'."

The 1972–75 Labor governments brought these political aspects into the public arena. But there is no doubt that permanent heads under previous Liberal governments were just as politically involved as they were under Labor. However under Labor, public servants at lower levels became involved in the work of parliamentary party committees. For many years MPs have had access to the advice of friendly experts in the public service on a background basis. What Labor did was to have its ministers authorise public servants to attend meetings of party committees to give non-political technical advice. Unofficially, if the public servant was friendly, he might go somewhat beyond this brief, however that was not his job. The government also made it clear that public servants could brief party committees on the opposition side, and this facility was used. The RCAGA reported on the practice, and at the end of 1976 Fraser issued his guidelines for public servants in relation to party committees.

Guidelines to Apply to Appearances by Public Servants Before Party Committees

1. Ministers may authorise officers of their departments to appear before Government and Opposition Party Committees to provide briefings or background material on Government or ministerial decisions and proposals, including details and/or explanations of proposed legislation.

2. Briefing of this nature will be authorised on the principle of promoting the freest possible flow of factual and background material to permit informed consideration by the committees and parties concerned of the issues involved, consistent with preserving the necessary confidence of Government and maintaining the traditional political impartiality of officials.

3. Committee requests for briefing in the above terms will be directed to the Minister concerned. If he agrees, the Minister will authorise his department to put the necessary arrangements in hand. It will also be open for a Minister himself to initiate proposals for briefing of committees, where he considers this to be desirable.

4. Officials will not be expected or authorised to express opinions on Government policies, policy options or matters of a party political nature. The discussions may, however, include administrative arrangements and procedures involved in implementation of the proposed policies or legislation.

5. If matters are raised which in the judgment of officials seek expressions of opinion on Government policies or on alternative policies, the officials would suggest that the matter be raised with the Minister.

6. Where considered necessary or desirable, Ministers may elect to be present at discussions with Government party committees, to deal with questions of a policy or party political nature.

7. Where the Minister does not attend the committee proceedings, he will have the right to be kept informed by officials of the nature of the discussions and of any matters not able to be resolved by the officials to the committee's satisfaction.

8. Where an official considers that questioning by a committee goes beyond the authorised scope of the briefing arrangements, he should so indicate to the committee, and before answering will be at liberty to raise the matter with his

departmental head and the Minister, and if he so desires, with the Public Service Board.

Under the Labor Government there was a greater tendency for backbench MPs and Senators to have access to public servants on an individual basis to follow up electorate matters or to research factual material for policy work. Parliamentarians found they could often get answers quicker and more accurately by contacting the responsible officers than they by operating through the formal channels of communication—which meant through the Minister. Labor MPs tried to keep these contacts after they went into opposition, and again Fraser, following on the RCAGA report, issued formal rules to govern the behaviour of public servants.

Guidelines Relating to Access by Members of Parliament to Public Servants

(a) Much will depend on the nature of the request. There will, for example, be occasions when a request by a Member of Parliament amounts to no more than a request for available factual information equivalent to any request from a member of the public. In these circumstances, the information should obviously be provided;

(b) there will be other occasions when the request is sensitive, or where answering it would necessitate the use of substantial departmental resources. In such cases it would be appropriate to suggest that the member write to the Minister requesting the information;

(c) the officer should, as appropriate, inform his Permanent Head or Minister of a request for information and of the outcome;

(d) care should be taken to avoid unauthorised disclosure of classified or otherwise confidential information, for example, where a breach of personal or commercial privacy could be involved.

The public service, as the instrument by which government policies are implemented, is inherently a political force. It is the instrument of government (not of opposition) and governments use it to provide themselves with resources of information and advice denied to political parties which are not in government. However as the range of public servants involved in political matters has increased, so too has awareness of their political function. There has also been an apparent increase in contact between public servants and politicians on an informal basis which has resulted in many senior and middle-level public servants becoming unofficially involved in party policy formulation. There has also been a great increase in the leaking of politically damaging material by public servants to opposition parties and to the press.

9 The Press Gallery

The press gallery's *raison d'être* is to report the debates of the parliament of the Commonwealth of Australia; but just as Parliament House has become the home of the national government and the focus of most Australian national politics, so the press gallery has come to be at least as much concerned with the activities of national government and politics as it is with reporting proceedings in the House and the Senate.

The term press gallery describes both a series of places and a group of journalists. There are two galleries used by the press in the House of Representatives, containing about forty-seven seats, and one gallery in the Senate with about twenty seats. There is also an organisation called the press gallery which consists of the journalists working for media organisations (and a few freelance journalists who work out of Parliament House). These journalists and the staff who assist them (mainly teleprinter operators and librarians) are issued with a pass by the officers of the House and the Senate which entitles them to use the facilities of the parliament and gives them entry to the galleries in the two chambers. Seats in the galleries are allocated by the gallery organisation, not the parliament. The organisation also allocates office space on the top floor of Parliament House near the chambers—an area which also has the title, the press gallery. It also determines whether newcomers seeking press gallery privileges should be given them. Other than access, the other important privilege is the allocation of a box in a series of pigeon-holes located in one of the corridors in the press gallery. All press releases issued by ministers, reports tabled in the parliament, and statements made by anyone wanting to get information to the national news media, can be placed in these boxes. Each week hundreds of handouts go into each of the sixty-five or so boxes to be processed by the 130 or so journalists who are the members of the press gallery and who work in the press gallery.

News organisations employ from one to a dozen journalists to report out of the press gallery. There are between thirty and forty one-man offices; two offices contain more than ten people. Most Sydney and Melbourne daily newspapers maintain offices of between four and eight journalists. Four of Sydney's commercial radio stations have one representative each and their employers try to sell their output to radio stations elsewhere in Australia. There are large and small service organisations providing news material to groups of newspapers and other subscribers. Work methods and work loads vary with the type and size of the organisation and the style of its product.

One of the largest organisations is the Australian Broadcasting Commission which provides a full parliamentary and political news service for radio and television and employs specialists to report for radio and television current affairs programs (such as AM, PM and This Day Tonight). Another very large organisation is the News Ltd Bureau, which provides a common parliamentary and news service to all the News Ltd publications. Several of the group's publications (like the *Australian* and Sydney *Daily Telegraph*) have additional representatives in the gallery who provide them with commentary and news exclusive to the particular paper. The Herald and Weekly Times has two similar bureau arrangements. Its two Melbourne papers provide services for all its morning and afternoon newspapers throughout Australia and in addition all the capital city papers in the group have their own political correspondent in the gallery working in co-operation with the bureau and providing material specially written for the particular newspapers.

Another large organisation is the Australian Associated Press (AAP). It provides a full parliamentary service to any subscriber—in 1978 to every metropolitan newspaper in Australia plus country newspaper networks in Victoria, New South Wales and Queensland. This parliamentary service generally provides over forty reports each parliamentary day covering all the questions asked in the House of Representatives and most speakers in major debates. It also provides a general political service covering routine departmental and ministerial news and political news to its country subscribers, and to radio and television stations which subscribe to it—in 1978 this service was provided to every metropolitan commercial radio and television station.

The television networks are mostly represented in the gallery by a reporter, a cameraman and a sound-man. Weekly newspapers and magazines have one- or two-man operations. Overseas newspapers and magazines are most frequently represented on a part-time basis by journalists servicing several such organisations.

The reporting of parliamentary events is left mainly to AAP. Except at question time or when major statements or debates are under way, it is rare to find more than two reporters in the gallery, one from AAP, the other from the ABC which is required by law to maintain an independent news service.

The political correspondent for a newspaper (normally the head of the paper's press gallery office) writes up the major speeches or questions if he considers them important enough to warrant front-page treatment. Otherwise he spends his time concentrating on political news—trying to find out what cabinet is considering, what the opposition parties are planning, generally what is happening in national politics. Several members of his staff are occupied almost full-time dealing with material placed in the press gallery boxes. This includes parliamentary reports, press releases from ministers and from the opposition, press statements from departments and official sources (including daily collections of statistical information released by the Bureau of Statistics), handouts from national employers' organisations and lobby groups, and information from anyone else who has discovered the gallery boxes.

Others spend their time following up queries from their head office, generally about stories which have appeared in other newspapers or about events occurring outside Canberra which need a "Canberra angle". Specialist writers on economics, defence or foreign affairs spend their time checking their departmental and other sources. All spend considerable time reading—mainly newspapers. The average journalist in the Press Gallery will, while parliament is sitting, produce a great deal more material than his counterpart back in the newspaper's main office. Even when parliament is not sitting, his workload is still likely to be greater and his hours of work longer than the average journalist working for a metropolitan newspaper.

The average press gallery journalist is better educated than most of his fellows, particularly if he is a head of bureau. The political correspondent often travels out of Canberra to cover major political events such as federal meetings of the parties and by-election campaigns. He will cover entire federal election campaigns with the aid of one or two members of his staff, and will frequently travel overseas to cover the Prime Minister's international visits.

The press gallery has undergone considerable changes in the past decade and a half. While it has not expanded as much as other groups employed in Parliament House, lack of space has been the main reason for this. In fifteen years gallery employment has probably trebled, while office space for the gallery has increased by about one-third. In the 1970s the parliament placed a complete ban on any increase in gallery membership, a ban which, while not strictly adhered to, has prevented as big an expansion as some news organisations would have liked.

With size, the gallery has undergone changes in personnel and style. In the final years of Sir Robert Menzies' reign, half a dozen political correspondents from the Sydney and Melbourne newspaper groups dominated the gallery and set the tone of its relations with politicians and the style of reporting politics. Mainly in their forties and fifties, they had spent many years in the gallery reporting parliament and politics. They had close contacts with politicians they had virtually grown up with and they had close contacts among senior public servants whom they socialised with in common golf and other clubs. In the late 1950s they were largely replaced by men in their twenties and thirties who had less political experience, more academic training, and who tended to be less respectful of the politicians and the public servants.

Another major change has been the increasing use made of the basic news coverage provided by Australian Associated Press. In the mid-1960s it provided a parliamentary service to four major newspapers and Canberra political coverage to a string of country papers. By 1978 it was supplying the parliamentary service to every major newspaper in Australia and its full service to every major radio and television station. The parliamentary service included coverage of every report tabled in parliament and all meetings held by parliamentary committees in Canberra, in and out of session, as well as the normal proceedings of parliament. Its non-parliamentary service comprised a coverage of all other national events about which the press gallery would be concerned.

In 1977 for the first time, all major newspapers took AAP's basic coverage of the election campaign—it covered the itineries of all the major political figures, providing a basic service covering speeches made and press conferences given. Its service for radio included a "rip and read" coverage, written in a form which allowed radio reporters simply to tear the copy off their teleprinter and read it directly on air without needing to rewrite or rephrase it. Its general service also included coverage of the overseas visits of the Prime Minister and important ministers—ten such visits were covered in 1977. Its Canberra office also provided the political coverage it supplied to three overseas news services, (Reuter, United Press International and Associated Press), as well as several specialist economic services. All these services were provided by a permanent staff based in Canberra of only six, plus five additional reporters operating while parliament was in session.

AAP's basic service was used in different ways by different

organisations. Some, like *The Australian,* used it only as a backstop, preferring to rewrite any parliamentary copy which was to be used. Others, like the *Sydney Morning Herald,* often made full use of the service, with its reporters concentrated on writing comment material to go with the AAP copy. In all instances the political correspondent was freer to go in search of exclusive political copy than he had been when he was responsible for also seeing that all the basic news was covered.

Another development in the gallery came with competition between newspapers, and radio and television. When television and radio began actively covering Australian politics from their own resources, newspaper editors began encouraging their reporters to write more comment into their reports. In the late 1960s and early 1970s, radio and television reporters moved into Parliament House, setting up miniature studios which drew the attention of politicians who preferred to be interviewed for media which were likely to present at least some of what they had to say without distortion. Television and radio began to make and break stories ahead of newspapers which concentrated more and more on explaining events.

The politics of the gallery change rapidly. From being predominantly Liberal in the mid-1960s it became pro-Labor (or at least pro-Whitlam) in the late 1960s and early 1970s. Then it became anti-Labor through 1974 and 1975 and then anti-Fraser after 11 November 1975. Fraser's successful efforts during the 1975 election campaign, and after, to bypass the press gallery and get his views across through editors and proprietors worsened relations between the gallery and the new government. They deteriorated further after the government's popularity had peaked and criticism of the government's handling of the economy was allowed to emerge in print.

The gallery is an extremely competitive place. In Canberra the Sydney and Melbourne morning newspapers are available early enough in the morning to be home delivered along with the Canberra paper. These editions are scanned to see whether any stories have been broken by the opposition—which in Canberra means by any other paper. Later the other capital city dailies are read and compared. Journalists in the non-members' bar compare the successes and failures of their colleagues. But it is through their writings rather than through bar-room gossip that reputations are established and styles of reporting temporarily established.

Political correspondents spend much of their time in contact with politicians, public servants and ministerial staff. They develop their special relations with individuals in all fields and in all parties. Sometimes this is on the basis of "home town" interests, particularly with politicians who are concerned with getting a good press back where it really matters, in their electorates. Ministers too are susceptible to this type of relationship but also look to the state of their image outside their home state. Sometimes relationships develop on the basis of the journalist's political leanings, sometimes because of his reputation and possible influence, sometimes because of shared social backgrounds, sometimes because of common social habits.

Occasionally a minister will give information to a journalist accidentally, not aware that when added to other knowledge the journalist has, the information will provide him with a story. But more often ministerial leaks are quite deliberately aimed at getting a particular piece of information into print, to try out an idea to see whether it can gain public or political acceptance, to damage an idea being floated by a colleague, or to damage a rival within his own party. Sometimes the leaking is done by a member of a minister's staff (not always his press secretary) and on the minister's behalf, though some ministers prefer to pretend they do not know what their staff do in this regard.

Reports which appear in newspapers suggesting that "sources" or "staff" have provided particular information, or that the minister is "believed" to want something or to think in a particular way, are often the result of breifings by the minister himself, who wants to get information across without being tied to particular quotes which the opposition can use against him. The use of large-scale background briefings by ministers, particularly Prime Ministers, at which most gallery services are represented has fallen off because some journalists have decided that they will not attend such briefings, but that they will try to find out what happened at them and report them as fully as possible, attributing the material to the minister concerned. However Prime Ministers and ministers still provide briefings on an individual basis to journalists which result in stories suggesting that "senior government sources" have particular views.

Occasionally the "source" will be caught out. In 1973, for example, Whitlam, when Prime Minister, was identified as having briefed journalists about the existence and activities of the branch of the intelligence services which operated a radio listening facility in Singapore. In 1977, Prime Minister Fraser's hint to the editor of the *Australian* that he might "spring an election" led to that newspaper insisting there would be a spring election—Fraser had summer in mind.

Most briefing is on a one-to-one basis, and the only people who can really be sure of the source of the story will be the reporter and the person who gave him the material. On very important stories, secrecy is absolutely vital. In 1976, for example, the *Age* broke a story giving an account of cabinet's discussions on whether the Australian currency should be devalued. The story revealed that the Prime Minister was wavering in secret despite the government's public assurances that there would be no change in the dollar's value. The publication of the story made it virtually inevitable that there would be a devaluation, and that it would occur within a short period. The "leak" in that case would not have kept his job had Fraser been able to identify him.

As Prime Minister, Fraser preferred to deal with newspaper editors and proprietors rather than press gallery journalists. He met the top people in the more important newspapers three or four times a year in his first two years in office, sometimes entertaining them at the Lodge, sometimes accepting invitations to their boardrooms.

A briefing may result from a journalist's efforts to get information about a particular story or it may originate with the "source" anxious to see a particular story floated. Sometimes the information is genuine, sometimes it is speculative, in the nature of a trial balloon to see whether the newspapers or the public would find the particular proposal acceptable, and sometimes the information can be false—disinformation, designed to mislead the source's political opponents. A journalist rapidly decides which of his sources he can trust to give him accurate information, and which he must be careful to check out with official sources who can be quoted. Some stories simply cannot be checked—the reporter has to either accept what he is told and print it, or do nothing with the information. That is often the situation with material supplied by the Prime Minister (whoever he is), less so with ministerial information. And if a journalist does not use information a source gives him, he runs the risk that next time the source will give the information to someone else, a rival in the gallery.

A person who has information to leak will probably be careful about who he gives it to. He must first choose a reporter he is certain will not reveal the source. Which reporter may depend on whether he is trying to make as big an impact in the news as he can or whether he is aiming at getting the story circulated in a particular area—perhaps just bringing information to the notice of his fellow parliamentarians. It will also depend on the type of story and the source's views about the quality of the particular paper or program he is dealing with. Or the information might be leaked to a particular journalist to repay a political debt—or to build up a bank of goodwill which might later be drawn on.

In the mid-1960s one of the political journalist's regular jobs was to find out what happened at the weekly meetings of Labor and Liberal parties. Some journalists had sources who blatantly took notes during party meetings, others used backbenchers who had reliable memories. Often a journalist would have to check with a dozen MPs, none of whom was supposed to provide such information, before he was satisfied he had a full account of proceedings. However the Labor

Party in 1967 and the Liberals in 1973 changed that routine by providing quite official briefings of the events at party meetings. Journalists then used their sources to check on the briefing and tended to concentrate their stories on those aspects of party meetings which the official briefing either played down or omitted altogether.

Another change during this period was the increasing ability of journalists to gain access to cabinet material. Far more accounts began to appear about items on cabinet agendas and about cabinet decisions which were supposed to be kept under wraps. It also became more usual for reports to quote directly from cabinet decisions. Governments have attempted to protect cabinet secrecy but the increasing numbers of ministerial staff, public servants and others who have access to these documents has made secrecy more difficult. And the more that is published, the easier it is for journalists to persuade ministers and others to provide information to help protect the standing of particular ministers, or the government.

Parliamentarians have been as much affected by developments in the media as have the journalists of the press gallery. Although parliamentary proceedings are broadcast by the ABC (the House of Representatives on Tuesday and Thursday, the Senate on Wednesday), MPs and Senators rely on the press, radio and television for news coverage of the issues they try to publicise through the parliament—the listening audience for parliamentary broadcasts is minute.

As mentioned before, (see p.69), the requirements of the media have changed parliamentary fashions. In Sir Robert Menzies' day, the best time for important announcements was 8 p.m.—the best audience rating time on the ABC, and a convenient time to catch all the morning editions of newspapers throughout Australia. Now the favoured time is shortly after 5 p.m. If the event has been publicised in advance, a Prime Minister can probably attract a reasonable audience on radio, and he will get good coverage on television news from 6 p.m., as well as coverage in the morning newspapers. If the occasion is one which would encourage television stations to use film or interview material in their newscasts, their timing requirements will be carefully attended to.

Just which media are favoured will depend on the individual politician's appreciation of the impact he wants to make (and the time he is prepared to put into creating news). Fraser, for example, would devote time to giving radio and television interviews on particular newsy topics, but not to giving general press conferences. Whitlam preferred the general press conference and could rarely find the time to give individual radio or television interviews to supplement a particular news item.

The media tend to dictate not only the timing of parliamentary occasions but also something of their style and content. Personification and simplification are regarded as essential. Political current affairs programs rarely extend beyond three-minute encounters (called debates) between political opponents. Point scoring is all that is attempted. Policy issues are rarely looked at in depth. A few newspapers devote feature space to examining political issues, but news editors prefer scandal stories about politicians. They are helped in their search for scandal by the politicians themselves. It is not unknown for a journalist with a juicy tale about a politician to go to a member of the other side to get him to "drop a bucket" on the MP during question time or in the adjournment debate—the information is then privileged, and a paper can print it without fear of a defamation action.

Don Chipp has described this parliamentary character assassination as a recent phenomenon. This is probably true of the deliberate use of privilege by MPs to attack their political opponents with the intention of getting the privileged smears published as widely as possible. Chipp went on to attack the gallery journalists.

> It is strange that there are very few articles written or allegations made about politicians breaking promises or engaging in internecine fighting amongst themselves for positions of power. The reason for this is that the press gallery is literally an extended arm of the parliament where its heavies *expect* politicians to be less than truthful, to be abusive, to behave badly, equivocate, to conspire and stab each other in the back. The one thing respected by the press gallery is power irrespective of how it is grasped. (*Dissent,* September 1976. Chipp's emphasis)

While it may be true that journalists expect politicians to behave as Chipp describes, this does not explain why they do not report such goings on (insofar as they do not). There are three points to be made. First, because of the very severe laws of defamation, much of this bad behaviour cannot be reported unless politicians themselves provide privilege by discussing the particular behaviour in the parliament. In stating facts about particular bad behaviour, a journalist faced with a defamation action will need to produce proof of the truth of his allegations—and in most cases he will not be able to do so as his sources will be informant politicians who will not make their disclosure in public. Second, those MPs whose behaviour should be criticised are likely to be "sources". While they should not be able to buy protection by leaking information, it is inevitable that to some extent they will be able to succeed in doing this. Journalists close to a particular minister or backbencher will usually be the last to criticise him for his errors— in part because those journalists will seek to get "both sides" when allegations are made against their sources.

Third, and most importantly, decisions about attacking individual MPs (for their behaviour, or for lying, or for damaging their party's interests by attacking it) rest finally with the editors of a newspaper, not with its political correspondent. The man in Canberra is not all-powerful. His copy is subjected to the usual run of sub-editors, news editors and editors. But if it is politically contentious, it will be given even closer scrutiny. The fact that a correspondent writes a story saying that a minister or the Prime Minister has been shown to be a liar does not guarantee that it will be published. It may be cut, or pushed to an inside page, instead of given the front-page treatment the journalist (and Mr Chipp) may desire. More likely it will not be used, particularly if the man under attack is a Liberal. Stories about bad behaviour among Labor politicians stand a better chance of escaping editorial censorship. While it is probably true that the journalists in Canberra are in a better position to assess the political significance of any political story, the fact is that such decisions are made in the newspaper's head office. The result is bias. Some newspapers are worse than others, some try very hard to prevent the appearance of bias.

With radio and television presentation, bias similarly intrudes. To some extent this bias is seen by the public. A survey conducted by the (former) Australian Broadcasting Control Board found that 20 per cent of respondents regarded the mass media as very biased in its coverage of politicians, and 46 per cent thought it was "somewhat biased". Only 27 per cent thought it was not biased. The survey was conducted for the information of the Joint Committee on the Braodcasting of Parliamentary Proceedings (and published by it) for its inquiry into the televising of parliament. The survey also found that about half the people approached thought some televising of parliament to be a good idea. But interestingly the survey did not suggest that people would view such parliamentary shows for the purpose of information. Two-thirds of respondents said they watched television for entertainment, and they, as much as those seeking knowledge, thought they would like to look at parliament on television. The committee recommended that edited highlights of parliament should be made available to television stations and should be shown once a week on the ABC, and also that questions time should be telecast and shown at night. However although the committee reported in April 1974, no subsequent government has bothered to do anything about implementing its recommendations.

What was absent from the report was any comparison with radio broadcasting, particularly the audience presently attracted and the effect of broadcasting on the parliament. The committee thought the main reason for televising parliament was to have more public access to the processes of parliament. There is no evidence, however, to suggest that radio broadcasting (which has provided some such access) has had any beneficial effect.

Ministers and members tend to resent their dependence on the press gallery to get information or policies or propaganda through to the public. From time to time, backbenchers suggest throwing the press out of parliament house so that members can walk the corridors without being button-holed. Backbenchers complain that political correspondents are paid more than they are (they generally are not, but most have generous entertainment allowances which permit them to live quite well), that they have better access to ministers and that they have more power than ordinary parliamentarians.

Proposals for the new and permanent Parliament House suggest that the press gallery would be restricted from entering large sections of the building—at present gallery members cannot go into the members' bar or, unless invited, into the members' dining room. They are also banned from the corridor onto which the Prime Minister's office and the Cabinet room open. Governments have rejected the idea of charging press organisations for rent and electricity for their press gallery offices on the grounds that this would create some kind of tenant right for the organisation. Nevertheless there is no prospect that the gallery will be divorced from the Parliament. The two are far too interdependent.

10 Responsible Government in the Australian Federal System

The authors of the Australian Constitution drew together two diverse concepts in their construction of a parliamentary and governmental system for Australia. They married a system of responsible government and a parliament based on federal principles. Some of the founding fathers were sceptical about the possible outcome: several warned that the two concepts were incompatible, that only one of them would survive.

There have been many changes in the first seventy-five years of operation of the Constitution in the application of both federalism and responsible government in the Commonwealth of Australia, particularly in the last decade of that period, and specially in the last year or two of it. In 1974 few would have disagreed with the verdict of Professor Sol Encel in the second edition of his *Cabinet Government in Australia* when he said

> The discretionary powers which are, by constitutional theory, vested in a governor or governor-general have been of little significance during the twentieth century. Only two exceptions to this general situation may be noted, and both of them are now of interest only to the historian.... (p.18)

> ...dissolution crises will continue to provide good newspaper copy, and may call forth weighty pronouncements on constitutional issues including vice-regal discretion. Politics, even more than other human activities, has its ritualistic aspects. (p.25)

After 11 November 1975 everyone was wiser.

The hazards of setting down an analysis of current conventions and practices are apparent. However, no book which seeks to deal with the way the Australian Parliament works can avoid trying to describe the way the most fundamental notions affecting the Parliament that are involved in the Constitution are treated in the Parliament. What the politicians actually say about these matters counts for less than the way they behave in relation to them: one does not need to be a cynic to appreciate that the brave words Australian parliamentarians are likely to utter about conventions and proper constitutional practices are likely to be influenced by the way in which they propose to act—and not vice versa.

Responsible Government

It would be useful to be able to give a strict definition of "responsible government", particularly in its application to the Australian Constitution, and then to analyse each aspect of the definition in relation to the way the Canberra parliamentarians actually behave. Unfortunately, providing such a definition has its problems. (See in particular Prof. R.S. Parker's "The Meaning of Responsible Government" in *Politics,* XI (2), pp.178–84.) Finding a simple textbook formula acceptable to theorists and practitioners alike is a near impossible task.

That task was made more difficult by the events of November 1975 when the actions of the Governor-General appeared to at least some experts in this area to be counter to what they believed were the principles of responsible government. In writing about responsible government post-1975, the concepts explored should take into account Kerr's actions as well as the way Canberra governments and parliaments normally behave.

The idea of "responsible government" appears to involve three elements. First, acts of the executive government, whether by the Crown or its representative, ministers or public servants, are not undertaken arbitrarily but in such a way that someone (generally a minister, or ministers) is answerable to someone else for them. The "someone else" to whom accountability is owed is supposedly the parliament, or a part of it (and through parliament, the people). Second, ministers collectively accept responsibility for all the actions of the government of which they are a part, and especially for those decisions decided collectively by the government, whether or not they have agreed with the particular decision. Third, ministers are individually responsible to the parliament for their own activities as ministers, for their relations with the parliament and for the actions of those of their subordinates (public servants in particular) over whom they have fairly direct influence.

The above description admittedly involves considerable question-begging. This is inevitable if one tries to blend the theory in with the many exceptions which Australian experience has produced.

The Crown and responsibility

Much of Britain's political history was concerned with setting limits: on the authority of the Crown; on the change from absolute monarchy to constitutional monarchy; on the transfer of the powers of the Crown to ministers responsible to the people (through the House of Commons) for their actions. Although the makers of the Australian Constitution sought to capture British practice in this regard, the very act of producing a written Constitution produced a more rigid relationship between the Crown and ministers which was less capable of adjusting to political and social developments (such as the growth of political parties exercising tight discipline over almost all members of parliament) than was the case in Britain.

Writing as an advocate for the adoption of the Australian Constitution, R.R. Garran (later Sir Robert Garran, first Solicitor-General of the Commonwealth) pointed to the desirability of flexibility in the operation of responsible government.

> We must not, however, attempt to fix the present pattern of responsible government as a thing to be clung to for all time; we must allow scope for its development—for its being moulded to fit the political ideas of each successive generation. Responsible government, as we know it, is a new thing, and a changing thing; it depends largely upon unwritten rules which are constantly varying, growing, developing, and the precise direction of whose development it is impossible to forecast. To try to crystallise this fluid system into a hard and fast code of written law would spoil its chief merit; we must be careful to lay down only the essential principles of popular government, leaving the details of form as elastic as possible. Some fundamental principles must be fixed by the Constitution (subject to a more or less difficult process of amendment); whilst the great mass of merely accidental, and not essential characteristics of government may be left at large, to be controlled from time to time by the Parliament and the will of the people, as is the case today in Great Britain and in every self-governing British colony. (*The Coming Commonwealth*, p.149)

In fact the Constitution did leave the details of the arrangements for responsible government fairly flexible. It required ministers to be members of the parliament (or become members within three months) and it required the Governor-General to act, in some instances, with the advice of his executive council. However, those who wrote the Constitution deliberately left some matters solely within the powers of the Governor-General in order to demonstrate that while they considered that he should act on the advice of his ministers in virtually all his functions, it was somewhat improper actually to bind the Governor-General by the words of the Constitution to take such advice in matters that fell within the royal prerogative—even where the monarch in Britain would only exercise that prerogative on the advice of ministers. As Garran and his co-commentator on the Constitution were to write after its adoption:

> Whilst, therefore, in this Constitution some executive powers are, in technical phraseology, and in accordance with venerable customs, vested in the Governor-General, and others in the Governor-General in Council, they are all substantially in *pari materia,* on the same footing, and, in the ultimate resort, can only be exercised according to the will of the people. (Quick and Garran, *The Annotated Constitution of Australia,* p. 406)

This doctrine has been said by some modern commentators even to exclude the possibility of the Governor-General acting on his own account to withhold assent from a bill—despite the words of the Constitution in section 58 ("...he shall declare, according to his discretion, but subject to this Constitution, that he assents...or that he withholds assent....")

Until 1975 there were two areas of minor controversy about the prospect of the Governor-General exercising his "reserve powers" independently of the advice of his ministers. One concerned the dissolution of the House of Representatives or both Houses simultaneously, the other concerned his choice of a Prime Minister. (These were not all the possible debating points about reserve powers: it is possible to argue about the extent to which the Governor-General could exercise influence as "Commander-in-Chief" of the armed forces in any matter concerning the armed forces; also the exercise of the prerogative of mercy as a reserve power might have become a debating point except that the "Royal Instructions to the Governor-General" make it clear that the prerogative is to be exercised only on the advice of a minister or, in capital cases, of the executive council. There are other matters too but only the questions of dissolution and the appointment of ministers have become at all controversial to date. But given that reserve powers, prerogative powers and constitutional powers do exist, other controversies may arise in the future.)

Dissolution
Since the consolidation of the present party system in Australia in 1909, Governors-General have not refused to grant a dissolution of the House of Representatives to a Prime Minister when he has asked for it. There have been some controversies in the states over Governors giving or not giving dissolutions (see Fajgenbaum and Hanks, *Australian Constitutional Law,* pp. 79–91) but generally the political situation in the House of Representatives has been such that the question had not been determined at the Commonwealth level before

1975. Nevertheless Governors-General in recent times have speculated about the power of dissolution and have held firmly that they were entitled to make up their own minds, independently of the advice they received from their Prime Ministers, and made it clear that they would reject ministerial advice about dissolutions in certain circumstances. Sir Paul Hasluck, as Governor-General, delivering the Queale Memorial Lecture in Adelaide on 24 October 1972, spent some time discussing this problem. He concluded,

> In crude terms, the case for dissolving Parliament in mid-term is that Parliament has become "unworkable". Among various reasons for this may be a conflict between the two Chambers (Senate and House of Representatives), the defeat of the Government on a major issue on the floor of the House, or difficulty of a Prime Minister with his own supporters. The key question is whether in fact Parliament has become "unworkable". Have all the proper steps been taken to resolve the conflict between the two Chambers; can an alternative Government be found without an election; can the Government party or parties find a new leader behind whom a majority will rally? There are good authorities to support a view that Parliament should not be dissolved and an election held simply to help a party leader or a party get out of their own difficulties but that the electorate should only be asked to overcome difficulties which Parliament itself cannot overcome. (p.19)

Sir John Kerr, as Governor-General, addressed the Indian Law Institute on 28 February 1975 in much the same terms. He concluded that "the essential question is whether the Governor-General can be satisfied that Parliament has in fact become unworkable" and he stated "The decision to dissolve Parliament in mid-term is one of the matters which the Constitution leaves to the Governor-General to decide on his own".

Nevertheless, a Prime Minister seeking a dissolution for purely "political" purposes (such as getting a bigger majority, or strengthening his leadership) is unlikely to have any real difficulty in persuading a reluctant Governor-General of the purity of his purposes. In 1963 Sir Robert Menzies called an election twelve months early despite his control of both Houses at the time. Admittedly he had a majority of only one in the House of Representatives (after providing a Speaker) but that had not caused him any real problems, only some inconvenience. In 1968 Mr Gorton considered holding an election twelve months ahead of time. He did not proceed with it for political reasons, but had he wished one it is difficult to imagine the Governor-General refusing to allow it. Although Gorton had a record majority in the House, he had become Prime Minister only twelve months earlier and he could have argued that he wanted a mandate to govern in his own right (and not on the majority earned by Harold Holt). In 1977 Sir John Kerr granted Fraser a premature dissolution of the House of Representatives when he had a substantial majority in both Houses. Publicly, Fraser said he sought the dissolution to bring elections for the two Houses back into line. No correspondence between Fraser and Kerr on this issue had been published at the time this book went to press. It would seem, however, that despite the public reservations of Hasluck and Kerr about early dissolutions, no Prime Minister would have any real difficulty thinking up a good excuse for an early election.

Double dissolutions

Each of the four simultaneous dissolutions of both Houses of the Australian Parliament (1914, 1951, 1974 and 1975) has involved the Governor-General who granted it in political controversy. Section 57 of the Constitution provides that the Governor-General "may dissolve the Senate and the House of Representatives simultaneously" under certain specified conditions which involve a deadlock between the two houses over legislation. In the 1914 double dissolution situation, the Governor-General consulted the Chief Justice of the High Court, with the permission of the Prime Minister, for advice on how he should determine the matter. Chief Justice Sir Samuel Griffith said the Governor-General was not bound to follow the advice of his ministers but was "an independent arbiter" in determining whether the conditions laid out in section 57 had been fulfilled. The Chief Justice advised that the Governor-General should grant a double dissolution only when he was personally satisfied either that the proposed law over which the double dissolution was to be granted was of such public importance that it should be referred to the electors through an election, or that there was such a state of deadlock between the Houses that only a double dissolution could end it.

In the 1951 double dissolution, Prime Minister Menzies suggested to the Governor-General that he was not bound to follow his Prime Minister's advice concerning the conditions of fact set out in the double dissolution procedure of section 57, but that he had to be satisfied himself that those conditions were met.

The 1974 double dissolution involved differences between the houses over six stated bills. Because the government failed to win control of the Senate in the elections, the double dissolution was followed by the first ever joint sitting of the two houses, called in order to pass these measures. The High Court also became involved, first when two senators tried to prevent the joint sitting from occurring, and then to determine whether bills passed by the joint sitting had been validly enacted. The High Court's rulings made it clear that double dissolutions could be granted for more than one bill, and that a government could accumulate a store of such bills before requesting the Governor-General to grant a double dissolution. The High Court later invalidated one of the double dissolution bills on the grounds that the proper conditions of section 57 (relating to the timing of the introduction of the bill) had not been observed. The Chief Justice, Sir Garfield Barwick, suggested in his judgment in the case to prevent the joint sitting of the houses that the Governor-General's decision as to whether particular bills satisfied the conditions of section 57 and warranted a double dissolution did not decide the legal fact as to whether the conditions had been satisfied:

> . . .it is not given to the Governor-General to decide whether or not in fact the occasion for the exercise of the power of double dissolution has arisen. In my opinion, only this Court may decide that fact if it comes into question. But, of course, the Governor-General must make up his own mind whether the occasion has arisen for him to exercise his power of double dissolution and he may recite that it has. But what he determines for himself is in no wise binding.

Thus the Governor-General makes an executive decision which has a political effect, but it is not a decision affecting the legal merits of the case. The Governor-General may be satisfied that the conditions exist which permit him to grant a double dissolution—and once he has dissolved the Houses an election must take place because his action cannot be "undone". But the High Court may find subsequently that the Governor-General's assessment was wrong. It will invalidate legislation passed at a subsequent joint sitting of the parliament if it determines that the double dissolution provisions of section 57 were not legally satisfied.

This seems to make it even more desirable that the Governor-General should not exercise his own discretion. Rather the Governor-General should act to grant a double dissolution only on the advice of his ministers, particularly his Prime Minister. In the 1975 double dissolution, the Governor-General had to dismiss a Prime Minister (who controlled a majority in the House of Representatives) and appoint another (who lacked the confidence of that House) to find an advisor who was prepared to recommend to him the course he wished to adopt—namely the dissolution of both Houses of Parliament under section 57.

Appointing the Prime Minister
Sir John Kerr's sacking of Whitlam and his appointment of Fraser as Prime Minister in defiance of the state of the House of Representatives demonstrated the reality of the reserve power of a Governor-General

to appoint his ministers in accordance with prerogative and with the words of sections 62 and 64 of the Constitution (giving the Governor-General power to choose members of the Executive Council to hold office during his pleasure, and providing that he appoints officers to administer departments of state to hold office during his pleasure). Normally the choice of a Prime Minister is dictated by the state of the parties in the House of Representatives and the Governor-General has no choice but to swear in the leader of the party which controls a majority in that house. Other ministers are appointed by the Governor-General at the direction of the Prime Minister and to the departments determined by the Prime Minister.

Even before Kerr's 1975 actions however, two Governors-General showed that they believed they could exercise some degree of independence over the ministers they appointed. The more important case was in 1967, following the disappearance (and drowning) of Prime Minister Harold Holt. The Governor-General, at that time, Lord Casey, consulted the Liberal and Country Party leaders and two days after Holt's disappearance he swore in the Country Party Leader, John McEwen, as Prime Minister. While it was understood that McEwen was to be "caretaker" Prime Minister, to act only until such time as the Liberal Party elected a new leader who would take over as Prime Minister, the Casey decision to appoint McEwen was decidedly personal, distinctly political, and had important political consequences.

In 1939, on the previous occasion a Prime Minister (Lyons) who was leader of a coalition team had died in office, the Governor-General of the time had also called on the leader of the minor party in the coalition (Page) to be caretaker Prime Minister. On that occasion, however, there had been no deputy leader of the major party because of a power squabble within that party. From his Prime Ministerial position, the Country Party Prime Minister of that time had tried to force his coalition partners not to choose R.G. Menzies (the former Deputy Leader of the UAP) as its leader by saying he would not serve in a cabinet headed by Menzies. Menzies was nevertheless elected and the divisions between the two parties increased.

In 1967, Casey appeared anxious to preserve the unity of the coalition partners. He was apparently aware that McEwen, leader of the minor party in the coalition, would not serve under a Liberal Party headed by McMahon, who was the Liberal Deputy Leader. It was felt that if McMahon became Prime Minister, his prospects of winning the ballot would be increased when the Liberals formally elected a replacement for Holt. By choosing McEwen as Prime Minister until the Liberals could elect a leader, Casey diminished McMahon's chances. McEwen then made it clear that he was blackballing

Responsible Government 171

McMahon. This time the Country Party succeeded in dictating to their coalition partners and the Liberals opted for Gorton as Prime Minister. Casey's actions contributed to this result.

A less significant exercise of authority by the Governor-General occurred after Gorton was deposed as Leader and McMahon became Prime Minister. McMahon had wanted to establish a new department to be responsible for various minor jobs, as they were considered, such as the environment, Aborigines and the arts. He decided that his Vice President of the Executive Council (a ministerial position carrying with it no department) should control a Department of the Executive Council, which would take from the Prime Minister's Department those officers responsible for servicing the weekly meetings of the Governor-General's executive council. The Governor-General (Sir Paul Hasluck) declined to sign the necessary papers, considering it in some way improper that there should be a department named in such a way and carrying out the duties proposed. McMahon at first considered summoning a meeting of the Executive Council to formally overrule Hasluck, but eventually was persuaded to concede the point.

In 1977 Sir John Kerr decided that it was improper for a public servant to be the head of two public service departments, though the government pointed out to him that such appointments had been made before. Eventually the government had its way, but only after it put through parliament a special act, the Public Service (Permanent Head-Dual Appointment) Act, to meet Kerr's objections.

The Governor-General and his Prime Minister

In normal circumstances the supposed conventional relationship between the Governor-General and the Prime Minister works: the Prime Minister (in consultation with the Queen) chooses the occupant of the Governor-General's post whenever it falls vacant, and the Governor-General acts only on the advice of his Prime Minister. It is only in exceptional circumstances that the "rule" ceases to be much of a guide to what will happen. Immense political powers are in the hands of the people involved: the Prime Minister can have his Governor-General sacked; the Governor-General can sack his Prime Minister and dissolve one or both of the Houses of the Parliament. Who acts, and in what way, depends on the reading by the individuals concerned of the political, constitutional and historical situation. And no one else can intervene once either of them has initiated his action: neither the High Court nor the Queen is likely to be willing to try to put Humpty Dumpty back together again.

The powers specifically given to the Governor-General in the Constitution are very great; they appear to effectively include the prerogative powers through the constitutional formula that "The executive power of the Commonwealth is vested in the Governor-General as the Queen's representative, and extends to the execution and maintenance of this Constitution, and of the laws of the Commonwealth" (section 61) even though this may appear somewhat qualified by section 62 in its requirement that "there shall be a Federal Executive Council to advise the Governor-General in the government of the Commonwealth...". It was argued in 1975 that the Governor-General had not just the authority but also the "duty" to use his powers to sack Whitlam, appoint the Leader of the Opposition as Prime Minister, and dissolve the House of Representatives or both houses of the parliament—that was the view expressed in the letter to the Governor-General from the Chief Justice of the High Court, Sir Garfield Barwick, on the day before Kerr acted. Not all members of the High Court would have agreed with Barwick's assessment of the legal situation, and of course political views about the Governor-General's actions vary greatly. What is important here is that the Governor-General did act against the elected government, exercising some of the inherent, previously untapped, powers of his office.

And while to many his actions might not have been acceptable, they were accepted, not least by Whitlam, the man Kerr dismissed. There were no riots; there was no blood in the streets. The action by Kerr prompted many people to seek changes in the system because they disapproved of the notion that an unelected person should possess enormous power over the fate of an elected government. The potential power of the Governor-General—all those references in the Constitution to what he could do on his own account or with the advice of his Executive Council—could be used by a Governor-General acting independently of, and perhaps contrary to the interests of, the persons elected to be his ministers.

To some people, the idea of a person "above" politics, keeping governments in line, was not unattractive, particularly if they could feel that "their" interests would thus be protected. Associated with this was the idea that it was somehow improper that the Governor-General, the representative of the Queen, should merely be a rubber stamp for the Prime Minister of the day, his servant rather than hers. It was considered improper that the head of state should be entirely a figurehead, with absolutely no discretion to act, as the Constitution seemed to require of him, as the upholder of the Constitution.

The contrary view was that the Governor-General was a figure-head only, just as the Queen was in Britain, and certainly not capable of exercising independent powers which the Queen no longer enjoyed. Although the first Australian Governors-General had exercised some real executive power, they had done so as agents and/or delegates of the British Government by whom they had been appointed.

Since the Statute of Westminster that position had changed. The appointment of Australian Governors-General on the recommendation of Australian, not British, Prime Ministers, had cut the ties between the Governor-General and the British government. Now the only allegiance of the Governor-General was to Australia. Democratic principles suggested that the Governor-General as an appointed person should not have the power to over-rule a democratically elected government. This is not to say that the Governor-General should have no independence at all—that he should not, for example, be able to refuse to sign documents if he considered them improper—that in those circumstances the government should be made to accept full responsibility for those actions. Rather it suggests that the Governor-General's independence does not (or should not) extend to dismissing a government which has been elected by the people.

Future Governors-General may be less adventurous in the exercise of their powers than Sir John Kerr. There seems little doubt that Prime Ministers will try to ensure that anyone they select to be Governor-General will act only on the advice of his ministers. But there can be no certainty about this. It was Whitlam who selected Kerr. The two men had had rooms in the same barristers' chambers in Sydney, and Whitlam thought he could trust Kerr to follow what Whitlam considered to be the conventions of responsible government: that the Governor-General acted only on the advice of his ministers. Future appointments will be made in the knowledge that in a crisis it is open to the Governor-General to tap the enormous powers which the law vests in him, independently of the wishes of ministers.

Collective ministerial responsibility

The idea of collective ministerial responsibility is that all ministers are responsible for all acts of government—the only way for a minister to avoid responsibility for a particular action or policy is to resign from the government. Among the rules derived from this are requirements that ministers should be prepared to speak in support of all government policies (including those which they personally might disapprove of), ministers may not criticise one another or their administration, ministers should not express personal views about policy matters which have not yet been determined by the government, and new policies should not be announced without cabinet approval (at the cost of the minister's job if cabinet takes a different line from the minister). The rules give expression to the political advantages of unity. Franklin's warning at the signing of the American Declaration of Independence that "We must indeed all hang together, or, most assuredly, we shall all hang separately" is not carved above the cabinet lintel in Parliament House, but it has been echoed by many an Australian Prime Minister trying to keep his government whole.

In the past decade and a half, four Australian ministers have lost their jobs in the name of (collective) ministerial responsibility, two under pressure and two by their own hands. In 1962 Mr Leslie Bury was required to resign as Minister for Air (he was not in the inner Cabinet) because he made a speech in which he suggested that Britain's entry into the European Economic Community would not affect the majority of Australians "materially". His statement upset the Country Party Leader, McEwen, who expressed shock that "a ministerial colleague should completely undercut the strength of Australia's negotiating position" in seeking concessions in trading arrangements. The Prime Minister, Menzies, took McEwen's point and required Bury to resign, telling him that his attitude was incompatible with ministerial responsibility and cabinet solidarity.

In 1971 the Minister for Defence and Deputy Liberal Leader, John Gorton, was required to resign over a newspaper article in which he was defending himself against attacks made on his Prime Ministership (which had ended six months earlier). Gorton had complained about ministers leaking from the cabinet room and being afflicted with a compulsion to try out ideas on their wives. McMahon declared this attack on ministers of his government as a breach of the "basic principles of cabinet solidarity and unity" and required Gorton to resign.

Earlier, in 1971, Gorton's loss of the Prime Ministership was associated with the resignation of his Minister for Defence, Malcolm Fraser, who claimed that Gorton had been disloyal to him and that Gorton was not fit to hold office. Fraser handed his resignation directly to the Governor-General and not to his Prime Minister.

In September 1977, Mr Bob Ellicott resigned as Attorney-General over the Cabinet's attitude to a private prosecution by a Sydney lawyer of Mr Whitlam and three of his former ministers over their conduct at the start of the loans affair. Cabinet, against Mr Ellicott's wishes, decided to claim Crown privilege and parliamentary privilege in respect of crucial documents in the case. The Prime Minister had also made it plain that he wanted the Attorney-General to take over prosecution of the case, and then to drop the prosecution. Mr Ellicott protested that as Attorney-General, he alone had the decision as to prosecution and he resigned on the principle of the independence of the Attorney-General from the political pressure of his ministerial colleagues. Mr Fraser returned him to the ministry after the 1977 elections as Minister for Home Affairs and the Capital Territory.

These four resignations/dismissals hardly amount to a strong tradition, let alone a convention, about the application of collective ministerial responsibility in Australia. Bury's and Gorton's sackings had less to do with ministerial responsibility than with attempts by the Prime Minister of the time to keep the lid on differences (about policy in Bury's case, over personalities in Gorton's) which undoubtedly existed within the cabinet. Blood-letting eased the pressure.

While Fraser took a stand on principle, in his resignation, he breached the same principle of ministerial responsibility by complaining, when he justified his resignation in parliament, about Gorton's actions in another matter that had been before cabinet (concerning a call-out of troops in Papua-New Guinea). The New Guinea affair would have been an appropriate matter for resignation at the time, but Fraser had not resigned over it. By not resigning he had accepted collective responsibility for what had, or had not, happened. Complaining about it later added to the breach with conventional behaviour.

In fact Fraser's resignation could be linked more closely with the resignation of another of Gorton's ministers in later 1969. David Fairbairn announced two days after the 1969 elections that he would not serve in the Gorton cabinet because of policy differences and complaints about the way Gorton ran his government. He then challenged Gorton for the leadership (as did McMahon) but Gorton retained it with ease. These resignations were thus attempts to depose the Prime Minister of the day (in Fraser's case, successfully). They did not involve the sort of self-consignment-to-the-backbenches spirit which is the feature of the not uncommon resignations from British cabinets (in the name of ministerial responsibility and on the grounds that those resigning could not stomach being identified with particular government policies—such as devolution, common market entry, trade union bashing and the like). Ellicott's resignation was in this British tradition. But the resignations of Fraser and Fairbairn were instead a method of making a challenge against the party leadership.

While collective ministerial responsibility was used as the excuse for the disposal of Bury and Gorton, their cases too can be better understood if they are considered in relation to the exercise of power. Bury's comments about the common market were no greater breach of ministerial responsibility than McEwen indulged in late in 1967 when he virtually criticised a cabinet decision not to devalue the currency. McEwen at that stage was privately chastised by Holt, the Prime Minister. He then issued a statement pointing out that he had two loyalties, one to the government and one as leader of his own party. It was probably in exercise of the latter of these responsibilities that he had pressured Menzies into forcing Bury's resignation in 1962. As for the Gorton case, it came as a great surprise to everyone that the Liberal Party had elected Gorton Deputy Leader after he had voted himself out of office as Prime Minister; as a result tensions within the McMahon government were very great. McMahon was ready to use any excuse to get him out of the government.

McEwen's 1967 devaluation statement demonstrates the difficulty of trying to apply the dicta of collective ministerial responsibility to the activities of a coalition government. McEwen thought one of his responsibilities was to his party which looked after the rural industries. He was anxious that "the views of the Country Party" should be "made known to the rural industries". The fact that in this case the two Country Party Members of the cabinet had acquiesced in the government's decision did not appear to embarrass McEwen. Apparently what was important was that the Country Party should be *seen* to be fighting for the interests of the primary industries, even if within the secrecy of the cabinet it was not doing so.

It is not only when there is a major crisis that the Country Party feels compelled to break with the ideal of cabinet unity. Country Party ministers frequently make sure that their electorate is aware that particular decisions of governments of which they are an integral part were stoutly opposed by them, or were watered down through their strong intervention or went through because of their initiatives— depending on whether the final result appeared good or bad for rural interests. In this atmosphere, Liberal ministers also indulge in the practice of associating or dissociating themselves from particular policies or proceedings in the Cabinet—though they generally don't do it as baldly as the Country Party ministers.

On the really important issues, however, the break with the ideal of collective responsibility becomes quite public. In 1971, for example, the McMahon Cabinet spent three days arguing about the need for devaluing the currency. Each day's proceedings was marked by newspaper accounts of the various "sides" of the argument—in particular the "rural" versus the "Treasury" lines—written with authority by journalists who obtained quite detailed briefings from ministers or their staffs.

On the Labor Party side, collective ministerial responsibility provides an even poorer description of the way Labor cabinets work. Labor ministers can appeal from cabinet to the caucus and cabinet divisions are readily discussed both inside and outside party circles. Whitlam as Prime Minister found it impossible to prevent ministers from talking about the subject matter of other ministers' portfolios. The fact that ministers are elected to their posts makes it impossible for a Prime Minister to discipline ministers. A Labor Prime Minister therefore has to find some other means of creating and nurturing a sense of collective responsibility among his ministers—the success of his government may depend on it.

Labor ministers are far more prone to behaving in a non-collegiate way than Liberal or National Country Party ministers. As well as being members of a cabinet, Labor ministers are also members of the caucus which ultimately exercises authority over the cabinet. As caucus members, ministers are expected to have views on subjects outside their own ministerial portfolios and they are not required to be silent about them. They are expected to argue about policies while they are being formulated, and the probability is that caucus discussions (or discussions within caucus committees) will become publicly known. Thus ministers will be seen to be interfering in the business of other ministers and policy differences between ministers will inevitably become public property. In 1974, for example, the economic committee of the caucus engaged in a wide-ranging semi-public search for an alternative (to the Treasury line) economic policy. During the course of these activities a number of ministers circulated their own plans for the economy and those of Cameron and Cairns became quite public. The committee's work did help determine the way in which the government then approached economic planning for the next six months—namely, in a mood of panic. Another example of interference by ministers in portfolios of other ministers concerns foreign policy. Whitlam kept most foreign policy issues out of the cabinet and because they did not involve legislation, caucus was never called on to approve particular policies. However ministers did not hesitate to express their own views on foreign policy issues if they felt like it, and they were able to do so provided their views fell within the very broad policy outlines contained in the ALP federal platform. Outside the parliament, ministers also felt free to advocate policies different from those of the cabinet, and even the caucus, while they were attending meetings of the party's national conference and helping to formulate the guidelines within which the parliamentary party had to operate.

Labor's rules of caucus control and ultimate party control over platform thus run quite counter to the spirit of collective ministerial responsibility. While Labor ministers are expected to be loyal to each other, they have other loyalties which are more important. This was recognised in the Whitlam government through the establishment of a rule that while ministers normally were expected not to oppose cabinet decisions while they were before caucus, they were quite free to try to overturn them in caucus if they told the cabinet they intended to do so.

Individual ministerial responsibility

Ministers are said to be responsible for their own policies and actions and for the actions of their departments. However, just what "responsible" means in each case it is difficult to say. It seems to mean at least "answerable in parliament for" but not in every case "liable to censure for". Snedden, as Attorney-General in 1965, claimed that a minister was responsible in that

> he may have to answer and explain to parliament, but not absolutely responsible in the sense that he has to explain for (is liable to censure for) everything done under his administration.... There is no absolute vicarious liability on the part of the minister for the "sins" of his subordinates. If the minister is free from personal fault, and could not by reasonable diligence have prevented the mistake, there is no compulsion to resign.

A more practical approach was expressed eleven years later by Garland, another Liberal MP. At the time Garland was resting on the backbench, having resigned his ministry when charged with offences under the Electoral Act. (The charges were dismissed by a magistrate and Garland was later restored to the ministry.) Garland, speaking at the 1976 conference of the ACT branch of the Royal Institute of Public Administration, to an audience consisting mainly of public servants, thought ministerial responsibility meant that

> the Minister is responsible to Parliament for his Department to explain, and where error is shown, he takes corrective action. He will only resign if the Prime Minister believes it is for the good of the Government but in most cases that simply admits error and party conflict being what it is, admission of error is more serious than the error itself. Such issues were the V.I.P. aircraft, Jetair, loans affair. "Constitutionally responsible to Parliament" means the Minister who explains the situation to Parliament, therefore, ministerial responsibility still protects the public service from Parliament without endangering the Minister at any rate immediately. The concept of course is clearly a changing one....

Once again, examples of resignations from the past decade or so do not help establish that the traditional idea of individual ministerial responsibility is flourishing in Australia. All but two of the incidents centred around whether the minister concerned had misled (that is, lied to) parliament. The case which involved the most academic discussion of the topic occurred in 1967, when the opposition was probing the use being made of the RAAF's VIP flights. The government, through the Minister for Air, Peter Howson, the Prime Minister, and ministers in the Senate representing these ministers, maintained that the records containing the information required by the opposition did not exist. When the Senate threatened to call the Secretary of the Department of Air to the bar of the Senate, the records were suddenly produced. Howson offered to resign over this incident, but the cabinet declined to accept the resignation, recognising that Holt was also to blame.

Several years later another Liberal minister offered to resign over the principle of ministerial responsibility. However, the "responsibility" in this case was for the actions and words of the minister's wife, not his department or himself. Andrew Peacock offered his resignation because his wife was photographed in an advertisement for printed sheets—and when criticised she in turn criticised members of the governing parties for their attitude. Mr Peacock's resignation was not accepted, and his offering of it was not taken seriously.

In the last year of the Whitlam government there were two cases in which ministers either resigned or were sacked for the principle of ministerial responsibility. Dr Cairns, then Deputy Prime Minister, was sacked by Whitlam because documents suggested that Cairns had misled parliament over the existence of a promise to pay a commission on a loan. There were also suggestions that Cairns had not properly controlled the activities of his step-son, who was a member of his staff, and who had appeared to engage in financial dealings which embarrassed the government. Then the Minister for Minerals and Energy, Connor, was persuaded to resign when documents showed that he too had misled the parliament, this time on whether negotiations for an overseas loan had continued beyond the particular point when his authority to raise the loan had been withdrawn.

In the case of these two Labor ministers, there wasn't much doubt about their individual responsibility for the actions which brought about their departure from ministerial ranks. In the Howson case, there was reason to believe that he had been misled himself by his department. As a result of the Howson affair, ministers tended to take an even narrower view of ministerial responsibility than that expressed in Snedden's 1965 lecture. Ministers were very ready to blame their departments when things went wrong (as McMahon did in 1972 when he was challenged over his responsibility for the purchase and disposal of aircraft which had belonged to Jetair). Ministers changed answers to questions on notice, adopting formulae like "I am advised that..." and "My department informs me..." as if seeking to remove themselves from the responsibility firing line.

One of the least controversial aspects of ministerial responsibility has been that ministers should at least answer for their departments in the parliament. Yet the whole nature of question time and its point-scoring techniques militates against even this: ministers tend not to answer questions; their concern is with either avoiding trouble by not giving definitive answers, or turning the tables on opposition questioners and not even attempting to answer questions. Genuine questions about administration have to be put aside to await the appearance before parliamentary committees of the public servants who at senior levels are seen to be "responsible" for the conduct of their departments. (This responsibility is so important recently that the new Expenditure Committee of the House of Representatives requires permanent heads to sign all submissions from their departments in order to sheet home responsibility to a particular person and prevent the permanent head from passing the buck onto one of his juniors.)

What is left of individual ministerial responsibility? Essentially a minister is responsible simply to the Prime Minister in the first instance, and then to his party (particularly in the case of the Labor Party) for his performance as a minister. That includes his administrative policy, parliamentary and general political work. How he performs will help determine the way he is promoted or demoted within the ministry, or even removed from it. The House of Representatives will have no say in the matter because the government parties, which control the House, will not allow a minister to be rebuked there.

Ministerial Responsibility—Canberra style

There are reasons for believing that Canberra's deviation from the Westminster ideals of ministerial responsibility will become more pronounced. These reasons concern recent developments in the public service and the peculiarities of the parliamentary situation.

If a minister is to be held responsible in any sense for the activities of his subordinates within his department, it is reasonable to expect that he has some authority over them. But public servants have virtually permanent tenure: they can be dismissed only after proceedings by independent tribunals. Ministers also have little real say in the way their departments work. Staffing is the responsibility of the Public Service Board and organisation involves the permanent head and the board. A minister who wishes to become involved in administration may have some input into the organisational system but his dictates will not necessarily determine the issue.

However, there has been an increasing tendency in the past decade for ministers to have a say in who the permanent head of their department should be. Along with the growing trend to identify senior public servants and their policies, this has resulted in changes within the public service in regard to the notion of responsibility, and between ministers and public servants. Ministers, as has been noted before, have not hesitated to blame their departments, and even individual public servants, for administrative and even political misdemeanours. Public servants have had to accept responsibility for their own actions to an increasing degree. As a consequence, many have felt freer to point out (privately of course) the faults of their ministers.

Since the war, the growth of Commonwealth activity has far exceeded any growth in the capacity of ministers to handle their workloads. Recent changes in the appointment of permanent heads and the lessening anonymity of senior public servants have caused the notion of ministerial responsibility to come under some examination. While public servants still tend to insist that the way they act is in accordance with Westminster conventions, it is likely that few senior men have any delusions about the very real powers that they themselves exercise, and about the comparatively weak position of most ministers.

Recognition of this changing situation led some ministers to try to ensure that the men at the top of the bureaucracy had their (the ministers) interests at heart. Under the Labor government from 1972 to 1975, this led to some ministers using their personal staffs to vet departmental work, to the appointment of a few permanent heads and other senior staff whose views were considered sympathetic (to the minister or the ALP) and to the appointment within departmental structures of advisors and consultants, sometimes on a contract basis, to become involved in the most sensitive matters. It led Liberal and National Country Party ministers who succeeded the Labor Party in office to clean out some of the Labor appointees and replace them with others whose attitudes were considered more acceptable to the new government (though sometimes that just involved having a solid public service background). This situation caused Labor to appoint the Coombs Royal Commission on Australian Government Administration, but the Commission skated around the issues Labor would have liked settled.

Parliament has also gone through changes which have affected the operation of ministerial responsibility. On the Liberal side, instability in party leadership after Menzies has led ministers to attempt to carve themselves out some kind of power base within the parliamentary party as the best guarantee of getting and retaining a portfolio—or even the leadership. The comparatively small size of the backbench in relation to the front (the ratio of backbenchers to ministers at most is 5:1 and can be as low as 3.5:1) and the intimate contact between the two, promoted by the geography of Parliament House and the way it operates, result in backbenchers being brought within the circle of ministerial intrigue. Cabinet disputes (which theoretically should remain secret), rapidly become the property of backbenchers as ministers seek to convince supporters that other ministers are incompetent or illogical or weak or stupid. Ministers compete for prestige among backbenchers, claiming credit for resisting unpopular policies or Country Party blackmail, or for initiating electorally popular measures. Some of it gets into the media, but a lot merely circulates among the backbenchers. Whether it becomes fully public or not, however, the lack of secrecy destroys the very basis of collective ministerial responsibility.

On the Labor side, the collective responsibility is quite undermined by the supremacy of caucus, and ministers hold themselves individually responsible more to the caucus than to the Prime Minister. For both sides, in practical terms, individual ministerial responsibility has come to mean what a minister must do to retain his own job, while collective ministerial responsibility refers to what he must do to help keep the government as a whole in office.

Responsible government and the Senate

The extent of changes which the exercise of Senate power has caused in any consideration of responsible government can be seen by comparing the following two passages from Odgers' *Australian Senate Practice*. The fourth edition, published in 1972, states:

> Substantive motions of no-confidence in the Government, and motions of censure, are not *usually* moved in the Senate *because, even if carried, they would have no real significance. Governments are made and unmade in the House of Representatives, not the Senate.* Whereas the passing of a no-confidence or censure motion in the House of Representatives could spell the doom of a government, a similar resolution in the Senate would not mean the fall of the government, *centred as it is in the House of Representatives.* (p.549)

The section is rewritten in fifth edition, published in 1976, where it appears:

> Substantive motions of no-confidence in the Government, and motions of censure, are not *frequently* moved in the Senate. Whereas the passing of a no-confidence or censure motion in the House of Representatives could spell the doom of a government, a similar resolution in the Senate would not *necessarily* mean the fall of the government. (p.617)

> [Emphasis has been added to demonstrate the differences between the two passages.]

Odgers' reformulation points to the changes which took place in 1974 and 1975. Motions of no confidence no longer lack "real significance" if carried in the Senate. It is no longer possible to state that "Governments are made and unmade in the House of Representatives, not the Senate" or that governments are centred in the House of Representatives.

As Garran wrote:

> That the parliamentary system for federal purposes may develop special characteristics of its own is not unlikely. Thus the familiar rule that a Ministry must retain the confidence of the representa-

tive chamber may, in a federation—where both Chambers are representative—develop into a rule that the confidence of both Chambers is required. (*The Coming Commonwealth,* p.150)

It took three-quarters of a century for the Senate to prove that Garran was right. But the fact that he was right in this regard has many implications which he did not bother to explore. Given the electoral system now in use for the Senate, the prospect is that many future Australian governments will not control the Senate. This means their survival will be dependent on the political will of the Senate majority (or even just the half of the Senate who can prevent the passage of financial measures).

While Garran called both chambers "representative", the Constitution provides that in the Senate the smaller states will have the same number of representatives as the larger ones. Thus New South Wales, with ten times the population of Tasmania, has the same number of Senators. With a proportional representation system, this means there will be political inequities introduced unless the political parties are able to attract similar levels of support in all the states— which they do not.

The use of the power to force a government to an election (at a time when it might be taking unpopular measures) was not justified in 1975 as an exercise of the power of the states represented in the Senate. Rather the power was exercised by political parties possessing control of the Senate. The only suggestion which Odgers makes that this power will not be used regularly to force governments which don't control the Senate into elections, is that the Senate will only act "in the public interest". In practical terms this means that no opposition will be likely to use its control of the Senate to dispose of a government unless it thinks it can win the ensuing election.

The Senate's exercise of its power in 1975 to bring about the dismissal of a government and the installation of an interim government which lacked the confidence of the House of Representatives demonstrated that the Senate not only has an equality of legislative power with the House of Representatives, but also has near-equality in relation to the executive government. According to the Constitution, Crown, Senate and House share the legislative power of the Commonwealth but the executive power is in the hands of the Crown advised by ministers drawn from the parliament. It is difficult to perceive any constitutional reason why such an executive government should not now be drawn from the party or parties which control the Senate rather than the House of Representatives when both have an equal veto power over finance. (It is true that the Constitution provides that financial legislation cannot be introduced in the Senate.

But it is irrelevant which Chamber a bill is introduced in if it is going to be defeated in either of the Houses.)

To put the matter another way: if a half Senate election produces a majority for the opposition parties and they then pass a resolution calling on the Governor-General to dismiss his House of Representatives-based government and hold an election for the House, and if the Senate persists in this attitude, an election for the House of Representatives alone seems inevitable. There will be no time, presumably, for the double dissolution procedures of section 57 to be brought into effect. In such a case the Senate majority could even argue that they represented the latest expression of the democratic will, and were thus entitled to force the Lower House to an election.

As well as possessing the ultimate power of life and death over governments, the Senate also possesses power (though it has not yet exercised it) over individual ministers whether they sit in the Senate or the House of Representatives. During the period of the Labor Government, the Senate carried motions of no confidence and censure in two Labor Ministers—the Attorney-General, Senator Murphy, and the Minister for Foreign Affairs, Senator Willesee. Neither minister resigned as a result of the motion and no question was raised as to whether the motion should be followed by disciplinary action against the particular ministers. However, the Clerk of the Senate prepared a statement which the President would have read out had either minister been challenged. The statement would have said that the standing orders did not require the President to take any action, and the President should not adjudicate on any matter concerning the executive government.

However, there is no doubt that the Senate could act to express its extreme displeasure against a minister it wished to censure. As far as a Senate minister is concerned, it could refuse to allow him privileges to which a minister is normally entitled under standing orders, it could refuse him leave to introduce any bills, and it could refuse to pass any estimates for the department of which he was the ministerial head. It could, ultimately, banish him from the Senate. The Senate would have less direct powers over a House of Representatives minister, but it could still refuse to consider any bills which he introduced into the Lower House, or pass any appropriations involving his department. That is, in theory, the Senate could veto the continuance in office of any individual minister.

Responsible government and the states

Although the Senate is sometimes thought of as the states' house, it does not provide for representation of state governments or state parliaments. It is simply a chamber in which electorates are based on whole states (or territories) and which provides for multi-member representation of these electorates. Whether Senators act as representatives of their state, or representatives of the political party under whose banner they were elected, or in their own or their party's conception of the national interest is for individual Senators to determine. But they have no direct connection with their states except as they see it.

The states, however, are given a role by the Constitution in connection with the Senate which can affect the composition of the Senate, and hence the life of Commonwealth governments. Until May 1977 the Constitution provided that state parliaments (or governments when parliament is not in session) should appoint replacements for Senators who died or retired before the end of their normal term. In 1975 two non-Labor governments used this provision to appoint men who were not supporters of the Labor government to replace a Labor Senator who had retired and a Labor Senator who had died. These two appointments made it possible for the opposition to muster the numbers to refuse to pass the 1975 Labor Budget.

In 1975 the Opposition parties also proposed that the state governments should make use of another clause in the Constitution to frustrate the Labor government and force it to the polls. The Constitution provides in section 12 that writs for Senate elections are issued by state governors. A normal Senate election (for half the Senate) is bound to take place in the twelve months preceeding the expiry of the terms of the relevant Senators. The practice has always been that the dates of the Senate elections are determined by the Commonwealth government and that state governors issue the necessary writs at the request of the Governor-General. However, in 1975 the Federal Council of the Liberal Party recommended to Liberal and National Country Party Premiers that they should not accede to any request to issue writs for a normal Senate election—and several Premiers made it clear they would do as the Liberal Party advised. In the event, they were not required to act in this matter, but the possibility is now very much alive that a state government can choose the time for the elections of Senators from the state at a time to suit its own convenience rather than that of the federal government. There is no requirement that all the elections be held on the same day.

In 1977 the Fraser government proposed constitutional changes to vary the requirements for the issuing of writs for Senate elections, the linking of Senate elections with House of Representatives elections, and the filling of casual Senate vacancies. The proposal for permanently linked House of Representatives and Senate elections failed to pass, however.

Conventions

Much of the political debate in the mid-1970s was about the breaking of conventions: the conventions of ministerial responsibility and responsible government, the convention that the Governor-General acts only on the advice of his ministers, the convention that those ministers must control a majority in the House of Representatives, the convention that the Senate does not reject money bills, the convention that states should replace dead or retired Senators with men selected from the same party as the departed Senator, the convention that the Commonwealth selects the day on which Senate elections are held, the convention that a government which does not have assured supply will resign, the convention that a Prime Minister defeated on the floor of the House will resign—and so on.

That all of these "conventions" were broken, or would have been broken had not others been broken, suggests something of the political turmoil of the time; but it also suggests that there could be something wrong with the terminology being used. For a "convention" is supposed to have some force; it is somewhere between customary usage and a law. Political conventions (of cabinet government, for example) have been recognised by the courts. They don't quite have the force of law, but the courts may be guided by them.

It is probable that in Britain, the important political conventions do have these qualities. In a situation which has swung from absolute monarchy through to the absolute sovereignty of parliament (i.e. where there is no restriction, as there is in Australia, on what laws the parliament may pass) the need for conventions is more apparent. It has been advantageous for all sides of politics to accept unwritten rules about the uses to which power might be put and the way in which it might be used. In the absence of a written constitution, conventions about, for example, responsible government, cabinet government, the rule of law, or the supremacy of parliament are inculcated through the educational system throughout the electorate, as well as being accepted by the political practitioners. A breach of the conventions won't just be railed against by the politicians who suffer from the breach; it is likely to be understood by the electorate at large, and possibly punished through the electoral system.

Australian politics has always been governed by enforced rules and laws, rather than by conventions. Appointed governors first made the laws, and then ensured that colonial parliaments did not go beyond what the British government was prepared to permit. When Australia federated it created a Constitution to govern and limit the law making of the Commonwealth and state parliaments, with a High Court to ensure that this law was obeyed by parliaments and governments.

The legal limits set by the Constitution do, as has been noted before, allow some flexibility in the system of government. However the High Court has rigidly enforced the borders, striking down Commonwealth and state legislation where the Court felt that the respective parliaments had exceeded the legal limits of their power. The Court's view of the boundaries of the power of the various parliaments and governments has changed over the years, though the court itself, by adherence to its own "conventions" has tried to avoid dramatic switches in its own treatment of parliament's legislation. In 1977, for example, the court rejected an appeal against Commonwealth legislation giving the territories representation in the Senate, having turned down a similar appeal less than two years earlier. The composition of the court had changed between the two appeals and although the new court favoured the arguments advanced against the legislation, it decided to uphold the law on the grounds that its previous decision had really settled the matter and it should not change its decision so rapidly.

Recent decisions of the High Court suggest that it is more than ever prepared to strike down legislation because of the way the parliament has conducted itself during the passage of the legislation. Its decisions in the cases arising out of the 1974 double dissolutions indicate that it will no longer abide by a decision of the court in 1911 in which the court effectively said it would not interfere in the internal proceedings of the parliament—a decision in accordance with the approach of the English courts. In England, however, the parliament may legislate to bind the courts; in Australia the High Court sees that the Parliament obeys the rules of the Constitution as the High Court for the time being interprets that document.

In such a situation, it is understandable that politicians have come to accept that in the pursuit of power they may do whatever the courts are prepared to let them do. Conventions, in the English tradition, have not been needed, as mutual restraint has not seemed necessary. Questions of (moral) right and wrong have been subordinated to questions of legality and illegality. There is no real place for conventions in a political atmosphere where the prevailing mood was summed up by Deputy Prime Minister Doug Anthony as: "In politics if you see a head, you kick it" and where the justification for lying during an election campaign was given (again by Anthony) as, "Well, we won didn't we?"

Of course, Australian politics is not like that all the time. Most of the time, Australian parliamentarians are cordial and civil towards their opponents, sometimes genuinely friendly. But when one individual (or a party) sees that he will be considerably advantaged in a particular situation by temporarily abandoning the accepted practices, he is more likely to abuse the "conventions" than not.

The political advantage to be gained does have to be considerable, because there probably is some electoral disadvantage in not following the "conventions". In 1974, for example, when the opposition decided to use the Senate to force an election by threatening not to grant supply, the Labor government appealed to the electorate in terms of this being a breach of all the conventions. This was put mainly (and to some extent successfully) in terms of the government not being given a "fair go". Come 1975 and the Senate argument was probably a little weaker—it is less horrendous to break a "convention" the second time around. The government's main electoral appeal was over the actions of the Governor-General in taking sides with the Liberal opposition to dismiss the elected government. Labor did very badly in the elections, but judging by the 1977 election result, it would have done even worse in 1975 if it had not had the Governor-General issue—had it simply stood on its record in government (at least in the terms which the public at the time appreciated that record) it would have suffered an even more disastrous defeat.

The 1974 and 1975 elections suggest that a party tainted with having breached conventions will suffer electorally to some extent (just how much is difficult to estimate given that both sides were accused of breaches of "conventions" in both elections). This means that a party contemplating a breach of the "conventions" would have to give some weight to the electoral cost of doing so. However it seems that that cost is probably fairly small. Since 1975 particularly, the "convention" terminology has probably lost much of the little force it had.

Few Canberra politicians would be likely to be persuaded not to adopt a course of action simply because that would break a particular "convention". In 1974 and 1975 (if not beforehand) the word "convention" was so over-used and misused that it took on the character of yet another meaningless piece of political rhetoric. In Australia a convention is nothing more than an established practice which remains a practice only as long as it suits the practitioners. That it is called, known as, or claimed to be a "convention" gives it little more respectability and force than any other political habit. In Australia the term explains nothing, and often only prevents a proper analysis of the particular practice and its place in the political system.

11 Parliamentary Reform

Ideas about parliamentary reform tend to vary with one's point of view. Backbench MPs who have given up any thought or hope of elevation to the frontbench are more likely than ministers to want parliament's power to be expanded, to make it a real power in the land that is able to keep a check on the way the nation is being run. Ministers and would-be ministers prefer a docile parliament which will wisely accept the correctness of whatever the government determines. Parliamentary officers, naturally anxious to stress the importance of the institution they serve, produce impressive lists of its supposed functions. Voters, reading about or listening to the way parliamentarians carry on, appear to expect something different from, and better than, what they see and hear. They seem to expect their politicians to be better behaved than they are, and to be more constructive than they are. Academics tend to measure the parliament against the performance of the mother of parliaments at Westminster, and find it somewhat wanting.

Ideals of parliamentary functioning have to be set against the political realities of the present Australian Parliament.

The most important fact of all is fierce party discipline which prevents the House of Representatives in particular from exercising any true legislative function. Other important features of the Canberra parliament are the intimate association between ministers and backbenchers, and the concentration by all MPs on governmental rather than parliamentary activity—on being in or getting into government, on having access to or sharing in governmental power, on conferring the governmental benefits on those who seek the help of their MPs. Ministers do most of their work in the same Parliament House building occupied by the backbenchers. Backbenchers have ready access to ministers in their offices, in the chambers, in corridors, restaurants and bars. The also have very real access to them in the party room where, irrespective of which party (or parties) is in power, government backbenchers can have very real influence over a minister's fortunes.

Backbenchers on both sides of both houses use their geographical proximity to ministers to push the interests of their constituents. Ministers, happy enough to provide some service to men and women with whom they are in such close juxtaposition, insist that their departments oblige MPs and Senators as far as possible. The backbench feels it is achieving something in providing these lobbying services for constituents. The same feeling of achievement is rarely possible from the work a backbencher does in the parliament itself. One result of this close association between the frontbenches and backbenches is the promotion of closed rather than open government. Government MPs learn enough about what the government does to satisfy their own curiosity and to persuade them that wider public knowledge of the way government is carried on will not necessarily benefit them in the electorate. Consequently, there is no common interest between the backbenchers of government and opposition in using parliament to force the disclosure of governmental information.

Another result is that the Australian Parliament tends to be pettifogging rather than principled. For the most part it is concerned with parochial rather than national affairs. Backbenchers devote most of their time to the demands of aggrieved constituents and it is considered a virtue in a minister if he devotes personal attention to constituency matters, irrespective of the effect this might have on his ability to manage his portfolio. The parliament is small and small-minded. It attracts few outstanding men or women into national political affairs—and very few rogues.

The usual recipe for parliamentary reform involves a major reworking of the committee system. The Senate did this in the late 1960s and early 1970s. But the members of the House have been unable to bring themselves to create an all-embracing powerful or effective committee system. Governments simply do not see it in their interest to have such committees in the House. Even a Prime Minister like Fraser, with a huge backbench to keep occupied has shied away from implementing the moderate proposals of the all-party Committee on Committees. In the Australian context reform of the committees of the House of Representatives is an unlikely prospect, at least while the ratio of backbenchers to frontbenchers remains so low.

Some changes are, nevertheless, in prospect. The most likely involve experiments with legislation committees to take over the committee stages of bills from the House of Representatives. However the establishment of such committees would be unlikely to loosen the government's control over the content of legislation. The committees could gain popularity in Parliament House if they were scheduled to meet at a set time and took the place of a regular meeting of the House (as happens with the Senate estimates committees). If, for example, Thursday afternoon were regularly set aside for the meeting of legislation committees, ministers who were not processing legislation through the committees would be able to schedule meetings and conferences in the knowledge that they would not be interrupted by divisions or quorum calls. However, moving committee debates from the floor of the House into the committee rooms would be unlikely to loosen party discipline, and while legislation might get more detailed attention than it presently does in the House, it is doubtful if ministers would permit significant amendments to be carried.

A less painful (for governments) reform would be to eliminate more of the "mumbo-jumbo" (as it has been called in Britain) associated with parliament in order to make parliamentary procedure mean more to the man in the street. Few people understanding the purpose of the business of going through a first reading, a second reading, a committee stage, a report stage and finally a third reading, before a bill is passed through one of the houses and sent off to the other. The procedures are mostly meaningless. Insofar as they are designed to ensure that members get a proper opportunity to examine and debate legislation, they simply fail. The way to reform here was demonstrated in the joint sitting of parliament in 1974: for each piece of legislation there was one single motion that it be affirmed.

Parliament has simplified much of its treatment of financial legislation, eliminating references to the ways and means committee for example, but a great deal more could be done. It should be no argument that "tradition" requires adherance to the old, often perplexing procedures. The British Parliament has gone a long way further towards reforming and modernising its procedures than the Australian. In some areas, such as in question time, the parliament in Australia has developed its own procedures which have had the effect of further protecting the already well-armoured executive from parliamentary inquiry. At quesiton time in the Commons, a minister regularly has to face three, four or five supplementary questions on every issue raised during question time, and he has fifteen minutes at a time to be asked questions. In the House of Representatives, a minister under attack can always count on friendly questions from his own side to interrupt the flow of proceedings, and the intervention of questions asked of other ministers who can give long-winded replies.

A Commons question time procedure which also makes sense is that the Speaker calls on the questioner by name. In Australia a member may only be referred to in the House by his electorate: he is the honourable (or right honorable) member for ... While it is true that most voters known the name neither of their member nor their electorate, parliament would probably seem less remote if the Speaker were no longer to call on "the Right Honourable Member for Lowe", but rather on "Sir William McMahon".

Another modest reform would be for the government to announce its legislative program at the beginning of each sitting. While the speech from the throne is supposed to give an outline of the government's intentions, it always consists of mere declarations of policy. Parliament and the public would be better off if governments were to announce which major bills were to be introduced in each session, when they would become available for scrutiny and when they would be debated. The very announcement of such a program would create priorities for legislative drafting which would help the government get through the business it proposed.

The parliament could also adopt another House of Commons procedure: at the end of each week the detailed program for the next week is announced and the Leader of the House is subjected to general questioning about the entire parliamentary program.

Most proponents of parliamentary reform, of whatever nature, appear to believe that parliament should meet more frequently. While the amount of work that parliament has been handling in the way of bills, questions and issues to be debated has increased, the number of days during which the parliament meets each year has remained fairly constant. In 1977 the House of Representatives sat for 676 hours. This compares with an average yearly sitting time by the House of Commons (the hardest-working parliament) of 1528 hours. European parliaments sit about the same amount, or less, as the House of Representatives, but do their most important work in committees. The US Senate, which is famous for its committee work, manages nevertheless to spend over 1100 hours a year in sittings of the whole Senate.

However while Australian parliamentarians are occasionally prepared to experiment with days and times of sittings, they are not prepared to sit longer than at present. Different groups among them have different reasons for this steadfast refusal to have the parliament extend its hours of sitting.

For ministers, parliament means a great intrusion into working time, interference with administrative work, interruptions to cabinet duties, and the risk (minor though it may be) that they will be found wanting in public. When parliament sits, they are subject to public criticism and questioning on their policies, and they have to exercise a certain amount of care to avoid mistakes. Parliament is necessary to them because of the need to have legislation passed. But most ministers would see little else in its favour.

The opposition frontbench is likely to look forward to parliamentary sittings with only a little more enthusiasm. It has a better chance of confronting ministers and showing their inadequacies when parliament is sitting. However, unless the opposition controls the Senate, its efforts generally prove disappointing to it, and oppositions tend to lose their keeness when a session is only a few weeks old. At the end of a 10-week sitting, oppositions are as ready to have bills rushed through the parliament as governments are, though they might make their ritual protests about "legislation by exhaustion."

Backbenchers on both sides show even less enthusiasm for parliamentary sittings than their leaders. It is only in the role of rebel that an MP or Senator is likely to attract much public attention, and that isn't a profitable exercise as far as promotion prospects are concerned. Most backbenchers would prefer to be back in the electorate with the comforts of home and a feeling of security that disappears whenever a member feels he is cut off from his home base. Most backbenchers see their best contribution to the government of the nation coming not from anything they might say in the parliament but from what they might achieve for individuals in their electorates. Most would believe as well that their work on behalf of their constituents is also likely to be more rewarding in terms of securing votes at the next election. Parliamentary committee work might have some attractions in terms of gaining publicity, but public sittings of committees generally occur only when parliament is not sitting.

Complaints that the Australian parliament does not meet frequently enough therefore draw little positive response from Australian parliamentarians. Most see little personal advantage in increasing the number of days on which parliament sits, and indeed they see positive disadvantages in terms of being separated from their homes or their electorates and from activities which will gain them useful publicity.

As for complaints that the parliament fails to utilise its time effectively when it does sit, that it wastes its efforts on repetitive debates, on meaningless procedures, on time-consuming divisions and quorums calls, these too receive little sympathy from the parliamentarians. Backbenchers rapidly become aware that they are not going to be allowed to contribute to legislative work, that if they put more work into speeches, and better preparation into questions, their efforts will probably go unrewarded. Ministers, resentful of the way parliamentary activity interferes with their time, don't particularly want parliament to be better organised as this will mean that they will have to contribute more, that they will have to take part in more debates or answer more questions about their administrations.

The atmosphere in Parliament House is quite cosy and stirrers who seek to have the parliament meet more frequently, or work more efficiently, don't get much support. Pressures for reform do arise periodically, particularly when a new batch of enthusiastic back-benchers enter the parliament. Their seniors encourage them to work out their frustrations in committees, to formulate their proposals, and then to try to put them into effect. Generally very little is achieved, however. And within a few years most of the would-be reformers are more intent on establishing their reputations within their parties in order to promote their prospects of being elected or selected for a ministry. Once they join the group from which ministers may come, their enthusiasm for reform tends to wane. On both sides of the House frontbenchers and would-be frontbenchers (say, two-thirds or more of the House of Representatives) accept that parliamentary reform will result in a minister's life becoming more complicated. So it is not only party discipline that keeps the House from pressing on with reform: there is a very large element of self-interest.

Self-interest has also helped prevent another important reform, a codification of parliamentary privileges. The Constitution provides that the privileges of each House shall be those enjoyed by the House of Commons in 1901, until such time as the parliament makes a law declaring its own privileges. None of Australia's thirty Commonwealth Parliaments to date has declared such a law although there is widespread recognition that reform is essential, if only to provide clarity in the law. Each house at the moment is judge and jury of the extent of its privilege. The courts cannot interfere to stop either house from gaoling any person the house considers has breached its privileges. The existence of this protective privilege inhibits criticism of parliament and parliamentarians. At the same time, politicians use parliamentary privilege to defame people who are not members of the parliament. Newspapers use the qualified privilege (which extends to reports of what parliament does) to print matter which they would otherwise be prevented from publishing.

While an argument can be made out that parliamentarians should be allowed to say whatever they like while they are speaking in parliament (in fact they put very strict limits on what they are allowed to say about one another), there seems little reason why their privilege should be extended to allow newspapers and other media to publish material which is blatantly defamatory. It is an easy matter for a newspaper with a juicy story to get a backbencher to put it on the parliamentary record so that the paper can print it. However it is unlikely that there will be any reforms in this area, apart perhaps from codifying the laws of privilege so that they can be better understood. Any real reform would have to be in the direction of reducing the powers and immunities of members of the parliament, and it is difficult to see a government or a parliament taking such a course.

Nor is it likely that there will be any legislative resolution of the conflict between parliamentary privilege and Crown privilege. This conflict arises whenever parliamentary committees try to question ministers or public servants on matters which governments claim ought to be confidential.

There is one important reform of parliament which a government considering its own (and the nation's) self-interest might implement. Given that one of the most important facets of parliament is that the ministry must be selected from its members, it is clear that one of the reasons why Australian governments have not been as good as they might is that the personnel available to form them is so limited. In the House of Representatives about twenty-two ministers have to be selected from between sixty-three and ninety government MPs. A bigger pool might improve the quality of the ministerial fish.

A larger parliament would have other implications for reform. It would increase the need for a better committee system in the House of Representatives and it might provide the potential for more independence of thought (and action) among backbenchers. In terms of the main functions of backbenchers at the moment, it would also mean better service for constituents—MPs looking after electorates of 100000 people would be able to provide better service than at present can be managed for electorates of around 160000 people. But whatever the size, no real alteration could be expected in the functioning of parliament without a change in the attitude of political parties towards the parliament.

Physical constraints, however, seem certain to prevent any meaningful change in the size of the parliament until a new Parliament House is built. MPs and Senators have already been told that they will have to wait for a new building before they get the additional electoral assistance the Remuneration Tribunal considers they should have. Improvement in office accommodation, library and other facilities will similarly have to wait. So, it seems, will reform.

The all-party, joint standing committee on the new and permanent Parliament House recommended in 1977 that the government adopt a timetable for the construction of the new Parliament, the target for completion being 1988, the bicentenary of the European settlement of Australia. The committee plans include provision for a 33 per cent increase in parliament's membership for 1988, and a doubling of the membership at any time from the turn of the century (or whenever the building was extended to meet the additional accommodation needs for such an increase). Increasing parliament's membership by a third won't bring about any changes in the relationship between government and parliament—by 1988 the number of ministers will probably have expanded by at least a third anyway, and governments may have again begun experimenting with the appointment of assistant ministers (at present a constitutionally dubious proposition) or parliamentary secretaries. This would reduce the ratio of backbenchers to front-benchers, further increasing the hold that the government has on the House.

The Whitlam government's misadventures with the Senate make Senate power an area of parliamentary reform more vital to the workings of parliament and government in Australia than any other. Given the impossibility of abolishing the Senate (a referendum would have to be carried in every state), it is probable that the ALP will concentrate on reducing the Senate's powers—and in particular its power to reject money bills. This is a reform which may gain support among the Labor Party's political opponents—it was advocated, for example, by John Gorton more than twenty years ago when he was a Liberal Senator.

It is unlikely that any attempt to reduce the Senate's powers over other than financial legislation would be successful. If it were, Australia would be left with a parliament totally subservient to the whims of the government of the day. This was the argument used (successfully) to defeat the Liberal–Labor proposal for bringing Senate and House election times together on a permanent basis: it was suggested this would allow the Prime Minister of the day to dissolve the Senate (along with the House) whenever it was carrying out its proper legislative duties.

A more useful reform might be the joining together of Senate and House election dates by fixing the time which each parliament must serve—that is, giving the House of Representatives a permanent three-year term. This would reduce the power of Prime Ministers to manipulate the parliament for political ends and reduce one of the threats that governments can use over their own backbenchers—the threat of an early election. Such a move might (and probably would) reduce the effect of party discipline on the consideration of legislation by the House of Representatives. It certainly would make less sense then to regard even the most trivial vote as a vote of confidence in the government. Fixed parliaments would have the incidental effect of removing the most far-reaching constitutional power of the Governor-General, the power of dissolution.

This is not the place to delve into reforms which would change the parliamentary system itself (see the author's *Elect the Governor-General!,* Nelson, 1976) though fixed parliaments could have the effect of making radical changes to the political system in Australia. But a fixed parliament and any other change which would have the effect of strengthening the parliament, inherently involve a weakening of the powers of the government or the Prime Minister. Governments are unlikely to agree to such changes in the existing balance of power unless they can be persuaded that such changes are in their interest. They are not going to make the changes because of some new-found academic interest in the merits of parliamentary supervision of the executive.

Political pressure for such changes would be internal or external. The internal pressures would come from a backbench revolt, generated by an overlarge backbench. There has been little evidence of the effectiveness of such pressure. External pressure would be in the form of a political campaign based on the proposition that parliament should be stronger and the executive weaker. There seems little likelihood that any party with a real prospect of gaining governmental power itself would promise to undertake such a program, or implement it if elected.

Select Bibliography

This is not a complete bibliography of material relevant to the Australian Parliament, but a selection of some useful books and articles.

The parliament itself produces a number of pamphlets, booklets and books describing the workings of the two houses and some of their history. These include:

J. R. Odgers, *Australian Senate Practice,* 5th edition, Australian Government Publishing Service, Canberra, 1976.

House of Representatives—A Short Description of Business and Procedures, 6th edition, AGPS, Canberra, 1975.

House of Representatives—Standing Orders as last revised 18 April 1972, AGPS, Canberra, 1973.

The Senate—Standing Orders as in force on 23 March 1977, Acting Commonwealth Government Printer, Canberra, 1977.

The Parliament is dealt with in a chapter or two in most of the texts on Australian politics. The best general and historical treatment of the subject is in

L. F. Crisp, *Australian National Government,* 3rd edition, Longman, Melbourne, 1973.

For a summary of the politics and legislation of the parliaments to 1948, see

Geoffrey Sawer, *Australian Federal Politics and Law,* Volume 1 (1901–1929), Melbourne University Press, Melbourne, 1956; Volume II (1929–1948) M.U.P., Melbourne, 1963.

Parliamentary Reports and Papers provide the most extensive review and record of parliament's activities. Reports of the Standing

Orders Committees of each house generally explain reasons for suggested changes in standing orders. The Report of the Committee on Committees contains an extensive review of the committees in operation in both houses in 1974–75. The reports of the Committees of Privilege of both houses, particularly in the past ten years, deal with clashes between the interests of individuals, the media, and the parliament. More general reviews of procedures of the houses are contained in the annual reports of the meetings of presiding officers and clerks of Australian parliaments. There is a basic examination of parliament, the executive and the press in the Commonwealth Parliamentary Association first Australian Parliamentary seminar in Canberra, September 1972, printed as parliamentary paper 283.

Articles dealing with aspects of the Australian parliament include:

F. A. Bland, "The Working of Parliamentary Government in Australia", *Parliamentary Affairs* (London), Vol. 4, 1950, pp. 73–83.

J. E. Edwards, "The Powers of the Australian Senate in relation to Money Bills", *Australian Quarterly,* Vol. 15, No.3, Sept. 1943, pp. 75–86.

Anthony Fusaro, "The Australian Senate as a House of Review. Another Look", *Australian Journal of Politics and History,* Vol. 12, No.3, Dec. 1966, pp. 384–99.

Jean Holmes, "The Standing Committee System in the Commonwealth Parliament from 1901 to 1950", *Australian Quarterly,* Vol. 38, No.4, Dec. 1966, pp. 29–49.

Jenny Hutchison, "Images of the Australian Senate", paper presented to Australasian Political Studies Association, Brisbane, 1974.

J. D. B. Miller, "The Role of the Australian Parliament in Foreign Policy", *Parliamentarian* (London), Jan. 1969, pp. 1–6.

Gordon S. Reid, "The Diminishing Freedom of the Federal Opposition—Social Services Legislation in Parliament", *Australian Quarterly,* Vol. 34, No.3, Sept. 1962, pp. 32–46.

Gordon S. Reid, "Parliament and the Bureaucracy", Australian Institute of Political Science, *Who Runs Australia,* Angus & Robertson, Sydney, 1972.

Gordon S. Reid, "Parliament and the Executive: the Suppression of Policits" in H. Mayer (ed) *Australian Politics: A Reader,* Cheshire, Melbourne, 1966.

Gordon S. Reid, "Parliamentary Politics", *Politics,* Vol. 2, No.1, Sydney, May 1967, pp. 76–90.

R. F. I. Smith and Patrick Weller "Learning to Govern: The Australian Labor Party and the Institutions of Government", *Journal of Commonwealth and Comparative Studies,* Vol.15, No.1, London, 1977, pp. 39–54.

For details of the history of Canberra and the building of the parliament, see
Lionel Wigmore, *The Long View,* Cheshire, Melbourne, 1963.

On the cabinet, and relations with the parliament, see
S. Encel, *Cabinet Government in Australia,* 2nd ed., MUP, Melbourne, 1974.
Earlier views may be found in
F. C. Green, "Changing relations between Parliament and the Executive", *Public Administration* (Sydney), Vol. 13, June 1954, pp. 65–75.
F. M. Osborn, "Australian Cabinet Government", *Australian Quarterly,* Vol. 34, No.3, Sept. 1962, pp. 83-8.

For a journalist's account of relations between prime ministers, ministers, cabinets and parliaments see
Frank Chamberlain, *Australia's Parliamentary System,* transcript of broadcasts issued by the Centre for Continuing Education, Australian National University, Canberra, 1976.
For recent developments,
R. F. I. Smith, "Australian Cabinet Structure and Procedures: The Labor Government 1972–75", *Politics,* Vol. XII, No.1, May 1977, pp. 23–37.

On backbenchers and parliamentarians, biographical material is contained in *The Australian Parliamentary Handbook,* compiled by the Parliamentary Library and published by the AGPS, for each parliament. Reports by various salaries tribunals have been published as parliamentary papers, while the present Remuneration Tribunal publishes an annual review, statement and determinations. Backbenchers use the estimates debates on parliament to discuss their own complaints and their assessment of parliament. Some of the papers written by backbenchers on their lot have been published in the various editions of Henry Mayer and Helen Nelson, *Australian Politics.* Three studies by academics are:
Helen Nelson, "Democracy's Dodo: The Back-Bencher", in H. Mayer, (ed) *Australian Politics: A Third Reader,* Cheshire, Melbourne 1973, pp. 558–79.
Julie M. Coates, "Liberal Backbenchers' View of the Liberal Party," in H. Mayer, (ed) *Australian Politics: A Second Reader,* Cheshire, Melbourne, 1969, pp. 473-4.
"Backbenchers", *Current Affairs Bulletin,* Sydney, Vol. 37, No.11, 1966.

On party discipline and the relationship between party and government, see

Patrick Weller, "Caucus Control of Cabinet—Myth or Reality", *Public Administration,* Sydney, Vol. 33, 1974.

Patrick Weller, "The power and Influence of Party Meetings", in Henry Mayer and Helen Nelson (eds), *Australian Politics: A Fourth Reader.*

Patrick Weller and R. F. I. Smith, "The Impossibility of Party Government", in Roger Scott and Jim Richardson (comp.), *The First Thousand Days of Labor,* Vol. 1, Canberra, 1975.

For the origins of party discipline

P. Loveday, A. W. Martin and R. S. Parker (eds), *The Emergence of the Australian Party System,* Hal & Iremonger, Sydney, 1977.

On parliamentary staff, see

F. C. Green, *Servant of the House,* Heinemann, Melbourne, 1969.

G. S. Reid, "Serjeant-at-Arms and Clerk of Committees in the Commonwealth Parliament", in *APSA News,* Vol. 5, No.3, pp. 6–10.

On Hansard

J. S. Weatherston, *Commonwealth Hansard: Its Establishment and Development* (3rd ed), AGPS, Canberra, 1975.

For different accounts of the roles of ministerial staffs, see

Roy Forward, "Ministerial Staff of the Australian Government 1972–74: A Survey" and J. M. Anthony, "The Politics of the Bureaucracy and the Role of Ministerial Staff", both in Roger Wettenhall and Martin Painter (comp.), *The First Thousand Days of Labor,* Vol. 2, Canberra, 1975;

R. F. I. Smith, "Ministerial Advisers", in Royal Commission on Australian Government Administration, Appendix Vol. 1, Canberra, 1976.

Sir Henry Bland, *Public Administration—Whither?* RIPA, Canberra, 1975.

The press gallery has been examined in a few unpublished theses. References to the relationship between the gallery and leading politicians may be found in all the books written on the 1972, 1974 and 1975 elections. See also the author's "The Press Gallery" in Henry Mayer (ed) *Australian Politics: A Second Reader,* Cheshire, Melbourne, 1969, pp. 550–5.

The best overall treatment of parliamentary privilege can be found in

Enid Campbell, *Parliamentary Privilege in Australia,* MUP, Melbourne, 1966.

The debate on responsible government and ministerial responsibility has heightened during the 1970s. For the view at the turn of the century see

Sir Richard Baker, *The Executive in a Federation,* Government Printer, Adelaide, 1897.

R. R. Garran, *The Coming Commonwealth. An Australian Handbook of Federal Government,* Angus & Robertson, Sydney, 1897.

Sir John Quick and R. R. Garran, *The Annotated Constitution of the Australian Commonwealth,* Angus & Robertson, Sydney, 1901.

For more recent contributions see

David Butler, *The Canberra Model: Essays on Australian Government,* Cheshire, Melbourne, 1973.

A. S. Cooley, "The Permanent Head" in *Public Administration* (Sydney) Vol. 33, No.3, 1974, pp. 193–205.

J. G. Crawford, "Relations between Civil Servants and Ministers in Policy Making", *Public Administration* (Sydney), Vol. 26, No.1, 1960, pp. 99–112.

H. V. Emy, "The Public Service and Political Control: The problem of accountability in a Westminster system with special reference to the concept of ministerial responsibility", *Royal Commission on Australian Government Administration,* Appendix Volume I, AGPS, Canberra, 1976, pp. 16–63.

Malcolm Fraser, "Responsibility in Government", Garran Oration, 1977, Canberra.

P. J. Hanks, "Parliament, Parliamentarians and the Electorate" in G. Evans (ed), *Labor and the Constitution,* Heinemann, Melbourne, 1977.

Sir Paul Hasluck, *The Office of Governor-General,* The William Queale Memorial Lecture, 1972, mimeo.

Sir John Kerr, *Address to the Indian Law Institute, India,* 1975, mimeo.

R. S. Parker, "The Meaning of Responsible Government", *Politics,* Vol. XI, No.2, Nov. 1976, pp. 178–84.

G. S. Reid, Comment on "The Double Dissolutions and Joint Sitting", in G. Evans, *Labor and the Constitution,* Heinemann, Melbourne, 1977.

G. Sawer, *Federation under Strain: Australia 1972–1975,* MUP, Melbourne, 1977.

R. N. Spann, "Permanent Heads" in *Royal Commission on Australian Government Administration* Appendix, Vol. I. AGPS, Canberra, 1976, pp. 222–75.

For a discussion of the constitutional aspects of responsible government, see

H. V. Evatt, *The King and his Dominion Governors,* OUP, London, 1936.
J. I. Fagjenbaum and P. Hanks, *Australian Constitutional Law,* Butterworths, Melbourne, 1972.
R. D. Lumb and K. W. Ryan, *The Constitution of Australia Annotated,* (2nd edition, Butterworths, Sydney, 1976.
W. A. Wynes, *Legislative, Executive and Judicial Powers in Australia,* (5th edition), Law Book Co., Melbourne, 1976.

The Royal Commission on Australian Government Administration (the Coombs report) discusses some of the aspects of these problems. For a discussion of the implementation of the report see the newsletters of the Royal Institute of Public Administration (ACT Group).

Reform of parliament has been a subject of interest for as long as there has been a parliament. Among contributions to the Australian debate have been:
D. M. Davies, *How Australia is Governed,* Melbourne Council of Civil Liberties, Melbourne, 1939.
Senator John J. Gorton, "Reforming Senate as House of Review", *The Age,* 25 August 1953.
Sir Isaac Isaacs, *Australian Democracy and our Constitutional System,* Melbourne, 1939.
The *Australian Quarterly* has provided a forum for parliamentary reformers for four decades. See, for example, John Curtin, "The Decline of Parliamentary Government—a Protest", Vol. 10, No.2, June 1938, pp. 5-9; H. M. Storey, "The Need for a larger Parliament", Vol. 18, No.4, Dec. 1946, pp. 80-88; H. B. Turner, "The Reform of Parliament", Vol. 37, No.4, Dec. 1965, pp. 56-65; H. G. Walker, "Presidential Government—A Cure for Political Malaise?", Vol. 41, No.3, Sept. 1969, pp. 43-9.

"The Westminster Model" is inevitably the standard by which the Australian Parliament is judged. For the traditional treatment of Westminster, see
A. H. Birch, *Representative and Responsible Government,* George Allen & Unwin, London, 1964.
Lord Campion, et al, *Parliament, a survey,* George Allen & Unwin, London, 1952.
Sir Ivor Jennings, *Parliament* (2nd edition), Cambridge, Mass., 1957.
Harold J. Laski, *Parliamentary Government in England,* George Allen & Unwin, London, 1948.
Lord Morrison *Government and Parliament,* (3rd ed), OUP, London, 1964.

More recent works, some dealing specifically with reform include

Humphrey Berkeley, *The Power of the Prime Minister"*, George Allen & Unwin, London, 1968.

Ronald Butt, *The Power of Parliament,* Constable, London, 1967.

Bernard Crick, *The Reform of Parliament,* (2nd ed), Weidenfeld Goldbacks, London, 1968.

R. H. S. Crossman, *The Myths of Cabinet Government,* Cambridge, Mass., 1972.

R. H. S. Crossman, *Diaries of a Cabinet Minister,* Volume 2, London, 1976.

Henry Fairlie, *The Life of Politics,* Methuen, London, 1968.

John Grant MP, *Member of Parliament,* Michael Joseph, London, 1974.

A. H. Hanson and Bernard Crick (eds), *The Commons in Transition,* Fontana, London, 1970.

Christopher Hollis MP, *Can Parliament Survive?,* Hollis & Carter, London, 1949.

Emrys Hughes, *Parliament and Mumbo-Jumbo,* George Allen & Unwin, London, 1966.

S. A. Walkland, *The Legislative Process in Great Britain,* George Allen & Unwin, London, 1969.

Woodrow Wyatt, *Turn Again, Westminster,* Andre Deutsch, London, 1973.

Index